ALRÉ

TEXAS FIELD

School house

Village hall

THE PILGRIMS' WAY.

Church Lane Cottages

BOUNDARY

The Keeper's Cottage

Church Cottage

Sedge beds.

TOP BEAT

Hornton's Cottage

fish ponds

drains

Time Waster's Corner

ditch

FIELD

FIELD

old hatch gates

ditch

J.M.B.

footpath To EASTON

The River Itchen at Martyr Worthy

"You Should Have Been Here Last Thursday"

The Life, Thoughts and Meanderings

of a Chalk Stream Riverkeeper

Ron Holloway

Ron Holloway

George Mann Publications

Published by
George Mann Publications
Easton, Winchester,
Hampshire SO21 1ES
01962 779944

A CIP catalogue record for this book
is available from the British Library

ISBN 9780954629991

First published 2007
Reprinted 2008
Printed in England

George Mann Publications

To
the two
favourite ladies
in my life,
my wife Paula
and
the River Itchen

Contents

Acknowledgements

Much of what I have learnt about the River Itchen itself and all the flora and fauna that live in and around it has been gleaned from my experiences working as a riverkeeper on the Martyr Worthy beat of the River Itchen in Hampshire for almost thirty years.

I am most grateful to the owner of the beat, Mr Simon Ffennell, and his father, Mr Denzil Ffennell, who employed me as their riverkeeper for all those years on such a wonderful classic chalk stream. It is impossible to list all the fishermen who fished the river during that time and with whom I spent so much time, forged so many lasting friendships and from whom I learnt so much. There are those who helped and encouraged me in my early years as a young riverkeeper and to whom I am especially grateful: Frank Moores my predecessor, Gus Headlam, Col 'Scrappy' Hay, Peggy Baring (Countess Malmesbury), Dermot Wilson, Commander Dennis Courage, Frank Sawyer riverkeeper of the Avon, Pat Fox riverkeeper at Easton and my many friends of the Hampshire River Keepers' Association.

Away from the riverside I thank all my friends in Canada and the USA: Chris Marshall who was instrumental in taking me to Canada and the USA for the first time in 1979; my great friend of twenty-five years and fount of knowledge of all things salmonoid and Canadian Dr Doug Dodge fisheries scientist at the Ontario Ministry of Natural Resources (OMNR) who has since hosted me on numerous working visits to Canada; Larry Solomon good friend and fly-fisherman extraordinary who keeps me updated on all things 'trouty' on the Catskill rivers; Marc Bale of the Sage Rod Company in Seattle who is a great fishing friend and fishing companion to me and supplier of some very special fly rods; 'Jock' and Anne Howat of New York for their friendship on and off the riverbank.

Grateful thanks also to my many fishing friends from far and near who have over the years taken me to fish on some wonderful rivers and at times in incredibly beautiful wild places: Peter Kane, John Winstone, Nick Measham, John De Mora Mieskowski, Derek Grayson, Hoagy B. Carmichael. A special thank you to the many fisheries scientists from around the world who have willingly answered my naïve questions and shared their knowledge with me.

Warm thanks are due to my dear friend Donald Downs for his great cartoon of my escapade with some bantam cocks. To my long time fishing friend and greatly respected fishing author, Peter Lapsley, who took the stunning colour slides of my long-tailed dry flies and has willingly given me such sound literary advice. To the late Tony Berry for his photographs of my spaniels. To Jean Amy Wheeler of Easton for her colour photographs of the river at Martyr Worthy. To Marilyn Bechely, the artist, who has captured so beautifully in her drawings the wildlife around the river and prepared the hand-drawn maps in this book. To George Mann, my unflappable publisher, who patiently edited my manuscript, advised and guided me through my inadequacies in the use of my computer and who encouraged me to write more.

Finally, my particular thanks are due to my understanding and loving wife, Paula, who for forty-two years has been so extraordinarily tolerant of not only the erratic hours kept by a riverkeeper but also the inordinate amount of time I spent during that time fly-fishing or in the company of fly-fishermen. Without her endless support and encouragement in all that I do this book would not have been written.

Preface

 book such as this, written about a riverkeeper's life around a chalk stream river should be read, partly perhaps for the sake of hints, information and instruction, but more so in the hope that the sense of pleasure that I have felt in recording these ramblings will permeate your mind as the reader.

The desire for solitude and peace is the most pleasant disorder of our times and it is man's natural balm to counteract the speed of modern life and to the many of the evils of the world in which we live. Solitude is almost beyond our reach today and therefore we seek it more eagerly. Some may find it only in dreams, others in the forests and mountaintops. I satisfy my craving, as do many others, by the side of clean, running water with a fishing rod in my hand, although I am no angling maniac.

In this tale there are no records of slaughter nor a tedious treatise on the mechanics of angling, rods, lines, baits, lures and all the other impedimenta that man in his genius has devised for the capture of fish. It is an appreciation of the beauty, pleasure, great humour and, not least, the lifelong friendships that have been found and made along the riverbanks of my beloved River Itchen and on the many other wonderful rivers of the world that I have had the good fortune to visit and fish.

It is my hope that this book may afford the city-dweller and countryman alike a brief insight into the fragile beauties of the chalkstreams and water meadows of Hampshire, with a hint of the scent and sounds of the seasons and also instil a sense of desire for contemplation which is so rare in this nuclear age.

Man, I believe, is the substance of the things he loves. From my earliest recollections, my love of nature has been paramount. Experiencing extremes of weather in all the seasons and observing its effect on the land and the rivers and attendant wildlife has been an all-absorbing lifetime interest. Even now, in the autumn of my years, I still enjoy venturing out in a snow or rainstorm, even in the most extreme temperature conditions, just to observe how Nature thrives. To observe the happenings of Nature at work takes time and practice and it seems such a pity that so many people who venture into the countryside, look, but never see the wonderful natural world in which we live.

Usually, we find our pleasures in our own way, we cannot always learn from others but trying to explain and share with others is as near as we can get. So in this book I try and share my love, enthusiasm and my own personal hopes and fears for the chalkstreams of Hampshire, and my beloved River Itchen in particular. Along the way, I have really enjoyed my work as a riverkeeper and treated the river work as a hobby as well as a job. Here I must take heed of Edward Grey's warning, that:

> *'When a man has a hobby, it is to be hoped that he will learn reticence and that he will never go out into the world without a resolve to not talk too much about what he cares for most. May he carry his delight within him like a well-guarded treasure and not ever disclose in all its fullness on any slight or trivial enquiry.'*

With this thought in mind there is, for me, yet another huge difficulty, that of expressing my feelings, thoughts and perceptions of the beauty of Nature, adequately in words. The English language seems to lend itself more readily to argument, disagreement and criticism than describing an atmosphere or one's feelings for, and perceptions of, the natural world.

I will endeavour to share the pleasures I have enjoyed over the years in my work as a riverkeeper on the River Itchen and in meeting the many people who have fished the river. It has been immensely enjoyable getting to know other members of the human race just as well as I got to know the native wild brown trout who live in the river.

Ron Holloway
Summer 2002

The Brook

I come from haunts of coot and hern,
I make a sudden sally
And sparkle out among the fern,
To bicker down a valley.

By thirty hills I hurry down,
Or slip between the ridges,
By twenty thorps, a little town,
And half a hundred bridges.

Till last by Philip's farm I flow,
To join the brimming river:
For men may come and men may go,
But I go on for ever.

I chatter over stony ways,
In little sharps and trebles,
I bubble into eddying bays,
I babble on the pebbles.

With many a curve my banks I fret,
By many a field and fallow,
And many a fairy foreland set
With willow-weed and mallow.

I chatter, chatter, as I flow
To join the brimming river:
For men may come and men may go,
But I go on for ever.

I wind about, and in and out,
With here a blossom sailing,
And here and there a lusty trout,
And here and there a grayling,

And here and there a foamy flake
Upon me as I travel
With many a silvery waterbreak
Above the golden gravel,

And draw them all along, and flow
To join the brimming river:
For men may come and men may go,
But I go on for ever.

Alfred, Lord Tennyson

One happy father with 5lb brown trout from Chew Valley Lake, 1962.

~ 1 ~
In the Beginning

I was born at Stockbridge by the River Test, as was my mother. I learnt years later that her father, whom I never met, had, in his younger days, assisted the original James Lunn in some river work at the famed Houghton Club waters on the River Test. I would like to believe that I might have inherited a few riverkeeping genes from that source.

After the untimely death of my mother in 1939 I was adopted and spent my formative years in the western suburbs of Southampton. I was fortunate to have a father who was a keen fly-fisher and, at the appropriate age, I was soon introduced to the delights of the chalk streams, to dry-fly fishing and to all forms of angling.

Among my earliest recollections of my paternal grandfather's cottage was the hall-stand that stood just inside the front door. It was a Victorian piece of little antique value yet for me it held a treasure trove of fishing gear as Grandad had stored all his fishing tackle in it and on it for fifty years or more. It was a big piece of furniture with two shelved cupboards, four good-sized drawers and two rows of hat pegs, one row each side of a misty mirror. As a young boy, already addicted to fishing, I always longed to have a rummage through the contents of this golden hoard of angling memorabilia whenever I visited my grandparent's cottage. I am sure it would have taken weeks of careful sorting to find out and identify all the goodies it held within its ample bosom.

From the odd occasions that I was allowed to look inside the hall-stand I remember it held a mass of fishing tackle of all shapes and sizes. There were various gadgets, parts of reels, floats and weights, packets of assorted sized Allcock's 'Hooks to Gut', skeins of Cuttyhunk line, reels of various strength plaited silk spinning lines and coils of sticky Kingfisher fly lines. There were scores of tobacco tins that held vast selections of spinners and spoons, weights and swivels along with many wooden cigar boxes containing a huge assortment of dry flies and masses of other fishy things and bits and pieces.

Standing next to this treasure chest was an umbrella stand that held a wide selection of walking sticks. There were walking sticks for every occasion with thumb sticks cut from the hazel coppice down the lane through to a gnarled old polished blackthorn stick cut from high up on the downs to a posh silver-topped cane for going to church. Stored with these walking sticks were odd sections of old cane fly rods that I knew Grandad kept to train lively springer spaniels and wayward grandchildren to walk to heel.

When not wearing it, Grandad's old dark brown Harris tweed jacket hung from the peg nearest the front door and even now I can still remember the smell of damp Harris tweed mixed with Ronson lighter fuel and cut plug pipe tobacco. Laid along the top of the stand with its tip resting on a picture frame down the hall was Grandad's pride and joy fly rod which was a Hardy Itchen 9ft 6in three piece cane rod with a Hardy perfect reel loaded with

Me, early 1940s.

a Kingfisher number two silk line. The cast attached was, of course, catgut as nylon had yet to find its way into the fishing world at that time. This tackle, a classic state-of-the-art combination for the time would now be an out of date heavyweight when compared to the feather-light carbon rods that are in use today. Yet to watch the owner deliver a thistledown cast 25 yards upstream with this rod to a rising trout was a joy to behold, even in his eightieth year.

A smartly rolled black silk gentleman's umbrella always hung underneath Grandad's jacket. This item appeared to me, even as a child, to be somewhat out of context with all the rest of the contents of the hall-stand but I thought little of it at the time. In retrospect, this object would not have been out of place on the 8.25am Winchester train to London or tap-tapping its way in a military manner along Threadneedle Street or across Horseguards. I soon came to notice that, even if it was raining when Grandad went out for his regular evening pint at the local, he never used the umbrella. His trusty old tweed jacket and his cap was all he ever used to make this regular journey no matter the weather conditions.

One evening, when I was old enough to accompany Grandad to the pub, I plucked up the courage one evening to ask him about the umbrella. With a twinkle in his eye and a wink to the landlord he said that he only took the umbrella out with him when he went eel quadding at night. Being in mid-gulp of my ale I exploded into my pint and drenched Grandad, the landlord and the barmaid in one go. I quelled my embarrassment while mopping up the mess and paid for drinks all round, just to keep the peace, I asked Grandad to repeat what he had said. Again he said he only took the umbrella out when he went eel quadding at night. Knowing his penchant for leg-pulling I dropped the subject and started up a conversation on fly-fishing.

On the way home from the pub that night Grandad asked me if I would like to go quadding for eels with him the following night as it was late September, it had been raining and, with no moon at that time of the month, he knew that the silver eels would be running down the river. I jumped at the invitation. I turned up at his cottage at the appointed time, dressed for the part, and we went off to the hatch pool below the mill.

I was fascinated to look at the tackle Grandad was carrying. It consisted of a eight foot hazel pole with a length of Cuttyhunk line wound around the top, a hessian West of England wheat sack, a tin of garden worms, an old woollen sock and, of course, the gentleman's silk umbrella. I watched Grandad closely as a sizeable pebble was dropped into the sock and with his pipe scraper he made some holes in the sock and threaded some worms through the holes. The sock was then gently rolled up, bound with some string into a round ball with the pebble at the centre of the ball and then tied to the end of the line at the end of the hazel pole. After filling his pipe and firing it up he slowly lowered the ball into the depths of the mill pool and gently bounced it along the bottom of the pool. After a couple of minutes he raised the pole and, lo and behold, there was a large silver eel attached to the woollen sock. As he swung the eel out of the water he instructed me to open the umbrella and stick the point of it into the soft grass so that it was upside down. Grandad explained that the eels were attracted to the worms and as they bit the worm they got their teeth caught in the wool of the sock. The eel was gently shaken off the line and dropped into the upturned umbrella. Whilst observing all this the penny finally dropped. I watched the eel as it struggled frantically to get out of the umbrella. I noticed that the eel was unable to gain any traction at all as the wet silk had become so slippery that it continually fell back into the bottom of the cup of the umbrella. Within a few minutes the umbrella was holding a dozen fat silver eels. I was then told to hold open the hessian sack and the eels were poured in and the top of the sack tied tight with a bit of string. That was it, so we packed up and swiftly made off to the pub where the eels were dispersed between the landlord and the regulars and so it was free ale for Grandad and me for the rest of the evening.

I now know why a silk umbrella is so essential when quadding for eels by oneself. So, even now, whenever I see anyone carrying a black silk umbrella I look closely at it to see if I can spot any evidence of illicit evenings quadding for eels.

One of my first solo fishing sorties was in the early 1940s to the Cemetery Lake on Southampton Common, some half a mile from where I was living, to catch 4-inch roach. An interest in water and fish was thus born which was further nurtured at the time by the damming of the feeder stream to the lake. The creation of mini-weir pools at high water and after rain made the release of the impounded water a real highlight for a young boy and from which grew a lifelong fascination with moving water.

Even at this tender age I was subconsciously observing and learning about the action and effect of running water on the banks of a stream and what affect the scouring action of newly released water had on the beds of gravel. The science of which I have since found out is called by the awful name of 'fluvial geomorphology'. From those early days, unbeknown to me then, was to flourish a lifelong love affair with the chalk streams of Hampshire.

One of my earliest recollections of the chalk streams I remember very well. I was 8 years old and standing on the crossbar of my bicycle peering over the hedge that surrounded the Drawing Room pool at Nursling on the River Test. I watched a fisherman as he played a huge spring salmon. Not only was it a big fish but the enduring memory of that day was in the huge volume of water that was flowing down the pool and that it was crystal clear even in the month of March (the keepers of that part of the Test will tell that the river rarely does not clear in most years now until late August at the earliest. Two things from that tale have changed, many big spring salmon and clear silt-free water).

I watched the fisherman as he played the fish around the pool for a good while before the fish decided to take off back to the sea from whence it had come. The angler had no option but to follow it down the river and, as he went, the fisherman beckoned me to follow. I hastily climbed off my perch, opened the wicket gate and followed him down, at a respectful distance, to watch events. After some time and many anxious moments the fish was eventually gaffed (which was legal in those days) and dispatched with a huge wooden priest. I was then offered the job of carrying the fish back to the weighing room in the keeper's house nearby. The keeper was away up the river tending to another fisherman. No wonder the fisherman asked me to carry it as it turned out to weigh 33 pounds. By the time we arrived back at the house I knew it was a heavy fish, particularly for a skinny eight year old to hump along the soft muddy riverbank.

In retrospect, I was grateful to that fisherman for allowing me to share in his triumph. To this day I often wonder who that gentleman was and what was his name. It is probably recorded in the catch records for March 1945. Now years on, with hindsight, I can understand why that fisherman asked me to come in and watch him grass that beautiful salmon because I believe anglers like to share such thrills as that salmon and all the memorable catches of our fishing lives with other human beings. To do it all alone does not seem quite right somehow as it leaves us with a feeling of a somewhat incomplete experience. Maybe it was satisfying a deep human genetic trait that is latent within us all, that of the returning successful hunter carrying home his quarry to feed his tribe syndrome or perhaps the fisherman wanted to be seen to be successful.

It was around that time that I was to catch my first wild brown trout. My father, being such a keen fly-fisher, went fishing whenever he could find the time, war duties permitting, and I was of an age to go with him although he had yet to give me my first fly-fishing lesson. My role, when we went fishing early in the trout season, was twofold, to net his trout and to search for and collect some coot and moorhen eggs for mother to cook, if it was spring.

I was very keen to catch a trout for myself so I took off one fine morning with my trusty whole bamboo rod and float and bait tin and headed off to the River Blackwater, a tributary of the Test, which runs off the New Forest. This stream was not a chalk stream as it ran over clay soil and its headwaters ran off the very acid forest ground. The run of sea trout up that stream was quite fantastic and even today many big sea trout are taken each year.

After I had stowed my bicycle out of sight I headed off into the backwoods where I had been told a good fish holding pool was located. After an hour or so without a touch, or even seeing a fish, I wandered downstream. As I went I casually fished each likely looking spot until I arrived at a sparkling run that had formed on a cattle crossing. The gravel was sparkling gold in colour and the water appeared to be gin clear so I trotted my worm down the run and almost immediately caught the bottom, or so I thought until the bottom got up and moved downstream. I lifted my rod and the bend in it made my heart leap as the fish leapt out of the water still attached to my line. The fish finally came ashore and as I unhooked it, the sun caught its flanks and for a few seconds I just held it in the water and marvelled at the beauty of the animal, the brightness of its spots and its dazzling colours. That picture of my very first trout was imprinted on my mind – a vision of beauty that has remained with me since. The size and weight of the many fish that I have been fortunate to catch over the years has never been so important to me as that trout and I suppose it was all of 8 inches in length. I do remember however telling and retelling the whole sequence of events that led up to its capture to a very patient father that evening over supper. I am sure that there was a happy smile on my father's face after I had been packed off to bed that night.

My father was an expert dry-fly fisherman and, when watching him cast, I would often inwardly marvel at his ability to place his dry fly so accurately and gently upon the water. His rods were all split cane and 9 foot plus so for a child of my age and stature these rods were far too heavy to use single-handed so it is only now that I can understand his reluctance to teach me the art of dry-fly fishing until I had at least grown a bit and developed sufficient strength in my right arm to wield one of his rods. Glass fibre and carbon fibre had not been invented at that time. Nevertheless I never refused the opportunity to accompany my father on any of his fishing trips and I would amuse myself by collecting coots eggs or playing in the edges of the river when the fishing was slow, besides it was always good to be alongside running water. The times I arrived home soaked to the skin with wellies full of water and the rest of me splattered with mud were innumerable.

One other memorable trip was to the River Stour in Dorset at a little village called Shapwick. It was a warm spring evening as we walked across the fields towards the river and there appeared to be a thick fog rising off the river. It soon became apparent that the rising fog was in fact a huge hatch of mayfly and before I even got to the riverbank I was covered from top to toe with live mayfly. I had to button up my shirt collar to stop them crawling down inside There were millions and millions of fly in the air and peering through the mist the surface of the river was seething with fish feeding frantically off this bountiful supply of protein.

I watched fascinated at this natural spectacle as my father hurriedly tackled up and ventured towards the river. His casting was as immaculate as ever but although he could catch chub that evening he did not fool any trout at all, his excuse being that there was too many fly on the water. I was so disappointed that he had not caught a trout that towards the end of the hatch I suggested that he caught another big chub to take home for me to eat. The look on my father's face was a picture. I shall never forget as he screwed up his face in mock disgust at my suggestion. I persevered with my request and, as he was playing yet another large chub of some four pounds, I badgered him to kill it for me to take home. My wish was granted, but this time I could not see the look on my father's face as I wrapped the fish up in a large dock leaf before placing it gently into my father's wicker creel.

On the way home I asked what was the best way to cook a chub. 'Leave that to Grandma' was all the reply I could elicit from my father. My wish was granted, for as I arrived home from school the following day I could discern a strong smell of fish being cooked long before I got to the front gate. That should have warned me. Not to be dissuaded I, for some reason, sat down on my own that evening to a steaming hot plateful of chub and chips. I was soon to discover that chub was absolutely disgusting to eat, although I thought the chips were not too bad. I had learnt my lesson and decided from then on that all chub were best left in the river.

During the latter part of the Second World War my school friends and I started our fishing 'careers'. Our movements were somewhat restricted due to the wartime regulations. We were soon introduced to the roach and gudgeon populations of the Cemetery Lake on Southampton Common.

An instance I remember very vividly was during another lone fishing visit to the Cemetery Lake in 1940s when the air raid warning siren suddenly sounded over Southampton. Within no time the anti-aircraft battery hidden in the trees beside the lake opened up with ground-shaking force and head-splitting sound. The ack-ack soldiers manning the gun were more concerned about my safety than hitting German aircraft. I had become used to air raids, air raid sirens, the sound of German aeroplanes, bombs falling, bombs exploding, anti-aircraft guns firing and I was oblivious to any danger. I was determined to stay by my favourite pitch beside the lake, especially as the roach had just started to feed. If I did have any concern at all it was that the ground vibration from the guns might frighten the roach out of my swim.

It was soon after this time that *Mr Crabtree* arrived on the back page of the Daily Mirror in the Friday edition. I started to cut out and collect the cartoon strips, written and drawn by Bernard Venables. So my serious angling education began. Little did I realise at that time that, many years later, Bernard Venables was to become a much-cherished friend and angling companion. It was from the many long fishery and fishing discussions I had with Bernard on the banks of the River Itchen that I soon came to count him as one of the most important

Two cartoons, from *Mr Crabtree Goes Fishing*, a cartoon strip published once a week by the Daily Mirror, written and drawn by Bernard Venables. They were the start of my serious fishing education.

(reproduced by kind permission of Mirrorpix)

Bernard Venables signing my copy of *Mr Crabtree Goes Fishing*.

influences on not only my angling life but also on my whole life in general. I'm sure many other anglers of my generation will also have similarly benefited from Bernard's great angling knowledge and love of angling all of which exuded from his informative writing and wonderful drawings of fish and waterside angling scenes.

With this newly acquired angling knowledge gleaned from *Mr Crabtree Goes Fishing* my confidence grew and I ventured further afield through water meadows greener. My adventures took me onto the hallowed banks of the Rivers Test and Itchen to try out my newly acquired expertise on the brown trout and other species of fish that inhabited these rivers.

The war meant that there were few active full-time riverkeepers about to deter an agile and keen youngster for very long from pursuing his love of fishing even if it were on some of the most famous beats of these two rivers. I must have poached nearly all of the quality beats on the Test from both banks all the way from Redbridge up to Stockbridge, usually in the company of my best friend at that time, Brian. We made a good team! Between us we constructed our own fishing rods that were made of a single bamboo cane. My rod was taken from the garden greenhouse where my father had used these bamboo canes to tie up his tomato plants. We crafted makeshift wire runners from unravelled paper clips and fixed these to the rod at the right intervals with black insulation tape. Pocket

Brian and me with one of our catches at Hatchet Pond, Beaulieu,1 September 1950.

money was saved and a small aluminium centre pin reel bought from Woolworth's for 2/6d also attached to the rod butt with black insulation tape. This reel was loaded with 30 yards of Cuttyhunk line and a supply of Allcock's size 16 hook to gut purchased. A selection of home-made swan quill floats and a supply of elastic bands, a match box full of assorted split shot and we were well tooled up and more than ready to fish our way endlessly up and down the River Test and Itchen.

We fished at weekends and all through the seemingly endless hot summer school holidays with little interruption to our sport, for sport it really was as only rarely did we take home a trout, if caught. We were fishing for the sheer love and thrill of it and the great uninterrupted pleasure of being in such glorious and peaceful, albeit private, surroundings.

Those unforgettable times were for me the halcyon, 'Darling Buds of May' days of my childhood just at the end of the war. My parents then were working long hours for little money and they had no fear of letting their eight-year old offspring cycle off for the whole day safe in the knowledge that little harm would come to me. Although I must admit we did not tell our parents all that we got up to.

Armed with a pack of brown bread, margarine, dried date sandwiches (a wartime favourite of mine) and a screw top bottle of Tizer, plus a few green apples scrumped from Joe Saunders' orchard on the way, we would be 'gone fishing' for twelve hours or more. Unbeknown to us we must have been two of the first fishermen to be engaged in the catch-and-release philosophy for trout on the River Test. I suppose we were poaching but only in the word of the law and, even now, having been a riverkeeper myself, I have a lot of sympathy for any keen youngsters of today who have a true love for fishing and yet have so few places to go.

It does seem a pity that some small parts of our chalk streams could not be set aside where young fishermen could be encouraged to start, learn and be taught the practice and the art. Even now, almost sixty years on, whenever I travel up and down the Test Valley I can still point out and identify many of the now well-hidden or barbed wire festooned access points to some of the prime river beats. These places were where Brian and I worked the river over with our worms, maggots and live mayflies. I often say to myself that I must go back to Nightingale Woods in the Test Valley just to see if that huge hollow oak tree where we found a barn owl sitting on two eggs is still there.

One very wet Saturday afternoon in the November of 1946, when the 'Saints' (Southampton FC) were not playing at home, I set out on one of my lone fishing excursions to the River Test. I cycled from Southampton and settled down to fish a newly formed back eddy just below Nursling Mill that had been formed by a huge chunk of riverbank slipping into the river. Sitting with my legs dangling over the bank, and with every sense concentrating on my swan quill float bobbing around in a huge circle, I was totally unaware that the riverkeeper had crept up and was standing right behind me. He made it very plain that I was on private property and poaching to boot.

Crestfallen at being caught red-handed, being reprimanded and being given a good clip around the ear, I made to run away, but his large frame blocked my escape. He asked me what I had been fishing for and at least I had the presence of mind to say, 'roach and dace, Sir' rather than 'trout', as it was November.

With my very first dog of my own, Rex, a cross Alsatian/black Labrador, 1953.

In no time at all, a huge pair of black rubber thigh boots dangled over the bank beside my small schoolboy wellies and I can still remember to this day the smell of his wet yellow oilskins and his broad Hampshire accent emanating from under his dripping sou'wester saying 'now' whenever my float dipped unnaturally in the water. The keeper had already checked my equipment and altered the depth of my bait and very quickly we started to catch some good roach of a pound plus and several nice dace and, all too soon for me, the keeper said it was time for me to go and that I would be in serious trouble if I was ever caught there again.

Even today, I can still see his wry smile and the twinkle in his eye as he put a large foot on the middle strand of the barbed wire fence and held the top strand up for me to exit the field. The keeper was Vic Foot who, though now long retired, is still going strong. It gave me great pleasure when he came to my retirement party some sixty years later.

This escapade and many others during those years of growing up taught me a good deal about the chalk streams, the fish and the people who together nurtured the intense love and fascination I have for these wonderful rivers. Once infected by the angling bug, fishing is an occupation that conjures up more dreams than any other. Years can flit by without a sortie to a favourite fishing spot yet dreaming about such a visit can be a salve to the soul when other and more mundane things in life are not going just as they should.

From August 1954 to August 1955 I was a student at Sparsholt Agricultural College taking a general agricultural course. The course put off my National Service call-up until September 1955 when I joined the Royal Army Service Corps (RASC) and was attached to HQ MLF GSD&Trg Department (General Services and Training).

I spent most of my time in the Army on active service in the Middle East in Egypt during the Suez crisis and also in Cyprus dealing with the problems there, either playing cricket or toting a sten gun. When the bullets had been flying and things were getting tough and some close comrades were killed or injured, my mind regularly took me back to the beautiful Test Valley and the wonderful childhood days spent along that river. Those thoughts helped me to get through those dreadful active service days.

School, college and two year's National Service rushed me through my late teens and early twenties. With the onset of girlfriends and a very active passion for cricket and rugby, fishing seemed to take up less of my time yet I

National Service with the Royal Army Service Corps, 1955-1957, serving in the Middle East in Egypt and Cyprus.

Wedding day, Christmas Eve, 1965, at *The Dry Fly Club*, Twyford

always planned and managed to set aside a holiday in July to go trout fishing.

By this time, all the good trout fishing on the Test and Itchen was not only well protected but quite beyond my financial means. However, this served only to broaden my fishing experiences as father took me to such places as Blagdon Lake in Somerset and the Elan Valley in Wales to fish with the Coch y Bonddu artificial. As I was now deemed strong enough, father had presented me with a beautiful second-hand split cane rod with a Young's Pridex Flyreel loaded with a Kingfisher Nº2 double-taper silk line. This rod was, and I still use it occasionally now, a Hardy Itchen three-piece 9ft 6in – a very heavy weapon when compared to the powerful and ultra lightweight carbon fibre wands that are now used on our river today. The tackle was the then state-of-the-art fly-fishing equipment and even today that rod delivers the most perfect gentle line to the wily trout of the Upper Itchen. With a high backlift, for which the rod was designed, it kept the aerialised line safely above the high reed beds common on the Itchen and the length and taper of the rod enabled a perfect gentle but accurate delivery to be made. A great deal of thought had gone into the design of that rod.

Although my love for fishing was great, at this juncture in my life I had an equally passionate, but very secret ambition, to become a professional cricketer with ambitions to emulate a Hutton or a Compton or an Edrich with the bat and also be a good seam bowler like Alec Bedser. I wanted to be the Botham of the fifties but, after some fatherly advice, it was decided that I was to earn a proper living in the pharmaceutical industry. This entailed working for Boots the Chemists in retail for a short spell and with J M Loveridge Ltd who were manufacturing and wholesale chemists in Southampton. During this time my very private dreams of becoming and being a full-time riverkeeper grew ever stronger.

I had by this time met and married my wife, Paula, in a whirlwind courtship as it all had to happen between the end of cricket season, the middle of the rugby season and the beginning of fishing season. We met in the September of 1965 and were married on Christmas Eve 1965 and made our first home in the New Forest in an idyllic forest village called Nomansland.

I was fortunate, while living in the Forest, to befriend a New Forest keeper, Harry Toombs, on a local estate that bordered the Forest. This friendship was to rekindle a love of nature and the great outdoors. At this time, during my travels servicing veterinary surgeons practices, I had also made friends with a riverkeeper, Frank Moores, on the River Itchen at Martyr Worthy. My first meeting with Frank was purely coincidental and totally unplanned but it was a meeting that was to subsequently change my whole life.

Often during my travels, visiting veterinary practices, I would pass over the Itchen road bridge at Easton as it was between the veterinary practices of Winchester and Alresford. With the fascination that rivers have always had for me, I would park the car and lean over the bridge and do a bit of fish spotting. I have always suffered from an affliction called 'river constipation' whereby I could never pass a river, without stopping to have a look.

One day whilst indulging in this pursuit, I spotted the riverkeeper wading in the river some fifty yards upstream and became fascinated as I watched him selectively cutting the river weed. Eventually he took a break and climbed wearily out of the water. He shed his chest waders and, after hanging them upside down from a tree to drain and dry out, he walked down the riverbank and over the bridge where I was standing in order to go up to his cottage for lunch. We passed the time of day, fell into conversation and, from that chance meeting, a friendship bloomed. For months afterwards, every time I was in the area, I would call in to Frank's cottage for a cup of tea and a chat about the river and fishing. I remember to this day standing on the bank of the river on a glorious spring day in a charcoal grey suit and city type shoes, wielding Frank's glass fibre Hardy Jet fly rod. As I made my very first cast of dry fly on the Itchen to a rising wild brown trout of about a pound, with that my mind was made up there and then that a riverkeeper's job was what I had always subconsciously wanted.

I tentatively asked Frank if he knew of any vacant riverkeeping jobs on the Test or Itchen. He explained to me that vacancies rarely came up and that experienced keepers or their sons usually filled the ones that became available. My heart sank. What hope had I with no keepering experience at all? I remember driving home to the New Forest that afternoon in a great, but private, depression.

At that time Paula was unaware of my thoughts or desires of changing my job though she was well aware of my love for fishing. She can recount very clearly one of our first holidays together after we were married which was spent at Mrs Fletcher's B&B cottage at West Harptree near Chew Valley Lake in Somerset. Whilst sitting on the bank of the reservoir watching me fish the evening sedge rise, she wondered whether we would ever get any supper before the pub closed at 10.30pm. Paula knew I was not particularly happy with my job. We were living in a big old flat in the heart of the New Forest and both working in Southampton. It was assumed that we would shortly be trying to buy our first house and make our way in the world.

The months dragged by and every trip to Winchester and beyond was planned so that I could lunch with Frank at his cottage at Martyr Worthy. Each visit culminated in me asking 'Any jobs going on the river?' Usually I had the same reply but one day, right out of the blue when asking the question, Frank told me that he was giving in notice shortly as he had agreed to take another job at the end of the fishing season. This job was to manage some newly constructed trout fishing lakes that were being dug at Fairoak near Eastleigh.

My heart leapt as I asked him if there was a replacement for his position in mind. Through Frank an appointment was made for me to see Mr Denzil Ffennell, who was then Frank's employer and the owner of the Martyr Worthy beat of the River Itchen. Fortunately, I had over the years read as much as possible about the chalk streams and so at least I did know something about them. I went home and told Paula excitedly that I had the opportunity to apply for a job as riverkeeper on the River Itchen.

Although Paula knew that I had met Frank Moores and had spent quite a bit of time with him at Martyr Worthy, she did not realise just how important the job was to me. We talked it over and went to Martyr Worthy to see the cottage which was a bit of a shock for her as it was quite old-fashioned with only a stone sink and an ancient Rayburn in the kitchen – nothing had been modernised. However, we agreed that it could be made homely and, knowing how much this job meant to me, Paula agreed that we should have a go.

The appointment day finally came and I arrived, after a sleepless night, an hour early and spent the time by the river just absorbing the warmth and atmosphere of an early spring morning. 'Please God, let this be the place for me' I whispered to myself over and over again as I walked up from the river past the village church to the 'big house' for my interview.

The good Lord was kind and must have heard me as I was offered an opportunity of the job. This was only after I had agreed that I would work with Frank for all that coming season, without pay, in order to learn as much as I possibly could about the river and how to look after it – with the added proviso that if I did not come up to scratch at the end of it I may not be considered for the position. That was a risk that Paula and I had to take and take it we did.

From March to the end of September may seem a long time to exist without any pay but to learn the intricacies of a riverkeeper's job it would have been impossible otherwise. However, Frank was marvellous and willingly told me all he knew and we talked for hours as we worked together, doing all the jobs a keeper does during that period. I was also so extremely grateful for Paula's full support as she was very aware how much I dearly wanted this job. Without her support and her income I could not have spent all those months at Martyr Worthy learning the profession from Frank. Each day I drove our Mini from our New Forest home to Southampton to take Paula to her work at a builder's merchants and then on out to Martyr Worthy to work on the river and then back again in the evening. The spring and summer months just flew past.

Frank left the cottage in late September and I was then offered the job.

Although I did not think much about it at the time I suppose if I had stayed in the pharmaceutical business I would have most probably have had a more prosperous life and may have ended up with a good house out of town and a good pension, three major things in life I was to learn a riverkeeper cannot expect. I did make a promise to myself on that memorable first day that whatever happened I would strive to the best of my ability to maintain the river and pass it on at least in the same condition as I received it. I think I just about achieved that promise to myself and given all that has happened in the thirty years at Martyr Worthy I would not have changed it for all the tea in China.

I shall always be indebted to Frank Moores for passing on his knowledge and the benefit of his experience. So when I did stand alone on the bridge and realised that the river was now my responsibility I felt as though I had just passed my driving test and the challenge ahead of me now was to learn how to drive.

~ 2 ~
Discovering the Heritage

nce Paula and I had settled into our new abode, №6 Off Church Lane, Martyr Worthy, and adjusted to the ways of the life of a riverkeeper, I set myself the task of learning all I could about how and what a chalk stream was all about. I spent my spare time researching, seeking out information and reading anything I could lay my hands on related to chalk streams and brown trout.

It soon became quite a time consuming occupation but it did provide a great deal of enjoyment and the more knowledge I gained the more I realised how much I had to learn if I was to survive as a riverkeeper and, more importantly, do a good job for the river.

Firstly, I had to learn what a chalk stream was, to learn how it was formed, to know how man had changed it over the centuries and to learn all about the native wild brown trout that lived in it. I spent many fascinating hours in the Winchester City Records Office delving into historic manuscripts, grasping snippets of information on the River Itchen. Besides my researches, I also visited the other riverkeepers up and down the Itchen and the Test, observing how each individual keeper went about his work, what he did and how and why he did it. I was to learn a great deal during these visits, picking up hints and tips on methods of river management.

Physically, or from a geographical point of view, the River Itchen is perhaps the best example of a chalk groundwater fed river that exists anywhere in the world. It rises on the upper chalk down lands just below Kilmeston Down in central Hampshire. There are three spring fed tributaries, the Candover Brook, the River Alre and the Tichborne Brook. R D Baird so aptly describes in his lovely book about the River Itchen, *A Trout Rose*, where he mentions the '*three princesses that having once found one another, journey together down to the sea*'. The accepted source of the Itchen is at the head of the Tichborne Brook along with the other two 'princesses' the Candover Brook and the River Alre. These three tributaries join together to form the true River Itchen just a few hundred yards downstream from the town of Alresford. The river flows west via those evocatively named trout fishing beats of Ovington, Avington, Itchen Stoke,

Itchen Abbas, Chilland and Martyr Worthy, Easton, Abbots Worthy and Abbots Barton to Winchester where it collects the Nun's Stream from the north-west. It then flows southwards through the town of Eastleigh where it collects the Bow Lake Stream from the north-east. The river enters the tidal estuary at Woodmill where it is joined by the Monk's Brook that drains the growing urban sprawl of Chandler's Ford.

As my knowledge of the Itchen grew I discovered how unique each river and its catchment was and that the Itchen was particularly so in that 300 sq km of its total 400 sq km catchment was over chalk. I studied the geology of the area carefully to understand why the river was so unique when compared to many other rivers.

The underlying chalk rock forms part of the northern flank of the geological structure known as the Hampshire Basin. Its rocks slope gently, or dip, from the north to the south. The oldest rock is what the geologists call Cretaceous chalk which is porous fine-grained limestone which outcrops over the whole valley to the north of the town of Eastleigh. Rain soaks readily into the chalk rather than running off and is filtered as it gradually percolates through the pores or small fissures under the influence of gravity until it issues forth from the myriad of springs along the valley floor. The chalk thus forms a massive natural underground reservoir of water or aquifer as it is called. The chalk rock is split into three main subdivisions these being what the experts call the Upper, Middle and Lower Chalk. Most of the catchment comprises of Upper Chalk but there is an inlayer of Lower Chalk in the St Catherine's Hill area to the East of Winchester, which can clearly be seen when driving through the infamous Twyford Down cutting. It is the very permeable nature of the chalk that gives it its tremendous capacity to store water and which in turn gives the river its unique character.

Rainfall on the chalk downland is just like a tap dripping onto an empty sponge. The river has but few tributaries and those there are seem to fall on a right angle grid pattern which reflects the structure of the underlying chalk. The shape of the rivers drainage pattern contrasts sharply with that of rivers on impermeable clay catchments such as the River Medway in North Kent for example where rainfall flows mostly over such land thus creating a host of tributaries with a branching pattern. The chalk streams of the Hampshire basin are therefore described as having a low drainage density whereby most of the rain soaks into the ground. North Kent rivers have a high drainage density where the rainfall does not soak in and drains straight off the ground via many little streams.

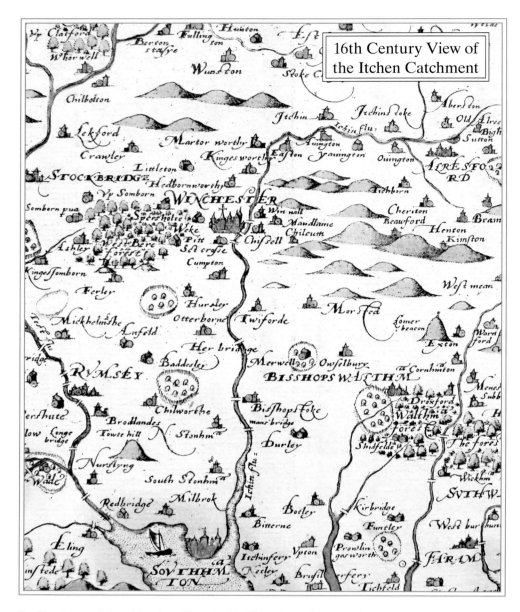

The River Itchen catchment, together with parts of the River Test catchment, as viewed in the sixteenth century. It is interesting to see differences in the names, such as the *Itchin flu (fluvius = river or stream)*.

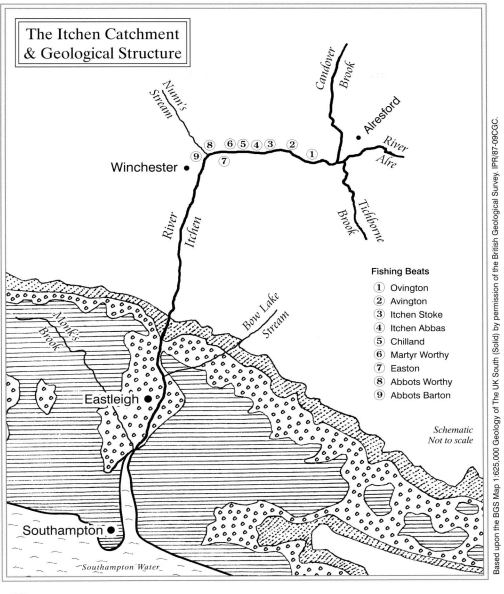

The Itchen Catchment & Geological Structure

Canlover Brook

Nunn's Stream

Alresford

River Alre

Tichborne Brook

Winchester

River Itchen

Bow Lake Stream

Fishing Beats

1. Ovington
2. Avington
3. Itchen Stoke
4. Itchen Abbas
5. Chilland
6. Martyr Worthy
7. Easton
8. Abbots Worthy
9. Abbots Barton

Monks Brook

Eastleigh

Schematic Not to scale

Southampton

Southampton Water

Based upon the BGS Map 1:625,000 Geology of The UK South (Solid) by permission of the British Geological Survey. IPR/87-09CGC.

London Clay ~ *Eocene* ~ *54.8 to 33.7 million years ago.*

Oldhaven, Blackheath, Woolwich & Reading Thanet beds ~ *Palaeocene* ~ *65 to 1.8 million years ago.*

Barton, Bracklesham and Bagshot beds ~ *Eocene* ~ *54.8 to 33.7 million years ago.*

Chalk ~ *Cretaceous* ~ *145.5 to 65.5 million years ago.*

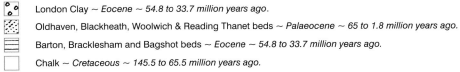

The numbered beats shown are those on the Upper River Itchen only and there are many famous beats below Winchester. The boundaries show the approximate location and name of each beat. The name of each beat originated from the nearest village or hamlet and, over time, boundaries alter with changes of ownership.

From the town of Eastleigh to the sea the Itchen flows over younger sands, silt and clay deposits of tertiary origin. These are more impermeable than the chalk. The whole landscape of the Itchen catchment was sculpted during and just after the last Ice Age. Although it is unlikely that the great ice fields reached so far south the ground would still have been frozen. Under these permafrost conditions, frost action along with rainfall and the run off from the melting ice fields would have carved and shaped the dry valleys that are so much part of the topography of the catchment we see today. It has been suggested that at that time the River Itchen would have been a tributary of the great Solent River which flowed from the River Frome in Dorset eastwards to Littlehampton in Sussex, when the Isle of Wight was still connected to the mainland. A sea level rise of some 15 metres around 10,000 years ago disrupted this river system when the sea breached the ridge between the Purbeck Hills and the Isle of Wight forming Southampton Water which is now a drowned low-lying valley that dates from that time.

The natural geological and hydrological elements of the river's make-up interests those who are employed and work in and on the river, particularly riverkeepers and fishery owners. The remarkably high water quality of the natural chalk streams owes much to the geology of the catchment. The many thousands of crystal clear springs that bubble up throughout the catchment discharge water at an almost constant temperature of 10°C (50°F) that varies little with the seasons. The quality of chalk water coupled with its hardness and alkalinity (ph 8.1 on average) accounts for its capacity to assimilate effluents but also affords such excellent and constant conditions for the natural production of fish food and fish. The average rainfall over the catchment is 875mm per annum, although the rainfall of late in 2000 and early 2001 was exceptional when this average figure was topped by at least 400%. In average years the summer evaporation tends to exceed rainfall levels, but in the winter the rain percolates down through the chalk and moves into the aquifers and through to the springs, a process that can take anything from 3 to 6 months. The maximum river flows in any one average year is typically only 3 to 4 times the minimum, unlike other rivers in the country where the ratio can be as high as 500 to 1.

This unique geology of the Itchen catchment which provides for a huge permanent reservoir of water that is stored underground the size of which is such that it is so large and widespread that it is almost impossible to measure. This enables the water supply companies to draw water for much of the domestic and commercial needs. These vast underground reserves also eliminate the need for any surface reservoirs to be constructed as all excess rainfall is naturally stored underground. Some holding reservoirs have been constructed in the lower Test Valley which, in my view, was only a public relations exercise to appease uninformed public opinion and was a waste of money as they only store about two day's water requirements for the immediate area. Given all these natural elements the river possesses, it became apparent as to why the Itchen had such great potential as a sporting trout fishery.

The salmon, sea trout and resident brown trout fisheries of the river are among the best in the south of England. History teaches us that the fine, world-renowned trout fisheries of the middle and upper reaches of the river have been managed by the riparian owners and their riverkeepers for several hundred years. These chalk streams are renowned for the abundance and diversity of water life that the fish require for food. Chalk streams, unlike the acidic waters of the clay and hard rock based catchments elsewhere in the country, provide ample calcium with which shrimps, snails and other creatures can build external skeletons. Studies have shown that within the Itchen eight species of stonefly nymphs, twenty species of *ephemeroptera* and *baetis*, including mayfly nymphs, thirty-eight species of caddis and sixty-seven other species of invertebrates have been recorded to date and I expect there are still more species yet to be identified by any one who cares to look.

I believed it was essential for me, as riverkeeper, to research the past if I was to understand and appreciate how the site evolved and how great has man's influence been on the environment by his past management and conservation of the river and its surrounds. I needed to know how, when and why all the ditches, streams and carriers that went to make up the fishing waters in the water meadow systems of the chalk stream valleys were created. I felt that an historical appreciation would be a valuable guide to my present management, otherwise many habitats would remain inexplicable. With that in mind I investigated how these man-made water-meadows changed the economy and ecology of the chalk land valleys.

The multi-channelled system of the river of today has evolved over the centuries. Before the first man stepped into the valley it was a heavily-wooded catchment with the entire flood plain appearing as an oozing bog with a heavily braided multitude of small silt laden channels seeping their way slowly towards the sea. These channels seeped their way slowly down towards the sea over layers of peat and through dense reed beds and mixed stands of native willow, alder, reed, carr and sedge. The flood plain must have looked like a steamy impenetrable Amazonian wetland jungle at that time.

With the arrival of man in the early Stone Age, followed by the Bronze Age and then Iron Age man, these populations gradually cleared the wooded hills to create grazing for their animals. Early man noticed that the greenery across the flood plain lasted well into winter whilst the cleared hill grasslands would stop growing with the onset of winter. To take advantage of this natural phenomenon and to provide watering areas for their live stock these early settlers began to clear the floodplain pushing many of the channels together to form larger man-made channels which tended to drain the floodplain leaving very fertile land to grow grass to feed livestock. The process expanded and many of the little silty channels were either filled in or closed off and the flows channelled into fewer and bigger channels thus speeding up the flow of the water towards the sea further helping to drain the land around and along the floodplain of the river and most significantly by lowering the water table.

The River Itchen today is not one stream but two, three or even more separate channels at times running almost parallel to each other. The River Itchen's banks are entirely man-made and the configuration of the water system is artificial. It is comprised of braided channels having a number of structures to regulate the flows and levels between them. The result is a very regulated river with very high water retention levels aided by the use of the sluices and hatch gates that are controlled mainly by the land owners although some are managed by the Water Authorities.

Three historic uses of the river gave rise to the maintenance of this multiplicity of channels: the harnessing of water power for wool washing, sheep dipping, milling, tanning and timber working; the use of water meadows systems to promote the early growth of grass for pastures; the development of the river for navigation. Further water-based industries that waxed and waned during the Middle Ages included wool processing, paper making, tanning, flour and grist milling as well as the more modern generation of electricity. The first mill was built in the 1300s and the last working mill closed in the 1960s. At one time there would have been a mill per mile of river.

One very interesting feature of the Upper Itchen is the huge causeway across the Alre Valley beside Alresford. This large structure that dams the River Alre was built on the orders of Bishop Godfrey de Lucy, the Bishop of Winchester in the Middle Ages in 1189 when Alresford was the centre of the wool trade in central southern England. This dam, when first built, impounded 200 acres of water from the River Alre which flowed into the main Itchen just below the town. The main purpose of this construction was to allow the wool to be carried downstream to Southampton where it was stored in the old wool shed, prior to the wool being sold and shipped to the continent – the wool shed is now a museum in dockland Southampton. The wool bales were stacked upon wooden rafts and after the rafts had been loaded, the hatches that impounded the water above the dam were lifted, releasing a huge amount of water and the manned rafts then rode this man-made flood all the way down the river to Southampton. This was long before the mills were built and any major river bridges that would have impeded the progress of these rafts. The dam, between New Alresford and Old Alresford, is still there today and is a causeway carrying a road along its entire length. The water impounded is now far less as the dam and its hatch system are not now strong enough to hold back so much water.

I learnt how and why the water-meadows were formed and operated in the preceding centuries and how man changed the valleys of the Hampshire chalk streams so dramatically. The term water-meadow is often used very loosely and can be defined as, 'a meadow which can be drained and flooded at the discretion of the farmer'. This can be distinguished from a flood-meadow, which was naturally flooded whenever the river overtopped its banks during high flows. The techniques of draining and flooding the water-meadows differed from one place to another, and from one generation to another, but it was clear that water-meadows were a form of irrigation. Today, these meadows are no longer irrigated, but the influence of man can still be seen.

Unfortunately, there was not a great deal of information on the meadows in the past, except for a few old maps and surveys that survived in the Hampshire Records Office, Winchester. I discovered other sources of information in the surveys of the Tithe Commissioners in the middle of the 1800s and in the records of the first Land Use Survey of Great Britain and in several books describing farming in Hampshire in the past.

I found it interesting to understand the management and use of water meadows, their appearance during their heyday and, most importantly, the effects of their decline on the ecology of the chalk streams as we see them today.

Farmers tried to accomplish two things in their water-meadows: first, they tried to drain the land of stagnant water; second, they irrigated the vegetation cover in times of water deficit. The techniques employed relied on the gradient of the land, the shape of the meadows and the timing of the irrigation.

Nearly all of the water-meadows in Hampshire were situated in chalkland valleys, or by streams which were fed by water which had already flowed through the chalk. Sandy soils with gravel subsoil formed the best sites and it is recorded that at Nine Mile Water at Nether Wallop in the Test Valley, where the water meadows were on hard gravels, were worth up to then £3 3s 0d per acre, compared to meadows on peaty soils which were valued at only £2 10s 0d per acre (Young 1795). There were therefore fewer sites with water-meadows on the Upper Itchen floodplain in the eighteenth century than elsewhere in the county because of the extensive areas of peat along the margins of the Upper Itchen.

It was found that the quality of the soil became less important after a few years of irrigation because the river water contained many nutrients derived from the chalky soils during run off and such nutrients as lime were also now being spread over the meadows. Thus, in time, the value of the meadows came to reflect the fertilizing qualities of the water rather than any inherent quality of the soil. On the other hand farmers required a free-draining soil so that there was no risk of the water stagnating on or beneath the meadow surface.

In order to keep the water moving a series of ridges and furrows were made. The ridges were usually 3 feet high and the water flowed into the meadows along carriers or trenches that were cut in the centre of the ridges. The water was allowed to run down the sides of the ridges into drains or channels made along the bottom of the furrows. The water came in at a 'trot' along the carriers and left at a 'gallop' along the drains and channels in the furrows. The secret of the success of this was in the experience of the men who operated this system who were called meadsmen or drowners. Their expert use of only the eye to determine gradients and their knowledge of the water flows of the river determined the width and spacing of the ridges. The drowners could regulate the input, throughput, and output of water through this system very accurately and hold the required flood level over a meadow to the fraction of an inch by the astute use of a cut piece of turf in the inlet or outlet channel.

The width of the ridges and furrows varied with the fall of the land and the free drainage of the soil. South of Winchester, ridges were low and simple, because there was a good slope, but north of the city the ground was very flat and so the ridges were massive and consequently became expensive to maintain. The remains of these ridges are quite evident and can still be clearly seen in many of the meadows that border the river between Winchester and Alresford.

Not all streams were fit for use as sources of irrigation of this type. Farmers generally found that a flourishing display of wild plants and animals in and around the stream often indicated that the water was suitable for irrigation. Yet some farmers expected dark, muddy water to be the richest in nutrients but that was not always the case. In 1810 a scientist by the name of Vancouver, showed that perfectly clear water was often very rich in nutrients and many other writers of the time commented on the clarity of the water of the Upper Itchen. Thomas Fuller in 1662 observed that no other county in England had so many 'clear and fresh rivulets of troutful water' as Hampshire. A sample of water taken from the River Itchen in the 1830s and analysed was shown to contain 2.5 parts of solid matter in every 10,000 parts, including chalk, gypsum and common salt. The farmers below Winchester found that as the use of irrigation grew above the city so the nutrient levels of the water they used decreased when re-used in their water meadows. To compensate for this the farmers turned to the Itchen navigation canal water that carried added nutrients of the sewage and run off of the roads and gutters of Winchester.

In its heyday the water-meadow irrigation encouraged the farmers to use every drop of water they could on their meadows and so became very skilled in exploiting the flows. To help them achieve this they dug and constructed many new high and low carriers and drainage ditches and, furthermore, built many hatch gates that created heads of water that would enable them to control very precisely the water levels in and out of these man-made channel systems.

A whole new system of high and low level carriers were dug, many of which can be seen today. The main benefits for the farmer were that on well-controlled meadow systems the land flooded with the constant 10°C (50°F)temperature spring water protected the ground from freezing, even in the hardest of winters. The water also deposited the required nutrients that encouraged grass to grow. The results were that the first growth of grass of the year would be available for sheep to graze in late February or at the latest early March. With a good rotation of flooding, grazing and fallowing, subsequent hay crops were prodigious and records of three cuts of hay per year with the maximum of two tons per acre were often recorded.

The start of the demise of the water meadow systems was first noted by Caird in 1852 when he observed that some of the water meadows were no longer receiving the attention as previously. There were several reasons for this decline. The work of operating the meadows was labour-intensive and the migration of manpower from the countryside into the towns and burgeoning cities was now increasing. The market for early lambs to London reduced and, as hay was the petrol of that age, the arrival of the steam train reduced the demand for year round hay to fuel horses. So farmers were unable to spend money working their marginal, less-profitable lands and so concentrated on the more manageable and easily workable downlands away from the labour-intensive flood plain operations.

The operation of the water-meadows affected the wildlife. Although there are few, if any, records it seemed likely that within these areas of intensely irrigated lands the incidence of wildlife was rather poor compared to the adjacent lands out of the floodplain. This would have been due to the heavy management by the meadsmen or drowners, the intensive grazing, the regular cycles of flooding, the draining and the ongoing clearing of the channels and ditches. Irrigation affected the bird populations and the ditches and channels were infested with rats and moles and farm records of the time recorded massive organised kills of these rodents. The impact of irrigation on the fish population received little attention but Berry, rather belatedly in 1935, stated that the water-meadows were blamed for serious losses in sport.

It is logical to believe that the water-meadows, when in full operation, may have taken a drastic toll on the numbers of migrating parr and smolts who lost their way in the rafts of cut weed and the regular clearing of the channels. Fish were diverted onto the flooded fields and left stranded when the water was released and, as these changes occurred rapidly, the avian predators and the rats had a bonanza. Any fish left in the mainstream would also have been deprived of a great deal of insect and plankton life to live on as much of this food was left high and dry in the drained meadows.

Today the water-meadows are ecologically very different from those of the early nineteenth century but on the other hand are not identical to the flood-meadows. It is highly likely that the old ridge and furrows, the now derelict carriers, drains and ditches still exert some influence on the micro habitat we see today in the Upper Itchen Valley. These old meadows are now in a transitional stage and are a relic feature that forms an extremely complex habitat. Each site is at a different stage of adjusting itself to the current conditions and knowledge of this ever-changing state is so important for the riverkeeper who now has the job of conserving this area of the Itchen Valley.

It is very interesting to note that in my researches I found that all the records that had been kept by the Avington Estate which dated back to medieval times and would have covered my area had been sold to a University in America. This occurred when the estate was broken up and sold in lots during and just after the last war. Within these records would have been a great deal of valuable information on the management of the River Itchen valley from early times. These records could explain a great deal about all that happened in and around the waters of the Upper Itchen over the last few hundred years. I would dearly love to be able to go to the USA and have a browse through those records because within them lies a great deal of valuable recorded history of the river that has been lost to the Itchen Valley and our nation. One of the many very interesting facts that came to light in my researches was that at Martyr Worthy the then glebe land that went with our local church of St Swithin and was called King's Mead is in fact the land that borders the middle beat on the fishery as it is now.

The revenue accrued from the hay crop taken from this glebe land was part of the incumbent vicar's stipend. The church records show that in good years two tons of hay per acre could be harvested from this area. Although there are now few, if any, rights to navigation on the river, historically there was a navigation channel between Winchester and Eastleigh which flowed parallel to, or coincident with, the river and for a short time was used by commercial craft. The coming of the railways put paid to the viability of this waterway. There is evidence also that the river was at one time navigable by small craft. The rafting downstream from Alresford mainly serviced the medieval wool and timber trade.

Owing to the unique nature of the geology within the river catchment, any rain, apart from that falling directly on the river and on the hardened man-made surfaces, soaks rapidly into the ground and in consequence, on average, there are only moderate major annual fluctuations in river levels. Historic records show that serious flooding has occurred in Winchester in 1852, 1903, 1928, and 1947 and to a lesser extent in the winter of 2001/2 where, at one time the river on my bottom beat was 200 metres wide and flowing over the Easton road. Fortunately no serious damage was done and all the footbridges survived. In the Upper Itchen again there was a bad flood in Kingsworthy in 1935, caused by the hatch gates of a river-powered sawmill becoming jammed shut which resulted in the river overflowing and flooding the village.

During this period of intensive learning about what a chalk stream was all about I also needed to learn more about the brown trout that lived in the river. I was fortunate to find a wonderful book, *The Trout*, written by those two renowned fisheries biologists Dr Winifred Frost and Dr Margaret Brown. Within this definitive work on the brown trout of the British Isles lay all the information I needed and even today this book is never far from my fingertips. To make it even more interesting a great deal of the research that went into producing that reference book was carried out by Dr Margaret Brown on my beat of the River Itchen.

As riverkeeper on the Itchen I had to be in a position to do a good job and have a good knowledge of the entire life cycle of the trout from egg through to five years old. By studying and understanding this life cycle and then observing all the life stages in my river I soon began to learn how to pinpoint and identify any bottlenecks that were controlling the survival of the fish at each of these life stages. At each life stage the trout require different habitats and there are certain natural or man-made events that control the survival at each life stage or are limiting factors. I had to acquire the ability to identify such factors and reduce their effect. Wild brown trout from swim up fry stage onwards require space, cover, food and protection from all forms of predator right through to good spawning and egg incubation conditions, all in good quality water. The more I learnt about the brown trout the more I became aware that this species of fish is quite remarkable in its abilities to adapt and survive in a variety of different habitats. I had to 'learn the life cycle of the trout and then think like a trout'.

I had only to look at all the introductions of brown trout by the trout fishing enthusiasts of the Victorian era to see that many of the countries of the world, which were once marked pink in our childhood atlases, had self-sustaining populations of brown trout in their rivers and streams. I learnt that sea trout were only brown trout that had decided to go to sea for a while before they came back to spawn. It is now known that only the female of the species produces a sea-going population and even if a female sea trout mates with a resident cock brown trout the offspring act like sea trout and return to the sea. A cock sea trout that mates with a resident brown trout female produces offspring which are predominantly river living.

Yet history taught me that the original brown trout that were introduced to the rivers of the Falkland Isles deep in the south Atlantic originated from an inland race of brown trout from England. It was only because the food availability in the Falkland rivers was so sparse that the rivers were unable to successfully support a large weight of fish and the species turned to the sea for their food in order to survive and only used the rivers at spawning time. The young that hatched out soon descended back to the sea to grow on, and so a wonderful sea trout population was created in the rivers of the Falklands from a so-called, inland strain of brown trout. The resident trout of these Falkland rivers rarely grow to any size but the returning sea trout do grow to prodigious sizes.

In Canada, where brown trout from Europe that were introduced to the rivers which flow into the Great Lakes, have, for similar reasons, established a 'lake run' strain of trout who come up the rivers to spawn and the young of the year return to the lake to grow on to maturity, thus using the Great Lakes as their sea. Scientists discovered that up to 15% of the Atlantic salmon that returned to the northern hemisphere rivers were the by product of a brown trout male fertilising a female Atlantic salmon. I can testify that could be the case as I have witnessed sexually precocious brown trout parr fertilizing the eggs from a 12lb mature Atlantic salmon in the Upper Itchen.

One remarkable recorded fact that always amuses me is that of a single brown trout who lived to the ripe old age of twenty-six years at the bottom of a shallow well in Hampshire and which on its demise had attained the length of only seven inches in all those years.

There are also the slob trout which are brown trout that have not quite made up their minds whether to stay in the river or go to sea so stay in the estuaries and come in and out with the tides as they ebb and flow.

My studies taught me that the brown trout was a most wonderful and valuable asset to the waters of this country in all its various shapes and forms. *Salmo trutta* was well worth all the effort people were devoting to its protection, enhancement and restoration. Wild and native populations of brown trout provided a wonderful barometer to the health of our rivers, streams, lochs and lakes and were in fact a measure of the health of our human environment.

The more I knew about the river system's state, evolution and history became essential knowledge that influenced and moulded my duties as a riverkeeper. It is a long story but such a very important one in the history and future welfare of the River Itchen.

~ 3 ~
Riverkeeper at Last

aving begun to accumulate some general knowledge about the river I started my work as a riverkeeper officially on the first of October, 1972. Through Paula's building merchant we were able to arrange for a new kitchen to be fitted in the cottage. We also arranged Sunday lunch parties for our friends when they were given lunch and then handed a paintbrush. That way the whole cottage was decorated from top to toe and when we moved in all was fresh and new. Then Paula started her learning curve as a riverkeeper's wife.

Paula had to get used to me being on the river most of the day and late into the night on summer evenings when the fishing continued until dark at which point everyone adjourned to the Chestnut Horse. Paula also got used to having the Rayburn in the kitchen draped with wet waders, boots and sundry clothing – though she had her own back in the winter when horse rugs would be drying on the boiler (the smell has to be experienced).

The benefits of life at Martyr Worthy were many. It was a wonderful place to live. Paula was able to keep her horse, Daisy, in the paddock next to the cottage and many residents of the village will remember her trotting by around the village. We reared spaniel puppies, Paula training the young dogs until they were, what I called, civilised and had a sufficient amount of discipline to walk to heel, sit, stay and come here. I took the dogs on and introduced them to the joys and disciplines of hunting and picking up game birds. Paula did the majority of the kennel work – washing muddy spaniels after a day's shooting, feeding and grooming – but they were very much a joint effort and we both enjoyed them very much.

After several years working in the pharmaceutical industry in the modernised, dusty, noisy and gridlocked traffic of Southampton, Eastleigh and Winchester it soon became apparent that there was not a more refreshing or peaceful place than the green, level valley of the River Itchen close by one of the quiet sleepy villages of the Upper Itchen Valley. Here land and water intermixed with the greenest of water meadows and the crystal clear currents of the river which divided and subdivided only to join again forming many an island and a long slip of meadow with streams on either side as it ran its 32 mile course from Alresford to Southampton.

The Keeper's Cottage ~ No6 Off Church Lane, Martyr Worthy.

I was among the most characteristic of small Hampshire villages with their old thatched cottages, mostly unalike, yet all harmonising in an irregular fashion along the roadsides. The village churches with their low towers and shingled spires surrounded by large trees of oak, ash, beech and chestnut. Alas, by this time, Dutch elm disease had taken hold and was decimating the large stands of the mighty elms that grew within the Valley.

After the traumas of moving house, I remember so well climbing into my new chest waders and stropping my scythe to Wilkinson Sword sharpness. I stood on the Martyr Worthy footbridge that very first early autumn morning pinching myself again to make sure it was really me who stood there as keeper of that wonderful beat of the river. Even now, 34 years on, it sometimes doesn't seem possible that it all happened in the way that it did and on one of the most beautiful stretches of chalk stream in the world that survives still on self-sustaining stocks of wild brown trout. I still now utter regularly a small prayer of thanks that I have been privileged to spend such a large part of my working life doing what I had always wanted to do.

As I walked downstream to the bottom boundary, to start the autumn weed cut, I was walking on clouds, so happy did I feel. Little did I know that the day was

Going weed cutting with my helpers.

to have a great influence on my early riverkeeping life. After a couple of hours cutting, just upstream of Easton road bridge which was the bottom boundary, a silver Simca estate car pulled up in the layby beside the bridge. A bearded figure walked out onto the bridge, leaned over the handrail and introduced himself to me as the riverkeeper, Pat Fox, on the beat below.

Pat Fox had been working on the river for about five years and had come from the River Kennet originally where his father had been gamekeeper for many years. Wanting to get on with my weed cutting I agreed to take up his kind invitation to join him at his local pub, the New Inn (now the Percy Hobbs) on the Alresford road on the other side of the village, for a pint at lunch time. Subsequently, this local pub became known as 'The Office' and many a visitor invited to meet us in our office soon found themselves in the bar of our local.

Thus, at that lunchtime, began a great friendship that has been fun and from which I was to learn so much about riverkeeping and chalk stream ways.

It transpired that Pat had served as an armourer in the RAF and, as I too had done my time in the Army, we had much in common. I soon found out that we also shared a similar wicked sense of humour, which at times over the years was to lead us both astray.

In those early days there were no colleges or schools to which I could go and learn about riverkeeping and riverkeeping skills could not be learnt from a book. All riverkeeping knowledge and experience was passed on by word of mouth, personal contact and hands-on tuition from a peer of the craft and from one generation of riverkeeper to the next. It was necessary to have the ability to accumulate carefully good knowledge and experience by actually working regularly all year round on a river. My formative years were guided by two of the greatest professional mentors a budding riverkeeper could possibly have had, Frank Sawyer and Pat Fox. I made it my business to be in their company as much as I could in my early years and hardly a week would go by when I did not pick up some nugget of information or tip which was then absorbed and retained by a very attentive beginner. I would spend many an hour over a pint discussing the aspects of riverkeeping, and weed cutting was a subject that kept us at the bar for a long time. I'm sure my wife, Paula, thought I only went to the pub for the beer.

There was also no better teacher than the river itself, simply by observing and learning how it worked throughout its annual cycle. To look, listen and learn costs nothing and as a dedicated disciple I set forth to try to put all this newly acquired knowledge into practice on my little piece of river.

One day, whilst talking about weed cutting over that lunch-time pint, I asked Pat about cutting weed in the deep water areas of my beat that could not be negotiated by wading to be cut by hand. Chain scythes were the answer he said but to operate a set of chains required two or more people. Pat volunteered straight away to help me cut the deep areas with a set of chain scythes that were hung up in my shed.

With Pat's experience of chain scythes on the River Kennet we set out to cut weed. Apparently, on the River Kennet where the river was deep in places, wide sets of chains were used that had twenty or more blades but the manpower needed to operate them was high. In these circumstances the local village tug-of-war teams were enlisted, for the price of a few pints, to pull the chains

At my 'office' desk in *The Chestnut Horse*.

Clearing cut weed after a weed cut.

upstream. This method not only cut a great deal of weed but was excellent practice for the tug-of-war teams and for the content of the till in the local pub.

The chain scythes were very awkward sets of equipment comprising twelve or more blacksmith-made scythe blades bolted together with a hinge between each join and lengths of stout rope attached to an iron D-loop and swivel at either ends. Each blade was slightly curved, the whole set taking on a crescent profile which, when sharpened, could be used in deep areas of the river to cut large amounts of weed. The blades were allowed to sink to the river bed and a sawing motion was achieved by alternate pulling by a man at each end of the ropes opposite each other across the river. The weed was cut by slowly moving upstream. When used correctly, they were very efficient at cutting weed but they did have one major drawback – they cut everything in their path with little or no selective cutting.

Chain scythes and motorised weed cutting boats could cut huge amounts of weed but unless they were used by experienced operators much damage could be done. Indiscriminate cutting encouraged the wrong sort of weeds to proliferate that, over time, affected the habitat of the trout. It was good advice for a young riverkeeper to consider.

The main objective of cutting weed in a chalk stream was to control the river level because a river channel of this nature could soon become choked with excessive weed growths and the resulting rising levels of water could very soon over top and undermine the riverbanks or, even more damagingly, flood valuable property. This high water could also make the soft banks impassable to fishermen. Weed was also cut and managed by the riverkeepers for the benefit of the fish, particularly where weed growth was strong and the fish species were brown trout.

Over the centuries riverkeepers learnt to identify all the various species of aquatic weed that grew in a chalk stream. By observation I also learnt which particular weeds the trout preferred as well as which were good for breeding and holding insect life which were the staple diet of trout in the chalk streams.

Frank Sawyer said to me one day, 'There is no bad weed it's just some species are better than others, and also bad weed is better than no weed at all'.

Living beside the Itchen and working in and around it for hours and days on end in my own company encouraged my mind to wander healthily which helped me to maintain a much saner outlook on life and enabled me to cope more readily with all the traumas of the growing, crazy, computer-driven age. No need for Valium or Prozac, the River Itchen was always there to calm frayed nerves.

In all our lives personal tragedy and worldwide happenings can and do become difficult to comprehend and cope with at times. At such times it was a saviour to me as a few hours spent alone working or just being by the river soon brought things back into perspective and gave me the mental strength to soldier on in a happier frame of mind.

As my keeper's experience grew over time I become very adept at utilising the current of the river to wash away accumulated silt. By carefully patching out the weed growth with a hand scythe I learnt how to manipulate and direct flows by judiciously leaving a bed of weed here and there and cutting through another to create a channel to speed up the current and direct it onto a silt bed. Moving water was the energy that I could harness to keep the bed of the river clean. The general principle was to cut the weed in such a pattern that the water flow spread equally across the channel so that it flowed at the same speed along the riverbank as it did in mid-channel. This weed cutting technique was called the chequer board effect where the black squares represented the trimmed weed beds and the white squares were the clean, weed-cleared, gravel river bed.

Where there were large silt beds it needed an area of weed of large proportions to deflect a sufficient volume of water to clear it. Again, experience told me how big this weed bed had to be and, most importantly, where it had to be located upstream of the silt bed so that the right amount of flow was diverted at the right angle. It was a good idea to keep an eye on the shape and positions of all the uncut weed beds upstream of the area that were being cut to assist in forward planning.

Cutting weed with a scythe was always carried out by working upstream and a start was made tight in and under the right-hand bank looking upstream. By working away across the channel and returning again to take a further swathe, slow progress was made upstream. In this fashion the cutter was always working in clear water so it was easy to see the weed underwater and the cutting action was downstream so that cut weed flowed away from the cutting blade and did not bind round the scythe handle.

While cutting it was important to keep in mind the creation of trout cover and trout feeding lies. Many times I observed trout taking up their feeding positions in front of a clump of weed and if that weed was not cut it would remain the trout's lie for the season. It was a simple exercise to move that trout to another lie by cutting out that clump of weed. I could, as I did many times, move trout about the river by just manipulating their feeding lies much to the chagrin of some of my fisherman. Cover was an essential consideration for trout and whilst weed cutting, tresses of weed were left to afford good hiding cover.

Weed cutting in a well-managed chalk stream was not just a matter of getting in and cutting everything in sight. By using good weed cutting practices the resident population of wild trout could be quite evenly dispersed throughout the river so giving more opportunities for fishermen.

Finally, I learnt to identify all the different species of aquatic weed and discovered which ones were beneficial. I used this knowledge to cut out the lesser weeds and thus encouraged the better species. I was underwater gardening.

~~~~~

My first autumn weed cut took me almost three weeks to complete on my own as the length of the main river under my care extended to approximately one mile (1.6 kilometres) upstream from Easton road bridge to the famous Chilland Shallows which at that time were owned by Major Allen and keepered by John Binns.

Besides the mainstream there was a carrier stream that came off the main river at the tail of the top beat just below the Chilland Shallows and meandered in a rough D-loop to the south side returning to the main river 50 yards (46 metres) above the bottom boundary of Easton road bridge. The bank yardage of this carrier was in the region of 1000 yards (914 metres). This beautiful little stream, despite being narrowed too drastically in the late 1980s, was the Upper Itchen in miniature and was, and still is, a wonderful trout nursery. The fishing upon it at that time was kept solely for the son of the owner to fish. This carrier took some time to weed cut and almost doubled the time I spent weed cutting during the rigidly adhered to weed cutting periods.

Besides this carrier there was a further carrier that entered the river at the very top of our water. At that time it belonged to Dermot Wilson, the doyen of dry-fly fishermen, who had agreed to pay a fee to our estate for me to tend this stream. Looking back all those years there was just one hell of a lot of weed to be cut by one person. However, being keen and very fit in those days I did manage most of the time to complete the job single-handed.

The July cut did cause problems at times as the allotted dates to cut were restricted to just five days during that month. It was the owners who dictated and allotted the dates when weed cutting could be done during each month with, at that time, little or no consultation with the keepers who had to do the job. If the weed growth was particularly strong, and it usually was at that time of year, to finish the job satisfactorily in five days, single-handed, was almost impossible. This was an ongoing bone of contention between the keepers and the owners and caused considerable dissent.

There were times when I got behind in my schedule to finish the July cut in the allotted five days, knowing that even if I started at 7.30am in the morning

The *Itchen Vale* springer spaniels almost behaving!
(*left to right*) Penny, Poppy, Lizzie, Snoopy, Sam Brown, Toby, Pixie.

and worked until 10pm in the evening I would still not be able to finish the job to my satisfaction. It was not possible to cut that amount of river regularly and single-handedly over a period of thirty years without it eventually taking its toll on the joints of the body. I know this for a fact from the screws in my hips, knees and shoulders. Experience taught me that no one in their right senses cuts river weed for more than three hours at a stretch without taking a break. Six hours hard cutting with a scythe is enough for anyone in one day. Riverkeepers did not get paid overtime in those days, it was all time off in lieu. Also to hire any help was unheard of unless the keeper himself was prepared to pay the helper out of his own pocket and on a keeper's wage that was highly unlikely.

During weed cutting times, I would be working all day in the river in order to cut the weed in the allotted time which, as all chalk stream riverkeepers will say, was never long enough. Around mid-morning Paula would trot down to the river armed with hot or cold drinks according to the temperature and with lumps of fruit cake to keep up my energy levels. Paula, when the occasion demanded and long before mobile phones, would stand at the top of the lawn and shout for me when I was needed urgently or if, as happened more than once, I went off weed cutting with both sets of car keys in my pocket and she had an urgent appointment.

A view of the middle beat showing the fringe at the river edge, the maintained path and one of the three fishing huts.

Anyone who has cut river weed for any length of time will appreciate that whilst in the river, weed cutting for days on end by oneself, the mind did tend to wander off into other, sometimes surreal, realms of thought. It was on one such day towards the end of my career when in the river weed cutting that I started to mentally calculate how many miles of river I had cut by hand in my time as a keeper. After some lengthy mental arithmetic the figure I arrived at was a staggering 246 miles (396 kilometres) of the Upper Itchen. I also then went on to contemplate how many tons of weed I had cut in all those years. A further rough calculation led me to think that in all those years I had cut around 2000 tons (2,048 tonnes) of weed. No wonder my joints are complaining these days!

During the first fifteen years I did become much stronger physically and with more experience became quicker and more adept at cutting. Thankfully the allotted weed cutting dates and times were eventually altered by the Test & Itchen Association, but only after long and protracted discussions via 'Scrappy' Hay and backed by a then strong Hampshire River Keepers' Association (HRKA). The then Southern Water Authority and the Test and Itchen Association were very reluctant to co-operate. Unfortunately some members of the board of the T&I even accused the HRKA of trying to be a dominant trade union but this accusation was dropped when common sense finally prevailed.

Being invited to join the Hampshire River Keepers' Association was the next milestone in my learning curve in riverkeeping. I had heard of and read about many of the well-known riverkeepers who worked either on the River Test or Itchen. I had not met many of them and I looked forward eagerly to the annual AGM of the Association where I was told that I would be proposed and seconded for membership. I well remember that evening when we all met at Leckford Village Hall and being proposed by Jim Collinson who was keeper on the River Alre at Alresford some four miles upstream of my beat at Martyr Worthy. My seconder was Jim Norgate who was keeper for the then Lord Ashburton at Itchen Stoke some one and a half miles upstream of my water.

I was so proud being in such illustrious company and being able to listen in awe to all the humour and pearls of riverkeeping wisdom from such well-known keepers as Ernie Mott from Leckford, Ted Clare from the Dever, Bernard Aldrich from Broadlands, Vic Foot from Nursling, Jock MacKenzie from Whitchurch, Dave Walford and Fred Kemp from the Test, Jack Jones and Mick Didlick from Eastleigh, Pat Fox and Joe Saunders and Jim Collinson and Jim Norgate from the Itchen and so many others who had spent so much of their working lives dedicated to caring for our chalk streams. Not forgetting the inimitable Mick Lunn from the Houghton Club, although not joining the HRKA he did support our aims and was always willing to help and advise on any river matters.

Over the years I have often thought that if only someone could gather, record and archive the combined knowledge and experience from all those men, what a wonderfully informative and very humorous book it would be. Sadly, as and when these knowledgeable men retired or passed on, so much invaluable practical riverkeeping experience and knowledge was lost.

~~~~~

For my first five years as a riverkeeper I was so fortunate in having such an excellent and knowledgable employer as Mr Denzil Ffennell. He was not only an excellent dry-fly fisherman but one of the most informed men on plants and insects I have ever known, in fact, on all forms of natural life that lived and grew in and around the river. He was also acknowledged as one of the country's leading lepidopterists. His knowledge on moths and butterflies was amazing. The stories he would relate to me of some of his escapades in his pursuit of a particular species of moth in some far flung corner of the British Isles would have me in fits of laughter at times. In his company I was able to learn so much about the insects and the wild plants of the Itchen Valley.

One morning on the river when Mr Ffennell had come down to fish and we were sitting on a bench waiting for the first trout to rise, he asked me to pace out ten paces along the river edge and then count how many different species of plant there were within those ten paces. I spent a good ten minutes on my hands and knees counting what I thought were every single plant species and came up with a grand total of twelve species some of which I knew by sight and name but had not a clue as to some of the others. Without leaving the bench Mr Ffennell said there were 26 species in the same area that I had paced out. The next hour we both spent on our knees as he pointed out, named and identified each species and he was right, there were 26. His enthusiasm for such things was infectious and from then on I made it my object to learn and identify as many of the wild plants that grew in the Valley as I could.

By looking closely at Mr Ffennell's fishing rod it gave me an excellent indication as to the best equipment with which to tackle the wild trout of the river. Although glass fibre was at that time the new revolutionary man-made material from which fly rods were being made in the early 1970s, being the traditionalist that he was Mr Ffennell still used a nine foot Hardy Triumph split cane rod. The reel was a classic Hardy Perfect loaded with a Kingfisher Nº 2 silk line, the leaders were of nylon which was about the only modern material he would ever consider using. I sat and watched him fly-fishing for many an hour and observed the way he approached and fished those gin-clear waters of the Itchen. He had fished this river since he was a boy and to me it was very evident from his tactics he was indeed an expert on the Upper Itchen and I knew I could learn a great deal if I watched him.

During those formative and learning years I soon became aware that the patterns of the work a riverkeeper engaged himself upon revolved entirely around the four seasons. More importantly I learnt that intertwined within those four seasons lay the life cycle of the wild brown trout.

One other thing for sure was that a riverkeeper's job was certainly not a nine to five occupation nor was it a five day a week job, or least it was not in those early days. When I came into the profession keepers were paid to do a job and, depending on the season of the year, the weather and what work there was to be done a working day could range from four to fifteen hours. If at times there was not much to do, which was a state that rarely occurred, I could take things a little easier and either work my dogs, go fishing, play cricket or even go shopping with Paula.

In my early days I would often go a couple of months without a day away from the river as I was expected to be on parade every week day and weekend whenever fishermen were on the river – I almost felt guilty taking time off to go for a haircut.

Weekends were particularly busy usually attending to guests of the tenants. Overtime pay and weekly pay-slips were unheard of in those days and right up to the time I retired. As the years went on I decided that weekends were for the family so, unless expressly asked, I did not appear for long on the river at weekends yet I was usually on call if there was an emergency.

During the trout fishing season, which in Hampshire commenced on the 2 April and ended on the 31 October, I had to be very aware that fisherman would be about the river at any time between those dates.

The 'carpet slipper' fishing, required by some owners, was to me the extreme whereby the riverbanks were made up and mown regularly to represent a well-manicured lawn. This produced a very pretty Victorian garden effect and, although this over-cultivated scene may have been aesthetically attractive to the uneducated eye, the wild trout did not always agree as their chosen and required habitat had been manicured out of sight. The riverside vegetation trimmed back to regimental box hedge standards and the in-river weed manicured like a well-managed herbaceous border with fishing huts decked out with hanging baskets of exotic flowers was not quite my idea of what a riverkeeper's job really was. Even by this early time in my career I had the view that a wild trout fishery had to look and even feel like a wilderness. The measure of the wildness of a fishery needed to be inversely proportional to its artificiality, so striking the happy balance between the both was my aim for all the years I keepered the Martyr Worthy beat. At the same time it was necessary to manage the wilderness to such an extent that allowed fisherman reasonably comfortable access yet without taking away the wilderness experience from the fisherman.

The topography of the Martyr Worthy water lent itself to being split up into three beats. Each beat had almost an equal diversity of holding cover and habitat for trout and for most of the time the catches from each beat would be very similar when taken over a whole season. To my mind the top beat was the best of the three, but if there was even a hint of wind then dry-fly fishing became very difficult as there was little protection from the wind that blew from any quarter. The middle and bottom beats were quite protected from the prevailing winds that come from the south-west and blew upstream as the river at this point flowed east to west and even in strong downstream easterlies a fisherman was still able to present a reasonable fly.

At Martyr Worthy in the early 1970s there were two full rods who were entitled to fish every day of the season if they so wished. They were allotted a whole beat each thus occupying two of the three beats. The third beat was shared between two rods; one would fish Monday to Thursday and the other

Friday to Sunday, The fisherman were also rotated around, the beats changing every Monday; each fisherman would have equal opportunity to fish each beat on a regular basis throughout the entire season. It all sounds very complicated but it worked quite well.

When I arrived at Martyr Worthy I inherited from my predecessor, Frank Moores, a wild flock of English game bantams which lived in the wild in the woods beside my cottage. Apparently they had been there for many years and the riverkeepers that had preceded me over the years had used these birds to furnish much of the required materials for the dressing of suitable dry flies for use on the Upper Itchen. I continued to do the same and as time went by I would cull some of these gorgeous cock birds when they were at their peak of condition. I would carefully skin them and preserve their skins for the wonderful range of colours and texture of the narrow feathers that some of the cock capes would provide.

Anyone who has ever reared bantams in almost wild conditions, as they were at Martyr Worthy, will agree that they are very independent creatures that will fend for themselves very well but most of all they are very early risers in the morning. Having arrived home rather late one night, at about 2am from over-celebrating a good win at cricket, I fell into bed. Despite the effects of the anaesthetic taken the evening before I was soon to be awakened from my deep slumbers at three o'clock by half a dozen mature cock English game bantams energetically welcoming in the dawn right under our bedroom window. As it was late June the dawn came rather early.

After nearly suffocating myself under a pillow and still not getting back to sleep, I jumped out of bed and, being summertime, was absolutely starkers. I stumbled off to my gun cupboard and took out my trusty twelve bore and a handful of light cartridges. As quietly as the squeaky stairs would allow I crept down and gently opened the ground floor lounge window and taking rather an unsteady aim proceeded to blast away at these noisy birds. I completed two clean right and lefts before they had a chance to scuttle off, but unfortunately the fifth bird was a runner which hobbled off down the lawn heading back to the woods from whence it came. Without a thought I grabbed my 'fore and after' hat from behind the kitchen door and put it on and jumped into my wellies that were parked beside the back door.

Out I went with gun under my arm and let out the spaniels from their kennel who were all by this time wide-eyed and wagging their tails with expectation from the hearing the shots. Together the spaniels and I walked down the lawn and with the commands 'Get on' and 'Hi lost' I sent the spaniels off to find the wounded bantam. My leader of the pack bitch soon found it and made the perfect retrieve and presentation to hand. Walking back up the lawn carrying a brace and half of bantam cocks I noticed Paula leaning out of the bedroom window crying with laughter. She was convulsed at the sight of me starkers wearing only a hat and wellies and a shotgun under the arm, carrying a brace and a half of bantam cocks and with three spaniels walking obediently to heel. What a picture! She said it would look good on the cover of the Shooting Times. I'm sure I had by this time also awakened the neighbours though I didn't see any curtains moving at bedroom windows but I did get some funny looks next day. Heaven knows what they may have seen.

Donald Downs

~ 4 ~
Maintaining the Status Quo

In the early years, the tenants, or rods as I preferred to call them, were somewhat typical of the clientele that one would expect to find on any beat of the exclusive waters of the Itchen and Test. An admiral, a newly retired captain of industry, another retired former naval person, a retired naval commander and an active man from the City who dabbled in stocks and shares made up the complement of rods who then fished my water. It did not take very long for me to get to know each rod very well although in those early days being called solely by my surname took some getting used to. I soon taught myself to accept this and even treated it almost as a compliment.

Fortunately, attitudes changed since those early days both in the fishermen, the owners and the keepers and Christian names were used more frequently. That old master and servant relationship, which existed when I started keepering, started to disappear and was replaced with a more humane friendliness that was better for all concerned. Any success in employer and employee relationships had to be based upon mutual respect for without it things can only disintegrate. However, being the early 1970s, it was still a few years off before things of this nature began to change. Coming into my profession as a riverkeeper, as and when I did, I was to witness several major social and cultural and economic driven changes in the countryside.

With the knock-on affects of World War II, and the post-war economic difficulties in the country's economy, many of the estates that had previously survived on inherited money began to feel the pinch. This started a landslide of nationwide changes in the countryside from which the Itchen Valley and Hampshire were not exempt.

Over the country some big estates either changed hands or were split up into smaller parcels and sold off. Pheasant and partridge shooting was an ideal example and acted as a barometer of the changes that came about. Private shoots, which for years had been very private, were no longer so and the guns were not necessarily all invitees and friends of the shoot owner.

During my first seven years at Martyr Worthy I was fortunate to have loaded (double-gunned) for Mr Ffennell on some of the most historically renowned

'Picking up' on a pheasant shoot at Easton Manor Farm.

pheasant shoots around the country. Together I believe we saw almost the last of the traditionally run big private shoots in Hampshire where all the guns were guests and where quality of the birds produced over the guns was far more important than numbers of birds shot. Many of these estates were increasingly forced to try to defer costs by letting days to shooting parties of strangers who could afford at least the cost of putting on the day. So the day of the let day and corporate entertainment shoot day commenced in earnest. In time the paying guns may have managed to shoot their allotted number of birds but quality of presentation seemed to be of secondary importance mainly because most of the shooters had no clue as to what a quality bird was. These new commercial shoots that for so long lived on their historical reputation of quality, found that the costs of producing a bird over a gun increased and their profits decreased. Some wonderful shoots around Hampshire, which were so well-known before the War and just after, soon became history themselves. To a shooter evocative names like Longwood, Tichborne, Hursley Park, Sutton Manor, Hackwood Park, alas are no more but sweet memories to the true sporting gun. The farmer's shoot and private syndicate shoots still survive on 50 to 200 bird days but even so many of these now have some paying guests to help defray costs.

Game fishing on the chalk streams was not exempt from the same malaise. Our fishery at Martyr Worthy was somewhat protected from the economic traumas under which shooting and other fisheries were then labouring. Fortunately it was decreed from my earliest days that the policy to be followed was that the fishery was run to break even over the course of one year and that while profit was not the initial aim neither was a huge loss.

The late Mr Denzil Ffennell explained to me, quite simply and clearly, that all the outgoings and costs of the fishery were to be balanced out by the income accrued from the tenant fishermen and their rents and that all the owners required from all this was that they were able to fish their own well-keepered and well-maintained water for little or no further major outlay. The costs of a full-time riverkeeper, a tied cottage and its overheads, repairs to and replacement of tools, the purchasing of materials for bridge and bank repairs were added up each year and divided between the number of tenants and the resulting figure determined the rental cost for each tenant. Quite a simple mathematical calculation and it worked for many years. The sums rarely balanced out exactly as there were usually unforeseen circumstances that were not budgeted for, such as a grass mower blowing up or a chainsaw being stolen or the natural disaster caused by the 1987 hurricane.

Although the policy of not making a profit continued for all the time I was keeper I felt, towards the end, that the owner wanted to make some profit upon which he could draw. Although the annual level of fees for a full rod on the river was directly geared to outgoings these naturally escalated in line with costs of living and ever-rising inflation. Rod fees went from several hundreds to many hundreds of pounds over the thirty years but there were always people out there who could and were willing to pay. The economic and related going rates for quality fishing was maintained and I always seemed to have a waiting list of half a dozen people who would have been happy to pay whatever was asked for a rod on my water. Even today there are probably few, if any, chalk stream fisheries that rely on fishing lets to generate sufficient income revenue to adequately covers costs, let alone make any appreciable profits.

~~~~~~

The accepted working year of a riverkeeper usually ended and commenced on the first day of October as Michaelmas was the traditional time for agricultural workers and riverkeepers to change jobs, if they were of a mind to move on to pastures greener. On the river these dates coincided with the ending of the permitted trout fishing season.

The legal fishing dates fluctuated over time but were fixed in law by the Environment Agency, the governing body, as the period from 1 April through to 31 October. As long as a fishery started and finished their season within these dates then all was legal. On the Upper Itchen where self-sustaining populations of wild brown trout predominated we started fishing on 1 May and finished on 16 October. The reason for this late start was that the spawning fish of the previous winter would have longer time to recover and regain body condition on the burgeoning insect life by 1 May and the ripening females in the back end of the year would be protected by curtailing the fishing on 16 October.

As the fishing season ended the autumn weed cut commenced which opened up and prepared the gravel for trout to spawn in December and January. Excess river weed was cut and any accumulated silt removed and withered bankside vegetation tidied up. Once completed the river was 'put to bed' until late spring.

From November through to the end of February the spawning gravels were checked and enhanced where necessary. Spawning trout were protected from predators and any untoward human interventions in the vulnerable areas. Structural repairs and new constructions were planned and commenced encompassing repairs to banks, construction and repairs to bridges and other general repairs. Trees had to be pruned, lopped and pollarded. During warm days in February there was some insect activity with large dark olives hatching out around midday and the odd trout rising to feed off the surface.

As days lengthened and day temperatures rose so the first signs of spring appeared around the river margins by which time, with luck, all of the major structural work was completed. The first signs of a successful spawning season were evident by the appearance of masses of young trout fry in the margins of the river downstream of the redd from which they had just emerged. If I observed that the swim-up fry mortality was too high, as a result of little or no fry cover at the margins of the river, I enhanced their habitat by setting twiggy branches into the riverbank to collect floating debris and provide extra cover and planktonic food for the vulnerable trout fry to allow these little fish to grow. I had learnt how to mitigate the identified bottleneck at this particular life stage. I became more conversant with all of the life stages and where they took place in the river so that the limiting factors became apparent and could be addressed.

Spring also heralded the first weed cutting period of the year and, in the years of strong weed growth, the April cut established the pattern of weed growth for the rest of the year. Weed was cut in most months from April onwards but only at set times, which were stringently adhered to by all riverkeepers. If this was not done then I would have been cutting weed somewhere on the river every day which would have ruined river conditions for all fishermen. In May the weed cut was restricted to 5 days only, and during the month insect life improved with the appearance of large dark olives and medium olives and sometimes iron blues at the latter end of the month on cold wet days.

The long warm summer days of June welcomed all the migratory birds back to the Valley. Such conditions caused the river weed to grow apace so that further cutting was required. The fishermen were out in force and rarely a day went by without a fisherman, somewhere on the river, requiring my attention. With vegetation running wild the bank paths around the river had to be kept open with regular cutting, as did the river margin vegetation to allow reasonable access to the water for the fly fisher. Insect activity was at its height during June with a full set of expected species and fishing went on well into the evening with some anglers not leaving until well after dark.

As the summer progressed things begin to quieten down for a while as insect activity waned during the day with some increased activity after the sun went off the water on hot days. The July weed cut was the heaviest of the whole year and the allotted days were seldom sufficient to complete the task. The blue-winged olive was the most abundant insect in July hatching from early morning through to late evening and sedge fly activity was apparent most evenings and good sport is to be had with this insect's imitation.

Late summer brought the 'dog days' with little or no appreciable insect activity to interest trout during the day. The remedy was to sit in the shade, read a book and drink river-cooled white Burgundy, although weed had to be cut and the footpaths kept open.

During September, as summer moved into autumn, the insect life re-awakened and hatches were expected each day increasing as the month progressed, similar to the pattern that of May. There was usually no need to cut weed at this time as growth slowed as the days shortened. The following harvest moons and mellow fruitfulness were often excellent for fishing, although the evenings were cool and the insect activity peaked around midday and early afternoon.

There were always things to do: there were fishing huts to make ready for winter; fences and signs required constant attention; preparations had to be made for the huge autumn weed cut. Invariably there was some unforeseen crisis during the season requiring immediate attention when trees fell down, a gale blew the roof off a hut or a tree collapsed into the river.

So ended my year – for everything to start and be repeated all over again.

One of the first major experiments I undertook was to try and increase the spawning potential of the resident wild trout. I had noticed in my observations that as each spawning time approached the hen trout would start to dig the gravel to lay their eggs. They did this in almost the same spot that trout had used the previous year. Many hen trout would try several places before one preferred area was chosen to dig the egg-holding redd. I was curious as to why this was.

I waded in to have a closer look at the gravel only to find that the trial areas were mainly composed of gravel that was very compacted by silt sand and calcium deposits that appeared to have welded the gravel together in an almost impenetrable crust. It was only the loose and clean areas of gravel the hen fish chose to lay their eggs. Once the area had been chosen the hen trout would guard it with her mate although several cock fish may eventually fertilise the eggs and the fighting between the cock fish vying for the hen's affections was often quite fierce and while all this was happening the hen continued to dig her redd As one mate fought off another a third suitor would pop into the redd and do the business with the hen.

On further observation of the spawning areas I became very puzzled as to why the hen trout did not readily use an area of gravel that I had spent a great deal of time and effort to dig over and rake clean of all silt and sand and which, for all intents and purposes, was identical in condition to the gravel they regularly used. I walked in to have a closer look.

As I entered the water I remember taking a cigarette out and while lighting it, I accidentally dropped my lighter into the water. I bent down over the drop zone and waited for the water to clear and as I went to pick up my lighter noticing as I did so that just beside the lighter the soft clean gravel was gently moving up and down. This immediately grabbed my attention and I looked even closer at the gravel bed with my nose almost touching the water. The gravel was indeed moving and every time I shuffled my feet over the spot the gravel soon cleared. Eureka! The penny dropped. There was a natural spring bubbling up through the gravel on the bed of the river.

From there on I went on and found many other little springs welling up all along a line about six foot out from the riverbank and it was on and over these springs that the hen trout preferred to spawn and I surmised they had possible done so on this spot for the past 10,000 years. Not all rivers have so many upwelling springs so trout elsewhere will use gravels that are not quite so suitable.

I also experimented by importing a few tons gravel of the right size, placed into areas where such gravel was short or had been washed away. This did eventually encourage trout to spawn but it usually took at least two years for the trout to use it because it seemed that it took at least a year for the imported gravel to weather in and take on the taste and smell of the natural gravels.

The use of water jets to clean potential spawning gravel could have been helpful when the gravel was silt laden or compacted but I had serious reservations on the regular annual use of water jets once the gravels were cleaned for the first time or the compaction was removed. The whole purpose of good riverkeeping was to encourage a natural method to keep the gravels clean. As soon as the gravels were used once successfully by the trout then that was all that was needed artificially. I found that continuous use by trout eventually moved the banks of good spawning gravel slowly downstream. This was a natural fluvial geomorphological event and the trout followed the gravel, although at times I had to consider replacing it.

One of the many highlights of my year was to watch the hen trout working the gravels and actually listening to the antics and fights between the sparring cock fish. If approached quietly and out of sight, it was possible to hear the cock fish thumping one another underwater as they vied for the possession of the hen. It was little wonder that so many cock fish died after spawning if the gashes and cuts a cock received during his nuptials were anything to go by. I never ceased to be fascinated by spawning trout and watching how a hen trout worked at digging her redd. The vigorous amount of energy expended by the hens in this operation was astounding. A one and half pound wild hen trout moved several hundredweight of gravel in the course of her egg laying. The hen gently measured the depth and shape of her redd between each egg laying session with very delicate feeling movements by her pelvic and ventral fins. Sometimes she left a large pebble in the middle of the excavated redd just as she finished laying her last batch of eggs. The reasons for this phenomenon I never discovered.

Over the years I came to recognise certain trout in my river and learnt where each one lived. The wild trout particularly were very territorial and once a trout established a territory it defended it vigorously from all-comers.

One friend in particular was a hen fish that lived under an overhanging willow tree. It would rise in such a spot where it was virtually impossible to present a dry fly. She managed to live there quite happily for several years only disappearing for the months of December and January to go upstream to spawn. Every spring I would look anxiously every day to see whether 'Prucilla', as she was called, had returned from her holidays and was on station once again under the willow. As soon as she was spotted I knew spring and the fishing season was not far off. Initially on her return Prucilla would be rather thin and lack-lustre, but as soon as the water warmed up a fraction and the insect life became more active she would rapidly fill out and take on a fine complexion. She was quite easy to identify because on her nearside she had a birthmark that was a dark patch or large thumbprint-sized spot in the middle of her flank that stayed with her all her life.

The last time I saw Prucilla was at the end of November just before she went off on her holidays. She was a fat fish of nearer four pounds than three. As much as I looked for her the following spring, she never returned. She was very much missed by myself and even by the fishermen as they would always doff their caps in a gentlemanly manner and wish her 'good day' every time they passed by her well-protected lie. I am sure she knew she was absolutely safe in her summer home as she would hardly move every time anybody passed by some four feet away on the riverbank.

I very much doubt that she was ever caught and am pretty sure that she did not recover from her final spawning endeavours. For several years after I would look hard to see if I could spot any trout with a black spot on its flank which I would have liked to think could have been one of the Prucilla's offspring. Alas, my efforts were of little avail.

A year that I shall remember for a long time was 1976 the year of the great drought and prolonged extreme heat. It was during that year when many rivers throughout the country really suffered with low water flows and high water temperatures and as the summer progressed there were daily reports of major fish kills and some rivers even drying up completely. Although the Itchen flows dropped back to 64% of normal summer flow the fish of the Upper Itchen were never in trouble.

One piece of fortune was that prior to this drought the water authorities had constructed the Candover groundwater compensation scheme whereby a series of deeply sunk boreholes had been drilled up in the Candover Valley through which a major tributary of the Itchen the Candover Brook flowed and huge ground water pumps installed and the summer 1976 was earmarked for the test runs. The whole idea was quite ingenious and far thinking, for the water authorities of that time anyway.

The geology of the Upper Itchen catchment was such that being over pure chalk many hundreds of feet thick and this chalk acted as a huge sponge and retained millions and millions of gallons of pure water. The idea was that in dry summers the stored water in this chalk sponge could be pumped up and discharged into the headwaters of the Candover Brook. It was then allowed to flow into the Itchen to do its natural thing all the way down the river channel to almost the end of the river where, just before it flowed into the saltwater, it was taken out to supply the potable requirements of Southampton and Portsmouth.

Using the natural river channel as an aqueduct was to me pure genius on someone's part, far better than just pumping the water out of the aquifer and piping it directly to the purification works; at least the water had a chance to do good within its natural course down the river. The worry at the time was how long would the cone of depression that was formed in the huge aquifer in the Candover Valley by this pumping take to recharge after pumping was stopped. Fortunately, when the drought broke in mid-September and the rains returned and the recharge rate was a great surprise to us all and relief to the water engineers who planned and built the system as the cone of depression in the aquifer filled up very quickly and ground water levels in the chalk returned to normal by the end of the year.

Since 1976 this compensation system has only been used for one very brief period in the 1990s other than the regular annual pump testing periods that only last for a week or so. I think that this system can be a great insurance for the future of the River Itchen although at the time some people were, and are still, not happy with the existence of such a system. It certainly helped the lower stretches of the river in that awful drought in 1976 and 1991.

Minor river bank repairs

[1] Occasionally an eroded river bank had to be regained. A river channel could widen by a metre or more over several years thus reducing the flow speed of the river, increasing the silt deposits and slowly changing the whole aquatic habitat along a stretch of river.

[2] During the winter, using a digger, wooden piles are driven into the river bed to re-establish the bank line. Brushwood bundles, or faggots as they are called in Hampshire, are installed behind the piles. These are fixed from the river bed to just below the average water height submerging them most of the time to prevent rotting. Once backfilled with chalk, soil and rooted vegetation faggots last a long time, some having been unearthed after 60 years as good as new. [3] Natural rooted vegetation is planted into the backfill and Nature then soon takes over and the new bank will start to blend in with the rest of the river habitat.

[4] Large tree trunks are used to re-establish a new bank line on a bend of the river on the bottom beat at Martyr Worthy.

Although the narrowing is minimal it will, when backfilled and planted, establish a firm bank line to protect against erosion.

[5, 6, & 7] The original river bank margins are being firmed up with a layer of heavy wooden slats which are over-topped with a layer of soil. The original peat river bank is very susceptible to erosion if not protected by a line of wooden piles and retaining tree trunks, set below the water level.

[8] Another completed bank restoration project whereby the river edge has been firmed up with wood and backfill has been over-topped with soil which in turn is planted up with indigenous vegetation. This represents about a month's work the result of which will last for about ten years.

Wherever possible all materials are obtained from local sources, except the wooden piles which are from a saw mill. To enable them to last in the water the piles are treated with a preservative that is quite harmless to any aquatic life.

In August 1977 tragedy struck the fishery when suddenly the owner collapsed and died one morning in his garden when he was checking one of his moth traps. Denzil Ffennell was only 56 and that was a very sad time for us all at Martyr Worthy. All our hearts went out to the family as they bravely came to terms with their very sudden and sad loss. The Royal Jubilee summer of 1977 will not be forgotten. The son and heir was serving in the Green Jackets and resigned his commission to come home and tend to all the necessary things.

By that time I had fortunately gained sufficient experience to understand how the fishery operated so I was instructed to carry on just as before as the late Mr Ffennell had always done. I had the confidence and the trust of the owners to do all that was necessary to ensure the fishery continued to operate in a satisfactory manner. For the following years this was the case, the tenants were content, the river was fine and the owners were happy. Life on the river returned to normal, more or less, and I was left almost completely alone for years on end.

As time passed, tenants either retired or went on to pastures greener so I was left to select most of the replacements. This I did with the greatest of care as it was essential in my view that we had fisherman as tenants who would not only care for the river and respect the fish but could be trusted implicitly not to break or bend any of the rules or etiquette of the fishery and got on well with all the other tenants.

From the outside it may have appeared to some that political cronyism reigned but this was just not the case as I selected and only recommended rods who fulfilled the criteria. If, as time and seasons passed, I became friends with them then so it was to be. This was the twentieth century not the dark ages of the eighteenth or nineteenth centuries when cultural and social conditions were quite different.

For a year or two after the tragic events of 1977 life on the river was almost perfect for me with a full set of tenants all of whom were regular visitors and who really appreciated the river, the way it was kept and the excellent but the very challenging dry-fly fishing it offered. It was indeed a great pleasure to work for them and to be really and genuinely appreciated for the work I did. I was also very fortunate to make some great life-long friends along the way.

One tenant who was a good fly-fisher and also another fishing book fanatic, as he appeared to have almost every book published on trout and trout fishing gracing his ample bookshelves. I never had chance to count them but he assured me there were over 500, mostly first editions and signed by the authors.

His pride and joy was a complete set of Frederic Halford's books, all first editions and all personally signed by Halford, and best of all there was a set of dry flies tied personally by Halford himself inlaid in between the sheets of text of one of the books. This set of books alone were to me pure chalk stream dry fly history in print.

~~~~~

The optimum spawning times for the wild brown trout of the Upper Itchen were the last two weeks in December and the first two weeks of January. The best years for spawning intensity, measured by the number of completed redds, appeared to occur when heavy autumn and early winter rains had lifted water levels, increased flow speeds, and the river was carrying substantial colour (fines) from the run off. My observations recorded that the swim-up fry survival of trout were far healthier in the spring following these conditions. Furthermore, insect life also improved or was stronger the following season after such a winter. The intensity of prolonged frosts during winter and water temperature regimes along with good high river flows with colour all seemed to contribute to not only good natural production of young of the year trout but also to the resident aquatic insect life.

It became very noticeable whenever there was a mild winter with low rainfalls, below average winter water flows, higher winter water temperatures and with few if any prolonged periods of frost both the young of the year trout survival and insect densities the following spring were much less strong.

In my researches to find some answers I came across some interesting work by Heede and Rinne (1989) regarding water viscosity in various temperature regimes and its strong affect on salmonoid and insect habitat. Cooler water temperatures affected the viscosity that in turn affected the sediment loading of the water. The conclusion drawn was that cooler water was advantageous for spawning salmonoids and insects.

Extreme climatic conditions were experienced in Hampshire from the middle to late 1980s when we struggled through a series of serious low water drought years through to the early to middle 1990s, accompanied by very high temperatures, low rainfalls and several very mild winters. The combined effects of these extreme conditions seemed to be contributory factors for the gradual decline in insect density and also be the cause of the problems associated in the perceived national decline in ranunculus that was reported by some during the same period.

The river substrates of the Itchen, prior to this period, were kept constantly cleaned by good, regular, high, cool, winter flows and insects would regularly be found living quite happily deep in clean, non-compacted gravel at depths of twelve inches, or even more. Today, on many waters, within the chalk streams and many other lowland rivers, significant areas of constant clean, silt free, non-compacted gravel with depths of one inch or more are becoming harder to find. Increasingly it will be found that these historic areas of gravel used for spawning and insect production which were once naturally kept clean and relatively silt free all the year round have now to be water-jetted or hand-raked to remove the excessive and more permanent quantities of fine silt that is now being regularly trapped in these substrates. The regular, annual use of water-jetting and hand-raking of gravel has yet to be assessed with regard to its affect on insect survival. This siltation problem in chalk streams was exacerbated by the natural calcification of these fines into an almost concrete like substrate which, if left undisturbed for longer than one year or more, became virtually impenetrable and less attractive to spawning trout and burrowing insects. My observations indicated, surprisingly, that wild trout spawning activity in the Upper Itchen was far more intensive when the trout were spawning in colder water from 2-5°C (36-42°F) that was carrying a deal of colour (fine sediment). In clear less silty warmer water of 6-10°C plus (43-50°F) trout spawning activity was found to be far less intensive or exuberant when these conditions occurred during natural spawning times. Furthermore, insect population strengths and young of the year trout survival following these latter winter conditions also appeared to be affected negatively.

Over the last 15 years or so it seemed that gravel substrates were not being kept naturally and constantly clean. Subtle, but important, changes in water temperature and rainfall regimes, an associated increase in fine sediment loading of the gravel substrate, plus the possible long term effects of chronic non-point source pollutants carried in surface and subsurface catchment run off, appeared to be possible contributory factors causing the perceived decline in insect density in the southern chalk streams.

Finally, the effects of the possible subtle climatic changes may have caused alterations in rainfall and temperature patterns. For example, although the actual 10 to 20 year average annual rainfall levels may not have altered significantly, the pattern of annual rainfall may show that the same amount of rain still falls annually, but in shorter and more intense periods. The effects of these changes could have significant impacts on the sediment loading of run off.

This was clearly illustrated to me in the Upper Itchen catchment where, due to the nature of the geology of the catchment, four inches of rain falling evenly over a period of seven days caused the river to rise by only an inch or two and yet it remained reasonably clear with little heavy sediment loading. In the latter years the general pattern of rainfall and temperatures appeared to change with shorter, but more intense, periods of rain with which even the unique geology of the Itchen catchment could no longer deal, without discharging significant amounts of heavy and fine sediments via the surface run off. The chalk streams started to show more spate-like characteristics rather than the traditional calmer spring-fed conditions of thirty or more years ago.

On many occasions I was privileged as a young riverkeeper to sit at the knee of Frank Sawyer and listen to his pearls of riverkeeping wisdom. Besides teaching me a great deal about practical riverkeeping, above all he taught me how to look into a river and to see and understand what was going on. Both the behaviour and life cycles of all the relevant insects fascinated me and I continued making observations over the next thirty years.

Over the years I certainly witnessed a decline in the densities of the invertebrate populations on the River Itchen. Although, throughout that time, the only species to have been extirpated on the Upper Itchen was the caddis fly, Grannom, despite my efforts to reintroduce the species by live imports from the River Test. Decreases in species density became more regular by the year, particularly to the more observant who well remember the annual regular and very prolific fly hatches of fifteen to thirty years ago. The iron blue has taken the biggest tumble in density to date, although all of the common aquatic insects that riverkeepers and fly-fishers cherish are still apparent on the Upper Itchen.

For so many years the insect activity on the Itchen was very prolific for most of the year. During many a Christmas afternoon, when it was Paula's and my habit after the lunchtime festivities to walk the river with the dogs, we would often notice a hatch of winter olives (large dark olives) that attracted the feeding attention of some of the non-spawning trout. In all my riverkeeping years I could count on one hand the number of days in a year when some upright-winged insects of some sort did not hatch out at some time during the day.

The best instance was one bitter winter's day, when working the spaniels through the sedge beds looking for the odd cock pheasant. I came out to the riverbank to wait for a retrieve and my eyes were attracted to a rise form and, lo and behold, there were a few winter olive hatching that a trout spotted and had for tea. The air temperature at the time was recorded at minus 12°C (10°F). This was vouched for by not only my two spaniels but also by two trustworthy guns who were also out to bag one or two of the old cock birds. How long the fly lived once it left the comparative warmth of the water I shall never know.

I developed a habit very early in my career of lying on footbridges with my nose six inches from the river surface catching nymphs on the back of my hand as they ascended to the underside of the surface film prior to hatching. I watched them hatch out on my hand observing every aspect of the whole hatching procedure right through until the insect had pumped up its wings and dried them off so that it could fly off to the cover of the bank side vegetation. I lay on the same bridge and watched with fascination the clouds of medium olives mating observing the females as they pitched onto the bridge piles from which they walked down into the water taking with them, as they broke and entered the surface, a globule of air that they had trapped between their wings. These insects laid their eggs some two feet below the water level on the bridge piles.

From these latter observations I experimented with the use of fly boards for collecting eggs from these medium olives. This simple Frank Sawyer idea was to attach a six-foot floorboard with a stout piece of cord to a footbridge so the board acted like a water ski on the surface of the water to avoid collecting any floating debris that drifted down. The board would be left in position for several days in June or July and, when lifted, the underside of the board was thick with medium olive eggs. Millions of them. This method of egg collecting gave me an opportunity to transfer insect eggs to other areas of water that was, for some reason, bereft of medium olive. The board, when loaded with eggs, was taken up and wrapped in a wet sack and taken to the new site where it was moored off in a similar position as before. It was essential to ensure that the board was not in contact with the riverbed to avoid the eggs being heavily predated before they hatched by riverbed crawling nymphs of caddis and stone-flies. The eggs were allowed to hatch and the larvae floated off and sank to the bottom to resume their normal pattern of growth, thus replenishing the stocks of medium olive in the immediate area. This method was used quite successfully for the introduction of insects to other watercourses.

Towards the end of my stewardship it seemed to me that even the Upper Itchen showed the first signs of deterioration in the quantity of its insect activity. I was unable to prove this scientifically but my instincts, backed up by my regular observations over the last five seasons, from 1996-2001, certainly appeared to corroborate these observations. Fly diversity was still fine but the volumes of each species appeared to be decreasing inexorably. My experience told me that there was a marked steady decrease particularly on the middle and lower beats of most chalk streams of most species of insects although the upper reaches of the main chalk streams still managed to maintain good diversity of natural fisherman's insects. It certainly followed the trend observed and recorded on many other chalk streams. Not only in the chalk streams was this occurring, it appeared to be a general trend on many other river systems around the country as told to me by many fishery managers, riverkeepers and fishermen from as far away as Cornwall and the Borders of Scotland. Fly life generally, nationwide was just not what it used to be.

After two day's fishing on the River Test in 2001 and two consecutive days on the Middle Test during early June, when the weather was just right for a good hatch of fly of some sort from about ten o'clock onwards through to close of play, I did not see one fish rise at all for the whole time despite there being plenty of fish in the water. There was virtually no surface fly life activity at all except for the odd desultory mayfly, which was snaffled by a small grayling.

Things have changed and are changing still, but not for the good I fear. What the cause is I know not although I do have a good idea, so I am glad that I don't have a regular rod on that water. Talking to the keeper, whom I respect highly, it appeared that he too was extremely concerned at this deterioration and that he was sure it had been getting progressively worse each year. I thought to myself how could it get any worse if there is no active fly life now.

It is senseless to act like an ostrich with its head in the sand as some keepers and fishery owners do. Not to even recognise the situation by saying things are fine and that there are plenty of fly, they are not only fooling themselves but, more importantly, their paying customers. Let us hope that the future will bring a change for the good, as and when proper assessment of the invertebrates that are being undertaken which, when completed, may at least identify the causes of the problem.

In the meantime lobbing large weighted gold head nymphs on 7lb nylon to bottom hugging stock trout is not what the chalk streams are all about but that seems to be the only way to fish if a trout is required to take home and all that for £200 per day. I was so glad I was not paying for the day.

DIARY
A Year in the Life of the River

OCTOBER

16 October fishing season closes (legal date 31 October). Harvest moons and mellow fruitfulness excellent for fishing. Evenings cool and insect activity peaks around midday and early afternoon. Autumn weedcut commences to open up and prepare the gravel for trout. Accumulated silt removed. Withered bankside vegetation tidied up. The river is 'put to bed'.

NOVEMBER

Spawning gravels checked and enhanced where necessary.

DECEMBER

Spawning trout protected from predators and untoward human interventions on vulnerable areas. Structural repairs planned and commenced: banks; bridge building; general repairs.

JANUARY

As December – plus tree management: pruning; lopping; pollarding.

FEBRUARY

As December. On warm days some insect activity with large dark olives hatching out around midday. Odd trout rising to feed off the surface.

MARCH

Days lengthen, day temperatures rise, the first signs of spring appear around the river margins. Major structural work is finalised.

APRIL

First signs of a successful spawning season observed by the appearance of masses of young trout fry in margins of the river below known spawning areas. Fry habitat enhanced by setting twiggy branches into the riverbank to collect floating debris for extra cover and planktonic food for vulnerable trout fry. Peak grayling spawning activity occurs during the middle two weeks of the month. First weed cutting of the year. In years of strong weed growth an April cut is required establishing the pattern of weed growth for the rest of the year.

MAY

1 May fishing season opens (legal date 1 April). Weed cut allowed for 5 days only. Insect life improves with appearance of large dark olives and medium olives and maybe some iron blue at the latter end of the month on cold wet days.

JUNE

Long warm days. Migratory birds back to the valley. River weed grows apace, further cutting may be required. Fishermen out in force requiring the my attention. Bank vegetation runs wild. Bank paths kept open with regular cutting. River margin vegetation trimmed back to give reasonable access to the water for the fishermen. Insect activity at its height with every expected species. Fishing goes on into the evening with some anglers not leaving till well after dark.

JULY

Quieter times. Insect activity wanes during the day with some increased activity after the sun goes off the water on hot days. Weed cutting heaviest of the whole year – allotted days seldom sufficient to complete the cut. The blue-winged olive most abundant insect hatching from early morning through to late evening. Sedge fly activity most evenings and good sport with this insect's imitation.

AUGUST

'Dog days' of summer. Little or no appreciable insect activity to interest trout during the day. Remedy: sit in the shade, read a book and drink river-cooled white Burgundy. Weed cutting. Footpaths kept open.

SEPTEMBER

Insect life awakens. Hatches expected each day increasing as the month progresses. Timing of insect hatches similar to that of May. Weed growth slows, little or no need to cut. Days shorten.

~ 5 ~
Life Along the Riverbanks

The more I learnt about the river, during those seemingly endless days, months and years I spent alone on and in the river and around my trout, the more I came to marvel at the intricate windings of Nature. The sheer beauty at times was overwhelming as on many occasions it was possible to almost be transferred onto another mental plane as the sights and smells seemed to take over my senses.

Living with, and so close to, Nature and witnessing the many wonderful things that happened and continued to happen almost every second of the day was indeed a very humbling experience. It made me realise how insignificant we humans really were. At times the profusion and splendour were more than human capacity could appreciate. The words of Sir Edward Grey reflect my feelings so much better than I ever could:

> *"The sight of all this beauty and the feeling of response to it in oneself gives assurance that God rules the universe and that evil cannot prevail."*

These are such soothing sentiments in the chaotic strife-ridden world in which we live in this twenty-first century.

~~~~~~

During those early years, as I felt my way along as a riverkeeper doing whatever jobs that had to be done, I often worked on my own for weeks on end for much of the time, especially out of the fishing season. The quietness of my own company meant that I very often came face to face with many of the wild animals that lived in and around the river and from these regular meetings I soon came to learn where each animal lived and what their habits and habitats were.

In the river I soon discovered the brook lamprey and in the spring I would lie flat on the footbridge watching with fascination as a group of these creatures went about their spawning activities. About a dozen or so would congregate on an area of clean, loose gravel and proceed to dig a hole. Each one would latch its sucker-shaped mouth onto a stone and wriggle hard and, using its body weight in the current, slowly lift the stone, drop it aside and then return to take the next stone. After a few hours activity they would all gather in the quite large depression they had formed and proceeded to do their reproductive business in one large heaving mass of squirming bodies. People passing over the bridge would have to step over me as I played the voyeur.

Back in the early 1970s the common water vole was so common and so prolific that its numbers were almost at pest proportions along the banks of the Upper Itchen. Their preferred habitat was around and within the many soft peaty banks of the river. The water voles' burrows honeycombed some riverbanks and in high water times these burrows would flood and, when the water levels receded, the burrows would collapse. Sometimes large expanses of riverbank would either slip into the water or collapse upon itself so lowering the height of the riverbank.

'Ratty' almost met its total demise when many feral mink suddenly appeared in the Valley in the late eighties. The vole population was the first species to suffer and was drastically reduced and in some areas completely wiped out in the matter of a few weeks. If it had not been for the long term and diligent trapping of these mink by some riverkeepers I believe the water vole would have disappeared completely from the Upper Itchen Valley.

My diary records that at Martyr Worthy alone I killed just over eighty mink in three years. Although the last mink is still yet to be killed on the Itchen the numbers have now been reduced to a tolerable enough level that has allowed the water vole population to recover quite well. Those mindless individuals who broke into mink farms and released thousands of mink surely could not be aware of the carnage that these released mink inflicted on the natural and wild inhabitants of the river and countryside that they purport to love so much.

At the height of the mink problem it was not only water voles that suffered, it was also the resident populations of coot, moorhen, little grebe, mallard and the reclusive water rail, all of which experienced a sharp decline in their numbers. Incredibly, so did the numbers of the stoats and weasels and whether they decreased because of the predation upon them as a species by the mink or because the mink reduced their natural food availability I never found out.

Fortunately our resident otters were not affected as they could very well see off a mink and a bitch otter could kill a mink quite easily, particularly if there were young otter cubs in the vicinity. At that time our otter population was growing which would have had some added effect on reducing the feral mink population.

I found that the most effective method for trapping mink was a cage type trap. These creatures have a very inquisitive nature so a strategically placed, well-camouflaged cage trap, giving the impression of an interesting dark tunnel for the mink to investigate, was the most effective way of reducing their numbers. I found that, when siting traps that way, any baiting was totally unnecessary.

Of all of the aquatic mammals the otter for me was the most enchanting animal to observe in its natural habitat and I was so fortunate to have had many, albeit brief encounters, with these most happy animals. On several occasions fisherman have said to me that they have lost trout after they had killed one and left it on a bench or on a tussock of grass whilst they went on fishing. It was not until one day when a fisherman actually caught an otter, red-handed, sitting up on a bench seat happily lunching on a pound and a half trout that the fisherman had caught earlier. Only then did the fisherman heed my warning not to leave dead trout around the riverbank.

One incident concerning an otter occurred at the time I had temporarily gridded off a section of the carrier stream to hold a batch of growing-on sized brown trout. One morning when I went down to clean off the grids I found about half a dozen dead trout laying up on the riverbank some yards away from the stream. Each fish had been killed by a neat bite out of the head. As it was long before the mink arrived in the Valley I thought it must therefore have been an otter, but I wondered why should she leave all these dead fish on the bank, as usually an otter would get into a stew pond, take a trout out and eat it completely before going back to catch another.

I talked it over with Pat Fox over our lunchtime pint at the pub and he came round in the afternoon to have a look and he agreed that all the evidence pointed to it being an otter. To make sure I went back to the river that evening and climbed up a tree so I could see into the area where the fish were yet be far enough away as not to put an otter off. Lo and behold, it was not long before I noticed a movement in the sedge bed beside the stream and out appeared a bitch otter with a couple of young cubs following on behind. I only wish I had a camera with me to record the whole incident. I was fascinated to observe them so closely and to see what they did.

It was not long before the mother slipped into the water and came out with one of my prize trout in its mouth which she killed and laid on the bank. She returned to the stream to do the same and soon the penny dropped with me, she was teaching her cubs how to fish and using my trout pen as a classroom. The young cubs then slid into the stream and proceeded to chase the trout about in their efforts to catch one. By this time, mother was standing on the riverbank watching and I am sure I could hear her tut-tutting as the cubs tried so hard, but unsuccessfully, to catch a trout.

Much as I like the otters I had to try to cure this problem without harm to them. After some thought I went off and 'borrowed' from some Council road works on the main road two battery-powered flashing lamps and set them up just at water level at each end of the gridded off area that held the trout. I turned them on at twilight and off at daylight. This ruse worked well. I did not lose any more trout and I was safe in the knowledge that the otters were deterred safely and without harm.

One of the most amusing incidents of this nature was not with an otter but a fox. One of the tenant rods had laid down two freshly caught trout and covered them with dock leaves in the shade of a tree beside one of the fishing huts. Why he had not put them in his creel in the hut I don't know. As the fisherman was walking back to the hut for a break along the narrow winding back path an hour or so later he noticed a fox with a lovely fat brown trout across its jaws walking towards him. I don't know who was the most surprised, he or the fox, because the fox leapt several feet into the air and while airborne turned and dived directly into the sedge beds without dropping the fish. The fisherman almost jumped out of his skin, as they were both only a few yards apart when they suddenly met head on.

Of the many creatures that lived in and around the river mention has to be made of the stoats and weasels as I doubt if there is a length of riverbank in Hampshire that does not have its own resident population of stoats and weasels. Gamekeepers I know treat both these species as vermin to be trapped and removed from the habitat as they predated heavily on the young of the prized partridge and pheasant broods the gamekeeper was protecting. As these animals did not predate on trout, and I believed stoats and weasels did little or no harm around a riverbank in a well-managed environment, they were left undisturbed and both helped to maintain the right balance within Nature's creatures in the catchment.

Over the years I have derived a great deal of fun and amusement from stoats and weasels, as I soon learnt how to 'squeak up' individual animals, by sucking on the back of the hand and producing a good sound imitation of a rabbit's panic squeal. Once this ruse is perfected it was possible at times to draw a stoat towards one from some considerable distance away. Many a time I have stood in the middle of a river footbridge and called a stoat up the riverbank and attracted it to cross the bridge for it to stop a foot away from my feet to then jump over them to continue its way over the bridge. These engaging little creatures with such bright shining eyes and pricked ears and cheeky character are for me great indicators of a healthy ecosystem. Some winters I would spot a stoat with almost pure white ermine fur, only the black tip of its tail maintaining its summer colours. This valuable white fur was used for the thick ermine-edged robes worn on state occasions in the House of Lords when it was chock full of noble gentlemen.

Weasels are, for all intents and purposes, just smaller versions of the stoat and can be found also in similar surrounding habitats. One warm summer's day a fisherman and I watched one particular bitch weasel's activities closely with great interest. We were both sitting beside one of the fishing huts quietly discussing fishing tactics for the afternoon when my eye was taken by a movement on the riverbank on the other side of the river. This turned out to be a weasel with a small baby rodent of some kind in its mouth. As we watched, without moving or talking, she hurried along through the dense vegetation to the footbridge just a few yards away. She came directly across towards us and disappeared under the stanchion of the bridge on our side only to pop out again a few seconds later minus the mouthful of food which was obviously for her hungry brood of youngsters encamped under the bridge. We watched fascinated for a good while whilst she regularly repeated the trip until an entire nest of six young rodents had been devoured. Each visit meant the weasel passed by our outstretched legs by only a matter of four or five feet so we had a perfect view of her on each trip to and fro.

There were many other interesting creatures I encountered around the river. With all the dense ground cover around my river some people asked whether there were any snakes. Where we had lived in the New Forest, the soils were quite acid and adders and various lizards were very common but in the Itchen Valley, where the soils were less acid and more alkaline because of the chalk, adders were virtually unknown. On many occasions I did see some very large grass snakes. I nearly jumped out of my chest waders one summer's day when waist deep in the river weed cutting on my top beat when I noticed a movement in the dense vegetation along the riverbank not ten foot away and to my astonishment at the time a huge grass snake flopped into the river and proceeded to swim very strongly across the river. This creature was all of five feet in length with a body diameter similar to a yard broom handle. Although I never saw a similar occurrence there were lots of grass snakes around the riverbanks that were absolutely harmless and carried no poisonous venom.

One other charming creature was the slow-worm or legless lizard. These were very common around the riverside in summer as were the common grass lizards that do have legs.

~~~~~~

During all these early adventures discovering the many and varied creatures around the river I very soon came to appreciate that one is never alone among the wonderful beauties of Nature. I soon found out each morning as I left my cottage and walked down my garden path to the river that I was becoming increasingly absorbed with all the natural things that the river environment offered. No two days were ever the same. As the seasons gently came and went so Nature continued to reveal even more of her wonders and secrets to me.

To describe that intimate and very privileged feeling one has of being in a position to share the company of these creatures that Nature provides is indeed wonderful and made me realise how human beings are now so unadapted to the ways of Nature. Even on a freezing day in January along the riverbank, when everything in the countryside appears to be in suspended animation, I would stop, look and listen and very soon something moved somewhere. I soon learned how and where to look and found that the countryside was very alive even in those frozen days of deep winter. It was on early mornings in winter, after a fresh snowfall, that the footprints of the animals that had passed that way over the last few hours were revealed. It was very interesting to identify the owners of all the tracks that these animals left behind. Reading tracks in the snow, or on the wet muddy banks of a riverside, was a wonderful pastime and I now do it subconsciously whenever I am in the countryside or beside a river.

In mid-winter the clear waters of the river itself appear oddly inky black against a background of snow-covered banks and yet within and beneath it harboured a wonderland of life and movement. Frank Sawyer once impressed upon me the need to train my eyes to look into and through the water rather, than as most people do, merely look on the surface. Frank demonstrated to me on many occasions his exceptional powers of picking things out on the riverbed that I had difficulty in discerning, even when using Polaroid glasses. I eventually managed to train my eyes which opened up a whole new world to explore. From watching a hen trout selecting and trying out various areas of gravel until she decided to dig her redd in the preferred spot through to selecting a square foot of gravel and watching from a prone position on a footbridge all the movements and habits of all the various and minute species of insects that lived on and in the gravel became an occupation that has absorbed and has so fascinated me over the years and still does today.

Besides trout, I had to 'land' and release for anglers an assortment of bats, swifts, swallows, house martins, not to mention a hedgehog and an eight hundred-weight short horn bullock. I can still hear the squeals and screams of fright from a visiting lady angler as she tried to reel in a short-eared bat as it flew around her head attached to a size 18 Lunn's Particular at the end of her fly line.

Hardly a season passed when swifts, swallows and a selection of martins were not recorded in the catch-and-release returns. Fortunately no birds so caught ever lost their lives for as soon as they were disengaged from the fishing line a gentle toss up into the air allowed them to fly off quite safely.

As for the hedgehog she was taken on a size 18 Greenwell's Glory whilst struggling to breaststroke her way across the river having for some reason fallen off a footbridge late one evening, it had probably been sniffing the empty wine bottles outside the fishing hut. Miss Tillywinkle was deliberately cast to and 'lightly hooked' in the dorsal fin by an angler who was concerned that she may not be able to find her way safely out of the river. Disengaging her from the meshes of the landing net took some time but eventually she toddled off somewhat cleaner and none the worse for her evening dip.

The bullock was however lost long before it was brought to the landing net. The Admiral had foul-hooked the animal on his back cast whilst fishing the top beat and as I arrived he was standing with his back to the river, rod held high, classically playing the animal off the reel as it sauntered off in high dudgeon into the middle of the field. I received rather a sideways look from the Admiral when I enquired whether his landing net could cope or did he need me to go and fetch the gaff and whether the priest he was carrying was adequate to deliver the last rites! Fortunately, the leader parted at the fly after a good fight and so the animal was lost to the record book – our catch weight average for that season was not to be enhanced.

~~~~~

It would be very remiss of me as a riverkeeper not to mention the wild bird life of the river and its catchment and to mention all the years of pleasure these wild creatures of the air gave me.

A riverkeeper has the finest opportunity to observe wild birds at any time of day or night or at any part of the year. Just being on or beside the river I was always in the company of wild birds. Undertaking my daily routines around the river I soon became accustomed to seeing certain species of bird in more or less the same territory day after day. As the seasons came and went so would the birds change their habits and it became a joy to count in the spring migrants as they arrived in the Valley and watch while they sorted out their own particular territory. Like that well-known remark from the Falklands war, 'I counted them all out in the autumn' and 'I counted them all back in the spring'. The late Mr Ffennell told me that the bird books said that swifts arrive in UK during early May. He said in the Itchen Valley they arrived in late April and each year I was commissioned to inform him when I first spotted the first swift in the Itchen Valley. This I duly did and each year he was right as I always spotted the first swift during the last few days of April.

In my early days at Martyr Worthy I was very fortunate to become acquainted with Michael Dann who had lived in the Valley all his life and had become the local expert on birds. His knowledge of wild birds was extraordinary and his hand-written records of the bird life in the Itchen Valley were fascinating to study.

My father had, earlier in my childhood, sown the seeds of my interest in wild birds. As a small boy I remember cycling out to the New Forest with him one day, just at the end of the last war, and spending the whole day identifying all the birds we happened to see in the course of our journey. From then on I have been an avid bird watcher although I must admit my father did also teach me the art of bird nesting. A great deal can be learnt about birds and their habits from watching them and then finding their nests. Even today I still find myself in the spring looking deeply into hedges and thickets, ivy-covered trees and sedge beds for bird's nests. Although egg collecting is now totally illegal, and rightly so, I remember clearly my grandfather and my father coming home from many a springtime fishing trip during the war with a dozen or so coot and moorhen eggs and mother producing a very nourishing omelette for our suppers that evening – jolly good it was too. Father explained to me that coots and moorhens would continue to lay if eggs were removed daily from the nest as long as at least three were always left. The hen would eventually lay twenty or more eggs and, with a dozen taken, would still bring off a natural healthy full brood of young. This old traditional country practice, once widespread among wild fowl species, is now strictly illegal.

The variety of bird life within the Itchen Valley was very impressive and Michael Dann and I set ourselves a task one year to count and positively identify all the residents and migrants that either lived in, or visited, the Valley in the course of one year. We would cross-check, if we could, each other's findings and eventually ended up with a grand total of 127 varieties of bird life.

At that time the meadows beside the river on the south side, laid very wet during the winter and spring and the temporary shallow lakes that formed on these old water meadows attracted large amounts of wetland birds and included a wide range of ducks and waders. The absolute tragedy of this area of the flood plain being infilled with many thousands of tons of chalk and soil to provide extra all year round grazing for the farmer's cattle, left these fields bereft of virtually all wild bird life. There was no longer winter habitat for mallard, shoveller duck, tufted duck, widgeon, shelduck, redshank, curlew and green plover, many of which are now rarely seen in any numbers today in the Upper Itchen Valley.

Wild flower diversity in these old flood meadows was reduced to zero in the monoculture of fertilizers and chemical weedkillers. Rye grass swards grew high each year as the farmer sold all his cattle. The ironic part of it all was that even with all the infilling and draining the fields, which must have cost thousands of pounds to do, still laid far too wet for any cattle to use it in the winter months as was the plan. The farmer received huge grants from government agencies to infill all these flood plain fields all for no gain and a great deal of loss of wildlife and wild life habitat.

It was not all doom and gloom as there were some rare and exciting wild bird sightings at Martyr Worthy over the years despite all this loss of habitat.

Grey phalarope on the river, 1990.

The most unusual visitor was the grey phalarope, a dainty little wader that has an extraordinary life cycle as it breeds on the arctic tundra of Iceland, Greenland and northern Norway and Russia and then winters down in the southern Atlantic at sea between South Africa and South America. To see this little bird, which is actually a member of the wader family, bobbing along on the surface of the Itchen was an amazing sight. It stayed with us for a few days and I was able to take many close-up photographs of it, as it was very tame and totally unafraid of humans. I sent the photographs to a friend who was the official ornithologist for the Ministry of Agriculture and able to positively confirm that the bird was indeed a grey phalarope, adding that in all his travels he had never seen one inland in this country.

We were very fortunate to have several pairs of that very shy water bird, the water rail, which skulks about among the reed beds for most of the time and very rarely ventures out into the open. To the casual observer these lovely little birds, if spotted, could easily be confused with the moorhen as to the inexperienced eye they do look quite similar from a distance.

The lesser spotted, great spotted and green woodpeckers were quite common. The little lesser spotted woodpecker caused us some problems when we put up a series of bat boxes, which were to attract the bats. The woodpecker loved these boxes and neatly drilled holes in each one. A bat box is solid on all sides and has a slit underneath that allowed the bats entry to roost inside. Although the woodpeckers did not nest in all the boxes the holes that they drilled allowed other birds, such as blue tits, to use them.

For years there were a pair of barn owls that kept us fascinated in the springtime as we watched them quarter the hay field in search of food for their young that they were raising in a large hollow ash tree in the woods. Unfortunately, the tree succumbed to the great hurricane of October 1987 and we never saw the owls afterwards, at least not on our patch. I put up some owl boxes in some tall silver poplar trees but those desirable residences were left unoccupied.

Another visitor that caused quite a stir in the Valley was the arrival one year of a pair of golden oriels. Although not as rare as the grey phalarope this very colourful bird with the distinctive call tended to be very elusive and although it could be heard distinctly at most times it was not visible. Usually when a rare species was identified in the Valley its presence was kept quite secret and only the knowledgeable would be told, but in the case of the oriels someone let the cat out of the bag and suddenly the Valley was inundated with TV cameras. Twitchers came from far and near and swarmed all over the place just to get a view of this elusive bird so they could tick the species off their list. It was no surprise that the birds soon disappeared never to be seen again.

During most springs and autumns it was quite reasonable to catch sight of an osprey wending its way along the river course and stooping down to catch an unwary trout. This handsome bird of prey would rest in the river valley for a day or so on its long journey to and from Africa to its nesting sites in Scotland. A pair of hen harriers were regular transient visitors but where they actually nested was not known.

There were the exotic escapees that always created a stir. For one summer a yellow crested cockatoo lived in a stand of poplar trees on the banks of the river. At that time I was rearing a few dozen pheasants under these trees and every morning, as I fed the pheasants, the cockatoo would flutter down on the feed and partake of its breakfast, although this exotic did not survive the winter. A pair of white egrets lived further up the Valley and survived for a number of years although they never appeared to have bred successfully.

Tragedy at times seems to accompany a rare visitor and this was born out when one morning while doing my rounds along the river one of my spaniels put up a bittern from out of a small reed bed. This was the first bittern that I had ever seen in the Itchen Valley and I was absolutely thrilled that perhaps one, or even a pair, had decided to visit the Valley and I hoped that if it was a pair that they would make their home with us. Alas, this was not its destiny as after spotting it on several more occasions I stumbled across its dead body one frosty morning, it was emaciated and I fear it died of starvation as it was winter and the sources of its food were most probably very limited at that time of year. One other species that turned up and has to date stayed in the Valley all the year around is the Cetti's warbler. Although not exactly a rare breed for the UK it was quite rare for the Itchen Valley. This drab looking little bird with the most distinctive song is very elusive and so difficult to spot as its favoured habitat is thick bushes and brambles and with its camouflage it becomes almost invisible.

One species that regularly caused excitement in the village was the arrival of the first nightingales. I have spent many a late night with various members of our village sitting on the handrail of the footbridge listening to the incredible song of this bird. One evening one lady villager came down especially with her mobile phone switched on talking to her daughter in Australia so she could hold up her phone to allow her daughter to listen to the song of the nightingale singing its heart out in the Itchen Valley.

Perhaps this brief description of the bird life of the Valley could not pass without mention of the mute swan, heron and the cormorant. These are three species of avian life that have historically given many a riverkeeper sleepless nights. I think these particular birds have, over the centuries, driven more riverkeepers to drink than any other species of bird, fish or animal and that includes the poacher.

The mute swan has in recent years become a real ecological problem mainly because its burgeoning population has risen out of all proportion and consequently their territory has broadened and now there is hardly an expanse of water in the whole country that is not home for a family or two of this most regal bird. From my point of view one family of resident swans was fine and would do little harm but it was the vast flocks of young and unpaired swans that cruise about the waterways like a band of Hell's Angels wrecking the aquatic habitat of the rivers of their choice that were a major problem with which I had to contend. I have seen a mile of once fully-weeded river totally stripped bare by a flock of several hundred marauding swans in the matter of a few days. This river channel when weeded up held a good population of fish of all types but as soon as the swans removed the weed so all the fish disappeared leaving a totally barren stretch of water. Any one who knows the Wylye Valley in Wiltshire will understand what I mean.

Modern legislation rightly protects these royal birds but surely some management strategy could be devised to mitigate all the expensive damage these birds can and do to fish and other wildlife habitat. Encouraging a breeding pair to take up residence on the threatened area was all that the expert advisors could suggest as a means of keeping the ever-growing marauding herds of immature 'hooligan' swans at bay. A flock of about forty immature swans that were pestering me by stripping my top beat almost bare of river weed did eventually get the message when I taught my pack of five springer spaniels to treat them as a bit of fun by putting them to flight each morning. Although it cured the problem on my beat it only moved it on to someone else on another part of the river. Again it was a matter of devising a method of maintaining a balance within a population.

At one time herons were present in large numbers. They were not usually a major problem once a pair took up a feeding territory. However there was one instance that did make me smile and indicated to me the naïvety of the then local RSPB inspector.

A trout farm had been constructed about a mile upstream and, as this farm had not wired in the stew ponds to protect the growing trout from the birds of the sky, so it soon attracted the attention of almost every heron in the south of England or so it seemed. One morning I took my camera up to a field next door to the fish farm and took a series of panning pictures of a group of herons sitting very contentedly dozing in warm morning sun in the middle of the field. When I had the pictures developed and laid them side-by-side I was able to clearly count 126 grey herons. The following morning I happened to bump into a gentleman on the footbridge, who was dressed like a member of the SAS in full camouflage with a huge pair of binoculars strung around his neck. I asked him casually what he was looking for. He introduced himself and said he was out on behalf of the RSPB to count the grey herons in Hampshire, as the Society was so very concerned about the very low numbers of this species in the county. I politely enquired if he knew how many they thought there were. He said there were thought to be only about twenty-six pairs in the whole county of Hampshire. I walked off smiling to myself saying nothing, as I did not have the heart to disillusion him.

The common cormorant has been with us since time immemorial and even thirty years ago I remember Pat Fox asking me when we met one evening in the pub whether I had noticed the '9.30pm' cormorant winging its way up the Valley. We both spotted this bird most evenings quite regularly.

There was one wonderful experience that I wish I could have shared with someone concerning a kingfisher. The Itchen Valley has a healthy population of these beautiful birds and hardly a day passed on the river when I did not hear that unmistakable short call of a kingfisher as it arrowed its way up the river.

One morning I was feeding some trout fry that I had reared from a few eggs I had taken from a few wild trout. The trough that held the young fry was set in a spring ditch with a steady flow of spring water flowing through it, a sheet of tin covered the top to keep the light out and a fine net mesh covered the tin. I had slid back the tin and folded back the mesh and was gently sprinkling some fine fry food into the head of the trough to encourage these swim up fry onto the feed. The whole process took about thirty minutes so I was stood quite still for most of the time and whilst standing watching intently at the reaction of the young fry to the food my attention was taken by a movement to my right and looking I spotted a kingfisher swinging on an overhanging twig of willow herb just a few

feet away. I froze and watched the bird in all its glorious colours that were reflected off the water by the angle of the sun. To my utter astonishment it then flew and pitched for a fraction of a second on my shoulder from where it then dived directly into the trough of trout fry at my feet, secured a beak full of trout fry and returned to its perch on the twig where it tapped the fry on the twig to stun them and then swallowed them whole, the bird then gave a kingfisher bob and flew off. I very often see the look of disbelief on people's faces whenever I relate this incident but it is absolutely true. I just wish somebody could have seen it all happen. It was one of life's unforgettable experiences.

Concern was shown by the experts who highlighted the worrying reduction in the population numbers of some well-known and well-loved species of birds like the house sparrow, the once common song thrush and green plover, that continued to heighten the fear that the quality of the environment in the Itchen Valley was not as healthy as it was in the time of my youth. I had not seen a grasshopper in the meadows around the river for many years. Thirty years ago a walk across a field, in early summer just before haymaking, caused thousands of the creatures to erupt under my feet. Thirty years on it was almost impossible to find one grasshopper in all of the forty acres of riverside meadows around my beat.

As the summer progressed so the numbers of crane-flies increased, although even their numbers went into decline. Somewhere along the line, man was breaking or interfering with the whole ecosystem and food chain the consequences of which reflected in the numbers and survival of some of our most common species of birds and insects. I did try to console myself with the old maxim that, 'there is nothing in Nature more constant than change'.

I had a growing concern about the rivers that led me to conclude that diffuse pollution was one of our main enemies of the twenty-first century. Point source, or pollution from a pipe, was easy enough to identify and control but other forms of unseen pollutants that spread over the catchment and eventually permeate down into the aquifers or were washed off the surface of the land were a problem. This was an aspect I felt we had to address if our aquatic ecosystems were to continue to survive and sustain healthy populations of fish and wildlife. Ratchel Carson's warnings of coming silent springs rang clearly in my mind as I thought about and listened to the ever-decreasing hum of insect life around the river.

No matter the season or time of year the Valley was still uplifting to the soul and very pleasant to dwell in and by. It was at its best in summer when all the greens were so deep.

I never ceased to wonder at the various colours and ever changing shades of green, of the bulrushes tipped with bright brown panicles, the grey-green Norfolk reed interspersed with the tallest of them all, the reed-mace, with its velvety brown spikes, all silhouetted against a background of tall willows and the ever shimmering silver poplars, set the scene. Under these trees lay thorns and brambles in tangled masses, and always in the foreground there were the brighter sedges, with wild yellow iris and purple flag mixed with great hemp agrimony with its flesh-coloured white powdered flowers and the big-leafed comfrey – so good in a pint of cold Pimms on hot day – and the fragrant meadow sweet, willow herb, purple loosestrife, yellow musk and the scores of other water-loving plants.

The crystal clear river flowed, cold and fresh from the chalk aquifers, through this array of vegetation, an infinite variety of greens. It was the most beautiful water with swaying tresses of water buttercup, water celery and starwort all rooted in the golden gravel river bed.

One morning, as I stood on the public footbridge at Martyr Worthy planning my day, I met our parish vicar, who was returning to the vicarage after attending to ministerial matters at St Swithun's church and, as usual, we stopped for a chat. Alec Knight was our newly-appointed vicar who was young and very keen to get to know all his parishioners, so we talked for some time about the weather and my work on the river. Before parting he asked me if there was any reason why he had not seen me in church. All I could say was that I had never been an avid churchgoer although I did have some very strong but very private thoughts on the subject. I went on to say that I attended *my* church every day of the year, at which Alec looked very quizzical. I explained that we were standing in the middle aisle of *my* church and, as I gestured all round, said that I gave thanks to the Almighty each day for all the beautiful things in and around this river. Alec smiled and said that he well understood my feelings on such a beautiful morning and that it was fair comment, so we shook hands on that and from then on we became very good friends and he never asked me the question again.

~ 6 ~
Dry-Fly Fishing

The late 1980s saw the start of a series of awful drought years when rainfalls diminished. At times the surrounding landscape became very parched and burnt brown with the exception of the margins of the river and the shaded parts of the flood plain which remained as verdant as ever as the cool springs of the Itchen Valley kept things green and healthy despite the prolonged periods of severe drought.

Although rainfalls were way below the average the river itself did not suffer particularly in the headwater reaches above Winchester. There were no reports of fish kills even during the height of the drought. The trout thrived although the fisherman found them extremely hard to tempt to a dry fly during the daytime and even the nymph, the use of which on the Upper Itchen was frowned upon by some, did not work very well.

Those hot lazy days of summer taught fisherman who had not a great deal of experience of these conditions something more about the river and the habits of the trout and the insects. In the normal course of events if a newcomer to the river who expected to fish regularly throughout the season was to ask me, 'what was the best time to arrive on the river' then my answer would be, when starting at the beginning of the season in May, 'Get to the fishing hut by 10am and wait! If there are no fish rising then just sit it out and certainly do not start to wander up and down the riverbanks looking for fish particularly on the Upper Itchen.' This sounded a bit Halfordian but just walking up and down the riverbanks of the Itchen at Martyr Worthy in such conditions is the worst thing to do as it would put the fish down for hours as the water was so clear and shallow. Patience and astute field craft were so important if any sport at all was to be experienced.

Until the fly life activity patterns started to change on the Upper Itchen in the 1990s the standard expectancy of fly activity on a spring day would be that the first trout would emerge from its cover and start to move off the river bed at about 9.30am and lift gently in the water column and would be on station in its surface feeding lie at around 10am. The large dark olive that had been hatching regularly each day from late February would still be active in early May and would usually be the first dun to show followed closely by the medium olive. At about noon the medium olives would be hatching and this activity would carry on steadily to about 4.30 to 5pm depending on the temperatures. At times in the spring the hatches of iron blue would be extraordinarily heavy, particularly if it was a nice cold wet day with a strong westerly wind blowing.

Very rarely did fly activity warrant staying on through to dark at this time of year. The only other insect that would interest the trout, and therefore the fisherman, was the terrestrial insect called the Hawthorn with a peak hatching time from 15-30 April which usually ended by early May, although some hatched well into May.

On the Upper Itchen the hatches of mayfly were historically very sparse, at least up to the last few years of the 1990s when, for some unknown reason, the intensity of the hatches began to grow and eventually the resident trout started to feed on the duns and spinners of this large fly. For years when the hatches of mayfly were going strong on the beats below Winchester we on the upper river would, at best, expect to see about half a dozen in the course of the day and then rarely would a wild trout take them as I believe the trout were so unused to feeding off the surface on such a big fly.

Many a time I watched as a mayfly hatched out and drifted down on the surface of the river, several hundred yards or more, drying its wings before it took off. At times it passed over many trout that were feeding vigorously on olive or iron blue duns. I saw wild trout shy away from a mayfly and actually go off the feed for a while until it forgot about that huge strange object that had floated over its lie. Hatching fly and surface feeding trout again sounds all very Halfordian but on the Upper Itchen at the Martyr Worthy water these general tactics evolved long before I arrived on the scene because during those years the dry fly was indeed by far the easiest method to catch the wily wild trout that abounded in the river. This was long before the arrival of the grayling and the steady trickle downstream of escapee rainbow and the upstream drift of stock trout from lower beats all of which had different feeding habits.

~~~~~

In the earlier days, as spring passed into early summer, fly activity patterns changed little. In the normal course of events a fisherman would be expected to arrive at 10am as usual and the activity go on till about 2.30 to 3pm. The activity, particularly on a hot summer's day, would generally peter out until the sun went off the water around 8.30pm. I never ever got it right when asked to say when was the best time for a fisherman to arrive on the river or asked to predict when *the* fly will hatch. Inevitably, it was the previous Thursday when not one fisherman had turned up to fish, and yet all the right flies hatched out, spot on the right time of day and continued to do so for hours. Sod's, or Murphy's,

Checking my tackle.

Law prevailed and from that was born the title of this tale – 'You should have been here last Thursday'.

The evening rise was to me a misnomer and was, on many occasions, a non-event, although on summer evenings what other place would one want to be than beside a chalk stream. In high summer the evening might have started off with millions of blue-winged olive migrating upstream to their egg-laying sites and a few clouds of olive spinners in the air but so many times the trout were not seen to be feeding, most probably because they were so stuffed full with the daytime bingeing on the varieties olive duns. There was possibly a saviour at such times as these and that was the good old sedge fly. It only took a few sedge to scuttle across the river surface during the evening for all hell to break loose, giving an hour's great and exciting sport well into the darkening night. In such situations I was, on many occasions, still netting trout for fisherman, repairing broken leaders and replacing sedge patterns that had either been lost up in the trees or in a trout's mouth long after darkness has fallen. It did not really get dark at that time of year and even if there is not a moon I soon learnt how to tie on new flies for a fisherman in the fading light. Holding up the fly to the west and threading some 6x gut through the eye and tying a good blood knot in these conditions was quite a frustrating exercise sometimes.

I was asked on several occasions by anglers whether trout feed very early in the morning in the spring and summer on the Itchen. One particular fisherman kept on asking me this so one day I suggested he tried it out and that I should accompany him on the following day so he could find out. We agreed to meet at the fishing hut at 4.30am next day. It turned out to be a beautiful soft but cool June morning. We sat and saw the sun rise and watched for almost three hours before one desultory trout rise was spotted. That was all we saw that morning until we went up to my house for breakfast at about 9am. I tried it several times over the years and but never found trout really up in the water and on the feed at that time in the early morning. The trout were certainly late morning risers on the Itchen.

Although the water temperatures of the river were relatively constant, due to the spring-fed nature of the river, there was a slight temperature change as the water cooled down overnight, particularly after a hot day, which then started to rise as the daylight lengthened in the early morning. I was sure that the insects adapted and responded to these subtle temperature changes. The trout also adapted to this and usually rested up during these morning hours. They lay in their resting lies or hid under some weed and one or two may have been roused from their slumbers by bouncing a heavy nymph in front of them but there again the best sport was with the rising fish and so to wait until later in the morning was the best ploy. As the summer blended into autumn so the fly activity returned to somewhat similar activity as there was in the spring.

Field craft, observation and delicate casting skills were the all important and essential skills required if a wily old wild Itchen brown trout was to be duped into taking an artificial dry fly. Thirty years on I may have refined my initial observations somewhat but not radically. All that I learnt from Mr Ffennell and my father about fly-fishing, plus my own fishing experiences, stood me in good stead over the years.

Whenever I talked to newcomers about the sport of fly-fishing, or the students who booked casting lessons, I asked them at some stage to try and define in ten words, 'What is dry-fly fishing?'

My general ten-word definition of dry-fly fishing was: *accurate observation; accurate identification; accurate presentation of the accurate imitation*. This may have sounded a trifle purist but it defined the basic principles of dry-fly fishing quite clearly.

Accurate observation involved spotting the insects on the surface of the stream to which the trout were rising and eating.

Stalking a rising trout on the River Itchen.

Accurate identification and imitation of the specific insects enabled the angler to select the right species of artificial from his fly box that was, as near as possible, the same size and conformation as the identified natural insect.

Accurate presentation was the ability to use the fly rod expertly, regularly casting a fly line fine and far off to present the artificial fly accurately and delicately just like thistle down upon the water so as not to alarm the trout.

I had a similar set of guidelines for the fisherman who tied their own artificial dry flies and the priorities to be considered when tying and fishing them. They were: presentation, size, shape and colour.

The presentation of the artificial was the most important aspect, even with the most perfect imitation of an insect tied on the end of the leader or cast. Success was remote if the fly was presented with a terrific splash or placed way wide of the mark or with a leader too heavy for the fly. Frank Sawyer put it in a nutshell one day when he said to me in his broad Wiltshire accent, 'T'aint the fly 'tis the driver.'

The size of the pattern of the artificial was also quite important, particularly when the natural insect that the fish were selecting and eating was just one of several different species that were hatching and appearing on the water. For example trout might have been feeding almost exclusively on medium olives when there were also large spring olives on the water. It always paid to have a range of different sizes of the more generic patterns of olives.

Shape, or more accurately the outline, and size were equally important. The impression, or the outline, which the artificial fly gave triggered off interest within the trout that it might be food. So often I saw experienced fly-fishers holding a freshly selected fly from their box up to the sky just to see if it had the right shape and that it would hopefully give the same impression when viewed from underwater by the trout.

I rarely had a major problem with colour when matching the hatch with artificials. As long as the colours were reasonably close to the natural shades of the live insect then that was fine, as in Nature the colours within the same species of insect can and do vary quite often. If an unused fly was taken from the fly box and held up to a bright sky the colours of the materials from which the fly has been constructed appear almost indiscernible and indistinguishable to the human eye against the bright background. At most times during daylight floating flies on the surface of the water were silhouetted against the brighter background of the sky so the same probably applied from the trout's point of view. I was aware that some expert fly-fishers had other ideas on these subjects but generally speaking these observations did hold true for much of the time. If one wanted to really get pedantic the pros and cons of light refraction, reflection off the underside of the surface film and low angles of sunshine could be brought into the equation. Messrs Goddard and Clarke discussed all this in depth in their fascinating book, *The Trout and the Fly*, as did Vince Marinaro in his book, *In the Ring of the Rise,* and Datus Proper in his *From the Trout's Point of View*.

Several thinking fly tyers have placed live insects onto the surface of water in a glass tank with the purpose of looking up from the underside, unfortunately most of these experiments were conducted by looking through the sides of the glass tank and up to the underside of the surface film that was holding the sample insect. What refraction occurred by doing this I am uncertain but I think it would be quite significant. I was led to believe from a leading eye surgeon that a trout's eye is fundamentally very similar to a human eye in construction but I still have to be convinced that fish see things on the upper side of the surface film in the same way as a human would if viewed from below from a similar position. From this the art of tying flies to fool trout into thinking they are real insects became another whole new can of worms.

Dry flies ~ Ron Holloway style

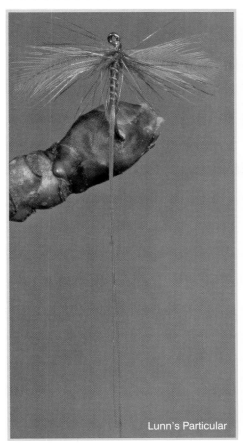

Lunn's Particular

Pale Watery Dun

Greenwell's Glory

Iron Blue Dun

Sherry Spinner

Caperer (Sedge)

Long-tailed Sherry Spinner

Medium Olive Spinner
(exaggerated long-tailed version)

A useful Sedge pattern

Iron Blue Dun (well used)

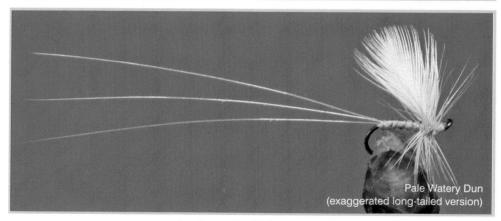

Pale Watery Dun
(exaggerated long-tailed version)

Dry flies ~ Ron Holloway style.

Emergers in and below the surface film.

Caddis fly.

A study in concentration as a fish takes on the River Itchen.

A typical wild Itchen brown trout.

(*above*) The old stew ponds alongside the river at the bottom of my garden where I raised trout with an old windmill header tank (*right*) employed as a sorting and temporary holding tank for grading out trout.

Twiggy branches set along the riverbank to provide cover for trout swim-up fry and young of the year.

Greater tussock sedge, commonly called 'bull's bums' by riverkeepers.

Norfolk reed in winter and (right) a brown -lipped snail.

A male Damsel fly resting.

Scarlet Tiger moth, an inhabitant of riverbanks and moist meadows and particularly fond of comfrey.

Marsh Orchid.

Comparison of stocked trout to wild trout (*see explanation opposite*).

Genuine wild male brown trout (*see explanation opposite*).

Stocked Trout and Wild Trout

The photographs opposite illustrate the subtle physical differences between stocked trout and wild trout.

To the inexperienced eye there may be little to choose between the four trout illustrated in the top photograph but a closer look reveals that three of the fish are stock trout and the fourth is the genuine wild trout. So which is which and why?

[1] This trout is a stock fish as the caudle fin (tail) is slightly frayed and the dorsal fin is well worn. Also the pectoral fins are not as pointed as they should be and are slightly rounded, all of which indicates wear from its time spent in a crowded stew pond prior to release into the river.

[2] This is a rainbow trout that had been stocked at some time, as are all rainbow trout. Although in reasonably good condition, apart from a slightly flabby stomach, its dorsal fin shows some excessive wear.

[3] This is the one genuine wild trout of the group. It has the typical markings and conformation of a wild chalk stream brown trout with perfect fins all round and no excessive wear at all on any of them.

[4] This is a stocked trout which shows typical stew pond wear on its dorsal and pectoral fins. Its conformation leaves a little to be desired as its body length is out of proportion to its depth which possibly indicates a minor genetic fault in that its backbone has one or two fewer vertebrae than a wild trout, which could account for its slightly 'humpy' shape. This phenomenon has been shown to be more prevalent in hatchery bred trout than in the wild and may be due to inadvertent inbreeding within the hatchery brood stocks.

As a matter of interest all four fish were caught on the same day in the month of May. The three stocked trout were caught on the River Test during the morning and the wild trout was caught on the Upper Itchen in the late afternoon.

[5] Illustrates the physical attributes genuine wild male brown trout with perfect fins, caught in late-September on the Upper Itchen. Note the complete absence of wear on the dorsal fin and the tail.

I was most fortunate and privileged to have met and talked to Vince Marinaro during my visit to Pennsylvania in 1979 and I learnt a great deal from his experiences during my short stay. Not wishing to delve too deeply into the history of our sport to find out who invented dry-fly fishing because I believe John Waller Hills answered this question quite well when he suggested that the invention of the dry fly was not complete until there was 'intentional drying of the fly by false casting'. In his *History of Fly-fishing for Trout,* Hills went on to state that the first mention of drying the fly occurred in 1851 and that the dry fly has a continuous history, but its use did not become common until 1860 and even then only on the chalk streams of the South of England. With accurate presentation being, to my mind, the most important aspect in dry-fly fishing, such presentation led to some very interesting events. The much discussed subject of purism and dry fishing is wonderfully discussed in Tony Hayter's recent book, *The Dry Fly Revolution,* published by Hales, where the life of Frederick Halford is chronicled and Halford's dictates from which the still controversial purist dry-fly revolution was brought about. For anyone interested in the history of fly-fishing this book is a 'must' read.

Peter Lapsley explained expertly, and dispelled in his inimitable style, many of Frederick Halford's rigid dry-fly doctrines that have dogged the chalk streams for so long, many of which were laid down well over a hundred years ago. The Halford doctrines were accepted at the time almost without question and religiously applied by owners of many chalkstream fisheries just as if these doctrines had been handed down from upon high as a set of 'thou shalt' commandments etched in tablets of stone. Even today some chalkstream fisheries still implement these archaic outdated ethics. However time is slowly bringing things around to more common sense thinking thanks mainly to knowledgeable chalk stream anglers and experienced chalkstream fishing writers as Peter Lapsley.

'No wading' regulations are common on many of the beats on the chalk streams and this seemingly arbitrary rule is made solely for the benefit of the fisherman. Any form of wading on the soft river bed of the Itchen can readily put a great deal of silt into suspension and often loosen quantities of aquatic weed, blanket weed and algae which will most certainly detract from the quality of the sport for whomsoever is fishing directly downstream. Being confined to fish from the riverbank only, may well test and challenge the casting ability of the fly fisher to cover some rising trout and it will invariably increase the incidence of drag but it all adds to the beauty and charms of the chalk stream challenge. A riverkeeper will usually turn a blind eye on the odd one leg in the water that enables a cast to be made to a trout that is tight in under the bank and there is dense overhanging vegetation along the riverbank. I have often seen sudden changes in the clarity in the River Itchen that, for no apparent reason, immediately put down any trout feeding off the surface. On investigation I have found the cause of the coloured water usually to be just one angler a mile or more upstream wading to and fro and up the middle of his beat. Even such apparent innocent minor in-stream disturbance can and does affect fishing for long distances downstream.

Fly-fishers should at all times commence fishing at the very bottom boundary of their allotted beat and work upstream. Working up a chalk stream in this manner with a fly rod is one of Halford's doctrines that will probably stand the test of time.

One aspect on this subject of fly tying is that the demand for quality imitative tied dry flies has diminished quite steadily over the last ten years. The natural fly life on the Upper Itchen at Martyr Worthy and the beats above right up to the source were, for most of my thirty years on the river, super-abundant with excellent strong hatches of all the common insects a dry-fly fisher would recognize. Seasonal shortages of one species was often balanced by megahatches of another.

During the late 1980s and even into the early 1990s the spring hatches of iron blue were extraordinarily heavy with a density at times of 60 to a 100 of these insects floating down on every square foot of river, which was a sight to behold, giving an appearance of the river being covered in fur. At such times it was very difficult to fish as there were just too many flies on the water and not only did it become difficult to pick out one's own fly but tightening into a trout was a chancy affair as one lost sight of the fly or mistook a natural for one's own artificial. What a lovely predicament and one that many chalk streams would envy these days. Each year I would use these megahatches of iron blue to measure the numbers of wild trout living in my beat as every trout from two to twenty inches in length would be feeding with great gusto so enabling me to undertake a head count.

Fly tying was, for many fishermen, an integral part of the enjoyment of fly-fishing and as far as I was concerned catching a wild trout on a dry fly that I have tied completed the cycle of enjoyment the sport offered. When I first arrived at Martyr Worthy I was taught the rudiments of dry-fly tying by Frank Moores that opened a further window for me on the appreciation of the wildlife of the riverside.

In those days the materials we used for fly tying were collected mainly from the riverbank and surrounding countryside. Whenever I went shooting I would scour the game cart at the end of the day for feathers and pick over the carcases of any vermin that had been shot for further supplies of the right coloured feathers and fur. Through all the years of looking I never did find that perfect natural honey-blue dun cape. Around the river the barbed wire fences were inspected regularly and hedgerows combed as it was surprising what could be gleaned from them. Driving about the countryside many a traffic jam was caused when I suddenly stopped to pick up the carcase of some wildlife road mortality. At one time the outer south wall of my work shed in the garden became lined with skins of many animals and birds that could or might be used in fly tying.

Man-made fly-tying materials were not common at that time with perhaps expensive capes, tying silk, cottons, wax and varnish being the only materials other than hooks and the strange things I was able to glean from my wife's sewing box, that were bought at the local tackle shop. The Wildlife Acts were also changing and afforded, quite rightly, stronger protection for the wild animals and birds of the air so that natural fly-tying materials became harder to come by in the shops. Starlings and coots were great sources of feathers for tying iron blue duns.

The increase in the use of man-made materials in all aspects of fly tying has been the major innovation over the past twenty-five years. The professional fly tyers experimented with the use of some of these new synthetics as the use of natural materials reduced. Considering that Nature has not invented or created any new species of insect for fly tyers to imitate and to which trout will naturally rise, all the artificial patterns for representations of these insects have long since been devised. It was only when the modern materials were used to create new interpretations that anything in the way of innovation was seen and without this spice fly tying would have been quite a dull exercise. Today, very few, if any, new dry-fly patterns are being invented although there have been one or two new methods of tying them using modern fibres and plastics. This, plus the more recent revival in the use of Cul de Canard feathers, has allowed dry-fly tying to move on, although some of its uses at times by some of the fly tyers defeats me. This was quite obvious from the patterns of bought-in artificial dry flies that decorated a fisherman's fly boxes and those that adorned the counters of tackle shops. Even so the modern fly-tying fishermen have yet to crack that eternal problem of designing and tying the perfect blue-winged olive dun imitation that actually works well.

Some people's conception of a medium olive or an iron blue, and particularly of the blue-winged olive, did astound me at times. James Lunn would scarcely recognise some of the modern tied representations of his famed Lunn's Particular pattern that can be found in many tackle shops and catalogues today.

Furthermore, the Reverend Greenwell may well revolve in his grave if he were to see some of the modern conceptions of his classic pattern. The same can be said for the Tupp's Indispensable.

The discussions we had on the merits of both accurate imitation and impressionistically tied flies went on for several years. Any fly fisher who experiments with new materials stimulates progress in the hobby. The best one can do is to concentrate upon reviving old patterns and methods and finding ways and means of improving them.

It is a worrying sign of the changing conditions on many waters today that surface activity by trout rising to natural insects appears to be diminishing. The fly boxes of today's dry-fly fisherman on the chalk streams are now reflecting these changes as they are increasingly becoming inhabited with complex ranges of nymphs and sub-surface lures and attractors. If we look further into presentation of dry flies to rising trout my feeling is that as long as the right size artificial is presented correctly without any unnecessary splash and as long as there is a significant trigger factor incorporated into the construction of the fly that encourages the trout to think that the artificial is real then there is more chance that the fly will be taken. I found over time that I tended to tie flies with extra long tails, using three long tapered micro fibbets, and as long as these tails laid flat on the surface they acted as the trigger factor, and even if the rest of the fly was a mess the better the chance of the trout taking the offering. Exact imitations of natural insects that are beautifully tied to perfection by some of today's very talented fly tyers do not seem to catch any more trout than do my very tatty long tailed 'hatching spents' as I called them. To call this fly a 'hatching spent' was possibly a paradox as it is neither one nor the other yet my innovative pattern caught many trout for me that were taking hatching nymphs attached to the underside of the surface film and also took trout that were homing in on spent olives floating in and on the surface film. As long as a fly was presented to a rising trout had some obvious or even exaggerated trigger factor, in this case long tails, then success was more likely. Furthermore having confidence in the fly also contributed to its success.

Some years ago I read an essay by the late-lamented fly-fisherman, writer, conservationist, Ed Zern in the *Field and Stream* on the subject of 'The Ethics of Fly-fishing'. That essay sowed the seeds within me from which over the years my present heartfelt feelings grew for the wonderful sport which has been such an integral part of my life for the past fifty years or more. It seems to me that all the problems of life are ethical problems and so to attempt to separate out

Tall tales being told of the 'one that got away'?

the ethics of fly-fishing I found rather difficult. Perhaps it was not really ethics but rather a one of attitudes, a code of behaviour, a concern for tradition, the preservation of fishing values and, above all, a desire for the conservation of our wild trout and the rivers in which they live.

The essence of our sport is skill, and the voluntary imposition or acceptance of arbitrary conditions demanding these skills. There is nothing illegal in shooting a pheasant on the ground, but the true sportsman will only lift his gun to pheasants that are flying high and fast and even then may even decline a shot which does not challenge his shooting skills.

Fly-fishing usually requires more skills than fishing with metal spinners or heavy spoons; fly-casting generally requires more skill than spinner casting or bait casting. Fly-fishing encourages the development of collateral senses and skills like the powers of observation and in the ability of the identification of insects and the dexterity of tying accurate imitations of the same. Dry-fly fishing also hones the skills in adept field craft and encourages a stealthy stream approach. Dry-fly fishing for me is a more sporting way of catching trout feeding off the surface of the water in which they live. It is irrelevant and unimportant if, at times, the spin and bait and the Czech style nymph fisherman catches more fish than the fly-fisherman because it could just be the other way around, but then who cares?

The sport of fly-fishing is not a game or a competition between fishermen, it is an end in itself. If we look at those great figures in the historical tradition of fly-fishing they are not the men who caught the largest fish or hold records of the greatest numbers caught. They are those men who like Ronalds and Francis, Mottram and Sheringham, Halford, Marryat and Skues, Lord Grey and Dermot Wilson, Theodore Gordon and Lee Wulff, Frank Sawyer and Vincent Marinaro *et al* who made lasting contributions to this sport, of thought and knowledge, of the fish themselves, of fly-fishing and fishing philosophy. All of which is set down in their writings and illustrated above all by their good sportsmanship. There have always been those who could accumulate more dead fish on the riverbank than anyone else. They belong to a fraternity who has that overwhelming desire to be seen to have caught the most or biggest fish because it is so important to them, but fortunately no one seems to remember who they were, or should. This begs the question what determines a good fisherman? Here I can only agree with the late Joscelyn Lane who wrote down his ideas fifty years ago on what made a good fisherman. I can only echo his thoughts when he asked what we meant by a 'good fisherman' and was the term 'good' synonymous with 'successful' in this case? This is not necessarily so if by a good fly-fisherman we mean an accomplished exponent of his art and all that entails. Let us take the analogy of the man on a shooting stick who brings down birds with the regular precision of a metronome He is undoubtedly highly successful at killing birds, yet he may know little or nothing of the work involved in producing those birds over his gun. On the other hand the man who achieves success through the less spectacular, through his knowledge of watercraft and through the habits of his quarry is surely a better sportsman for that. There are in my mind several fly fishers who will be long remembered as masters of their craft while many of their contemporaries who were more successful numerically in the taking of fish remain unhonoured and unknown.

I further agree with Lane that the inventory of the gifts and accomplishments of a finished fly-fisherman was a formidable one. At his best he was expected to display more than a fair share of skill in casting, have keen eyesight, perseverance, guile, extensive knowledge of weather conditions, of the ways of the fish and their natural food and its imitation, backed up by boundless enthusiasm and unflagging powers of concentration. If the fly-fisherman possessed all these qualities he was indeed a paragon yet there was one negative to add to the list and that was the absence of the competitive spirit. Competition necessarily forms the basis of many games we play but for me competition in fly-fishing tends to lead to discontent which in turn can mar the full enjoyment of fly-fishing.

The more I read about trout and trout habitat and trout rivers and trout fishing, the more I wanted to learn so the more books I collected and my modest fishing book library began to grow.

Many fishing books mainly written about how to catch, what with, how many and how big the fish had very little interest to me. The books that interested me were those that taught me more about other rivers of the world as well as the chalk streams and the fish that lived in them. There have been many books written about the famed chalk streams of this country over the years. Some are considered classics that are read and re-read, time and time again, for their information and guidance upon the wiles of chalk stream trout and their capture. Of course, the classics of Skues, Halford, Ronalds, Wilson, Waller and Hills were musts for any chalk stream riverkeeper along with, *Where the Bright Waters Meet* and *A Trout Rose*. Skues, Waller and Hills, Col Harding, Plunket-Green all wrote wonderful informative books. The list is endless. Several very interesting American books chronicled the events that led to the evolution of dry-fly fishing in the USA on the Catskills rivers of upstate New York. I acquired books and articles by such people as Theodore Gordon, Roy Steenrod, the Dette's, and the Darbee's those dry-fly doyens of the fly-tying bench.

I very much doubt that any of the classic fly-fishing authors were qualified entomologists or fishery biologists and therefore all of their ideas stemmed from their astute observation and personal interpretation of all the natural things that occurred whenever they were at the riverside and actually fishing. The so-called doctrines laid down by some of these gentlemen have, through time alone, become the cornerstones of much of the fly-fishing ethics that still hold sway on so many of our trout fisheries to this day.

Although there have been many books written in more modern times, few of these have attained the literary and informative heights as did these older and much revered classics. That is until Tony Hayter recently published his book, *F.M. Halford and the Dry Fly Revolution,* in 2002. Hayter's painstaking research and well-written interpretation of the happenings within the fishing lifespan of Frederic Halford, which he has set down so exquisitely, sheds light on aspects of Halford's life and describes the vital part he played in the evolution of the so called 'dry-fly revolution' that until then was unknown to many within the fly-fishing fraternity.

Many of the interesting discussions I had with fisherman over the years revolved around the so-called ethics of dry-fly fishing on the chalk streams. Whenever this subject is brought up then the well documented, and to my mind grossly exaggerated, feud between Frederic Halford and George Skues crops up somewhere in the discussion. The so-called contentious issues that set Skues and

Halford apart according to some have become etched in tablets of stone over the years and it is not until one reads carefully Tony Hayter's book that these issues really reveal themselves as being of no great relevance.

Most fishermen continue to read about fishing and fishing tackle until they die. It seems to me, from the copious reading I have done over the years, that some of the best fishing ever has been done in print. I believe that no other sporting activity has produced such a distinguished amount of literature nor has attracted so many literary people. Of all the fishing books that I have read the best, in literary terms, has to be Lord Grey of Falloden's, *Fly Fishing,* so beautifully written and takes a lot of beating particularly his chapters on dry-fly fishing. No angler worth his salt should shuttle off his mortal coil before he has waded through Izaac Walton's *The Complete Angler.*

Frank Sawyer was the first to agree that his books were not classic literary works but the information contained within those pages was, and still is, for me just one huge mine of riverkeeping knowledge that I have for so long had at my fingertips.

~~~~~

GEM Skues through his lifetime of observation eventually experimented with soggy dry flies when trout were observed feeding just under the surface on hatching nymphs. From this he went on to experiment with adding some heavier materials to his artificials to make them sink a little lower in the water. I have done similar things many times by taking my scissors to an overdressed dry fly to make it sink a little lower within the surface film or with the aid of a bit of spit make it drift down just sub-surface in an effort to take the eye of a trout that was feeding off the underside of the surface film or even an inch or two below it.

Frederick Halford had fished mainly with dry flies for trout for most of his later fishing time and was the first to admit that he had blank days when the trout were feeding sub-surface and he freely admits he even tried the nymph on several occasions with little success so he was not the exact purist that history makes him out to be. He admits, somewhere I believe, that he was just not as good a nymph fisherman as Skues.

Skues, I believe, was the more astute observer of trout habits when they fed sub-surface and, having such an inquisitive and inventive mind, devised a method of tempting these trout by offering them his soggy hatching nymph in, or just beneath, the surface at a level the trout were seen to be feeding. Halford and Skues did fish together on several occasions and I am sure Victorian gentlemanly conduct was maintained at all times. It was only in their writing did the two giants come to literary blows and as Halford was getting on in years and Skues being younger and a very articulate lawyer so the word war began. However, as age tends to encourage cantankerousness in all of us, I feel the 'dry-fly versus nymph' discussion was a verbal war of teacup proportions. It has only been others later who began to read in more than there was and so enlarged upon the subject which has since encouraged fisherman over the years to take one side or the other in the debate. Over the years it has at times developed the 'us and them' attitude in the use of the dry fly and nymph.

I remember talking to a friend of my Grandad who had met Skues on several occasions when Skues, in his later days, was living in a hotel in the Wylye Valley. His recollection of the late 1940s of Skues was of an extremely polite man who was rather short-tempered and very fixed in his ways and ideas. It must be remembered that at that time Skues was in his eighties and had lost his access to his beloved River Itchen so he had the right to be a little tetchy.

It must not be forgotten that Skues was, in my view, one of the greatest observers and innovators within the evolutionary history of our sport and he gave us all so much richness within his writing. Marryat was another but unfortunately he did not publish his findings although he I am quite sure contributed a great deal to Halford writings. It is suggested that Marryat was among if not the greatest contributor to the dry-fly revolution. Halford in his way comes across firstly as a loving family man who has a good sense of humour and who adored to be in fishing people's company. He too was an avid observer of insect life although at times tended to become rather dogmatic over certain aspects of trout fishing, this aspect to my mind was his Achilles heel.

Between them and together I believe Halford and Skues and Marryat have contributed more to the evolution of fly-fishing than have all the previous or present fly-fishing greats put together. Our sport is so much the richer for all their knowledge and expertise that they set down in all their writings for future generations to pore over. No doubt many times in the future the debate over dry fly and nymph will be resurrected, debated and then be put to bed once more.

There is one aspect of the Halford story that many do not realise. Halford, produced all his books from the researches and observations he undertook from his fishing experiences, mainly on the Hampshire chalk streams. It must be remembered that virtually all the various stretches of chalk stream he leased over the years and upon which he undertook his studies had to be heavily stocked each and every season with stew bred trout to provide any sport. From this many, if not all, of Halford's researches and conclusions on insects and the artificials he devised to imitate them to catch his trout were undertaken using and fishing for and over mainly stocked trout. This alone made me wonder if Halford's findings and doctrines would be any different today if all his research work had been carried out in the company of genuine wild trout?.

I have been privileged to look at some of Halford's original tying of dry flies and without exception almost all of his artificials were in my view over-sized and over-dressed if compared to the dry flies of the same era tied by Hammonds of Winchester for use on the Upper Itchen where wild brown trout were very prolific. I believe that Halford once politely declined a day's fishing at Chilland on the Upper Itchen as he deemed the wild trout of the Itchen rather too difficult to catch. He did however fish the Itchen around Winchester regularly but on stretches below St Cross that were stocked. Whatever history teaches us I believe the hands of Frederick Halford, George Edward Mackenzie Skues and Mr Marryat together rocked the cradle of dry-fly fishing.

The rivers Test and Itchen are so similar in character albeit the Test is much bigger and longer that comparisons are frequently made and although there has always been that friendly rivalry between riverkeepers on both rivers the Test is recognised as the 'King' of chalk streams and the Itchen the 'Queen' as is her want of being more gentle and, dare I say, more feminine in character.

Both rivers have witnessed the birth pangs of dry-fly fishing and upon their banks men like Halford and Skues were to shape the methods and ethics of the sport I love and who plied and honed their expertise that has over the past 150 years or more given these rivers their sporting notoriety worldwide. Fly-fishing developed at or about the same time on the other side of the Atlantic and America too had its own fly-fishing giants. The history of the rivers of upstate New York catalogues the renowned Catskill trout rivers: The Beaverkill, the Willowemoc, the Neversink, the Delaware, Esopus, and Scolharie. Rivers hailed by generations of that country as 'the birthplace of American fly-fishing'. It was beside one of these rivers that George LaBranche, who in the words of Sparse Grey Hackle, 'adapted the dry fly to fast water and started an angling revolution'. This revolution attracted into the Catskill Mountains a group of fishermen who further shaped and moulded the American dry-fly revolution. It was here where the great anglers, fly tyers, rod makers, entomologists, and angling writers gathered together. It was here that Thad Norris and Seth Green trout breeders plied their trade where Theodore Gordon cast his delicate dry flies and wrote letters to Halford on the River Test. It was here too that rod building became art with Hiram Leonard, Ed Payne and Ed Garrison producing their exquisite split cane rods. It was here where Roy Steenrod, Ed Hewitt, Sparse Grey Hackle and Preston Jennings fished, philosophised and wrote about it. It was here where Art Flick and Harry Darbee and Walt Dette tied up their wonderful dry flies. Between them and together the chalk streams of England and the Catskill rivers of New York have contributed so much to the evolution of dry-fly fishing as we all now know it and love so dearly today. Nobody can be said to have invented dry-fly fishing, it evolved by itself with the help of all of these men mentioned along with many others.

~~~~~

Fishing and dry-fly fishing is such a contemplative and tactile occupation which is why, I suppose, it appealed to literary sensibility. One other reason for the vast amount of writing about fishing is inculcated in that first theorem of fishing that states, 'No fisherman ever fishes as much as he wants to'. Perhaps the next best thing to fishing is to read about it which usually means reading the same story line, over and over again, in the latest 'How to and how I did it and with what' fishing book.

There is always the multitude of fishing magazines that pop through our door regularly every month. *Trout and Salmon* is not exactly *Harpers and Queen*, *Country Life* or *Hello* magazine but it does, for the deprived fisherman, satisfy the urge to experience vicariously what one cannot go out and do, which most times it does very well.

For most game fishermen the *Trout and Salmon* magazine is for game fishing enthusiasts, and when one is an enthusiast any magazine as such and any others similar like *Fly-fishing and Fly-Tying* and *Today's Fly-fisher* are read over and over again, every article and advert including all the classifieds at the back, are usually visually devoured and mentally and inwardly digested. I know – I have, like so many others, done it every month for the last forty years or more.

Many of my fishing books were bought second-hand from one of the best bookshops in Hampshire, Oxleys of Broad Street, Alresford. Lawrence Oxley, now unfortunately no longer with us, was a keen fly-fisherman which helped, and he was also one of the most knowledgeable people that I knew on the subject of books, especially fishing books. His shop sold newly published books and many book launches were held at his shop. The shop contained a vast array of second-hand books which kept me occupied for many a long hour on many a wet winter afternoon. There was a large section that contained second-hand fishing books to which I always made a beeline. Over the years I got to know Lawrence so well that he would hide away any second-hand book on trout or trout fishing so I could have first refusal to buy whenever I called in.

An old book shop such as Oxleys with every shelf crammed full of books

Happy fly fisher, Mr Noel Rice, with his first catch of the day.

ceiling to floor on every subject under the sun has that delightful musty old book smell which for me creates an aura that is unique and so evocative that once experienced it is never forgotten. I do love books.

Over the years I had a chance to study fishermen rather closely and by doing so it was surprising what I could learn. A few minutes in the company of a fisherman gave me a very good idea what he or she was all about. I tended to judge a fisherman by their approach to their fishing and the way in which they actually used a fly-fishing rod. A fisherman who had fished for most of his life was usually experienced enough to accept that even the best fishers had a bad fishing day. It was usually those people who came to fishing late in life who found it harder to accept a bad fishing day and even more so with those types of people who expected the regular and instant success in their business life to be reflected in their sporting endeavours. It did not take many minutes for me to work out whether the fisherman was enjoying him or herself. Body language was easily discernible in the action of casting a fly rod and this alone told me a great deal about the mental attitude of the fisherman. By reading the client's body language I could as a riverkeeper decide whether to stay or retire discreetly from the scene.

Unfortunately there were some fishers who found it very hard to accept failure and a blank day to some was deemed a sign of total personal failure. On the other hand I remember the late Dermot Wilson fishing his favourite beat on my water and having a blank day and, as was his way, he raised his trilby hat in a gentlemanly fashion to the river as he left saying that the river and the trout were too good for him that day. I did comment to him that he should have learnt one thing and that was not to fish on a scorching hot cloudless Thursday afternoon in August in a downstream wind over low water on the top beat of the Martyr Worthy water. We both had a chuckle over that.

Some found it hard not to be seen as a successful angler and some found it so hard that they at times resorted to devious methods to fill the creel just to maintain that aura of unfailing personal success. I felt so sorry for those people as they had surely lost something so precious from the fishing experience.

There is a saying, which must originate from a non-angler, stating that fishermen tend to be liars. This is not true because I do know of one great fisherman who never ever told a porkie pie and his name is mentioned in verse one of the first chapter of the gospel according to St Matthew. In fact game fishing and the church have gone hand in hand throughout the ages as I have noticed that there is hardly a salmon river in the land that has not got one or more pools called the Minister's Pool or the Bishop's Cast and in trout fishing we have many a Church Pool on many rivers. Besides there is the Rev Greenwell who gave us that wonderful general imitation of a medium olive called a Greenwell's Glory.

In all forms of fishing but particularly game fishing I have found that our sport is such a great social leveller. This was brought home to me when for a period of seven years I ran an annual fishing school on the River Spey back in the 1970s based from the Boat of Garten hotel. There would be fifteen people booked in for a week's casting and fishing tuition. The very first evening would be a formal social event to introduce myself and for all to get to know one another. Universally it will be found that such fishing schools attract people from many different walks of life and social classes and this is so easy to see on this first evening when observing how everyone is sizing up everyone else, including the instructor. Yet without fail, week in and week out and year in and year out, by the second evening the renowned barrister from Lincoln's Inn will be discussing casting techniques with the plumber from Bolton and the consultant surgeon from Winchester will be talking dry flies to the carpenter from Glasgow. The so-called social differences just seem to melt away as the common subject of fish and fly-fishing took up every minute of the time. Fish and fishing and learning to cast brought together regularly a complete cross-section of people and for me these were some very memorable days spent on the Spey in company that was single-minded on my favourite subject. Teaching people to cast a fly can be very rewarding and many of the students I have taught over the years have since become lifelong friends of mine. I find it so rewarding particularly when an ex-student contacts me some years later just to thank me and tell me of his fishing exploits experienced through their new found sport.

I believe that the Martyr Worthy beat is one of the last beats to insist upon upstream dry fly only on the chalk streams of Hampshire. From the very first day of employment I was told in the strongest terms that this was the code of practice on the beat. This policy was clearly illustrated to me many times by the then owner in my first year as keeper. Absolutely no nymphs and or use of a wet fly or wet fly techniques. If there were no trout rising then no one would fish – that was the form for thirty years.

The rods over the years were hardly ever disappointed with the fishing as the resident trout on the Martyr Worthy beat were always very ready and willing risers and hardly a day in the year passed when trout could not be seen taking something off the surface at some time of the day. The insect activity on the Upper Itchen was, during most of my experience on the river, most excellent as all the well-known traditional flies would regularly hatch in great numbers at the right time of year and at the right time of day. On most days nymph fishing was totally unnecessary as the surface activity was at most times quite frenetic. That did not mean that the trout were easy to catch, far from it. Except for the duffer days of early spring, when the first huge hatch of spring olive came off or the river was coated with iron blue and the trout were feeding gang busters, the Itchen trout could be very particular and choosy towards the artificials offered by the fisherman.

These trout could be extremely spooky and could and would dart off even before the fly was taken out of the fly box let alone presented onto the water. At other times they would continue to feed ravenously on naturals and take little notice of the fisherman on the bank casting away to them or even the splashes over their head as a succession of artificials were plonked upon their heads in an effort to attract attention from the trout. The same fish on another day would bolt for cover and hide for the rest of the day at the twitch of a fisherman's eyelid and even before the artificial fly had been taken out of the keeper ring. That is the obtuse character of the wild Itchen trout at Martyr Worthy.

Many an expert fly-fisher retreated to the hut fishless, and many were at a loss to explain why they had a blank day when the trout had been feeding so well off the surface for most of the day. The Itchen was such a great leveller and deflator of fishing egos and I have often chuckled silently to myself as some of the so-called experts have retreated to the hut, tail between the legs, having been completely bamboozled by the trout. Even the great Frederick Halford records in one of his fishing reports that he found the Martyr Worthy beat of the Itchen too difficult to fish.

One final illustration of the contrary nature of Itchen trout was the evening when two well-known fly fishers met on my middle beat bridge at the end of a fruitless day fishing together. They had fished over trout that had been rising consistently all the day. Whilst discussing between them the possible reasons for this, one fisher took out his Wheatly fly box that held around fifty dry flies, he proceeded to open each section and promptly tipped the entire contents onto the surface of the river. This hatch of artificial flies was directed over a number of rising trout that they both had been fishing for all day. Believe it or not 75% of these flies were taken off the surface by the trout, the fishermen were dumbfounded. The Upper Itchen has this reputation and long may it continue but I am afraid 'things – they are a changing'. The natural conditions, clear water plenty of food good cover and the fact that all the trout are from genuine wild stock that have been born and bred naturally and have adapted to these conditions over hundreds of generations has produced a stock of trout that are now as fickle as they can be. Educated I think is the word to use when describing Itchen trout they certainly have their BSc's, PhD's and QBE's in survival!

There has been so much sense and uncommon sense written and talked about over the years around the subject of the ethics of fly-fishing. For one who has spent the majority of his life around the chalk streams it is inevitable that I would have been brought up to abide by the ethics that have historically evolved on these streams. Not wishing to resurrect the Halford versus Skues story again we must however remember and accept the fact that it was Halford who was most influential in creating a set of general rules pertaining to dry-fly fishing on the chalk streams to which so many fly-fishers have adhered. Prior to this event the rules and ethics pertaining to fishing on these rivers were very flexible to say the least as the use of various bait forms and subsurface attractors including live mayfly on blow lines, was the order of the day.

Looking back and reviewing the evolution of fly-fishing from the early 1800s and charting its progress through these years it will be found that it was improvement to the equipment used for fly-fishing that contributed most to its progress. Rods evolved from hickory to greenheart, from whole cane to split cane, from tank aerial steel to glass fibre, and from carbon fibre to titanium. Lines have evolved from plaited horsehair to plaited silk through to the now sophisticated multi-profiled plastic floating and sinking lines. Co-polymers, fluorocarbon and other man-made materials have now superseded catgut and so it goes on.

All of these improvements have enabled and encouraged some major changes and improvements in the efficacy of known and allowed methods of fishing particularly in fly-fishing. Coincident with these changes was the improved access availability to the once exclusive fisheries allowing a wider range of anglers to fish many and most of these once exclusive waters. These changes brought a broader spectrum of angling thought to our rivers; it was the catalyst that introduced some so-called new methods to our streams.

I fished with Frank Sawyer after he had devised his Chadwicks 477 grayling bug and he demonstrated how to catch the grayling on his shallow waters of the Upper Avon in Wiltshire. It was not long after that when anglers discovered that this grayling bug pattern also readily took trout and that bags of trout increased further when the bug was tied up on a larger hook with more weight added and it was accurately cast and fished from the riverbank. Frank skilfully fished this bug down narrow runs between thick tresses of ranunculas and in the deeper areas of the river and the trout were mainly taken on the lift. I could not see this method ever being recognised as acceptable let alone becoming an allowed method of catching trout or grayling on the Test or Itchen. If this method were to become part of the armoury of the chalk stream angler then it would need to be adapted somewhat. Frank Sawyer devised many years ago a successful method of catching grayling that other trout fishermen have adapted to something similar to this new Czech style fishing.

The now popular method of salmon fishing with large gold heads dressed as gold ribbed hare's ears using a sink-and-draw method was not a new innovation as so many people claimed. Frank Sawyer described it accurately in one of his books catching Atlantic salmon back in the 1960s and 1970s on the River Avon at Ibsley above Ringwood with his weighted Chadwicks 477 grayling bug using the identical gold head sink-and-lift approach.

It took the Czechs some time to hone this fundamental method from its early beginnings some fifty odd years ago into the so-called sophisticated and now much vaunted new Czech style of nymph fishing, or Eastern European method, we see promoted and so widely used by the angling experts of today and expounded by some of the experts and given much coverage in the angling media.

In my opinion the method was not new and had little to commend it, if it was used as described by some of these experts on the chalk streams. The method entailed standing almost right on top of the quarry and dangling a steeply tapered length of leader with a bite indicator attached off a very short heavy fly line carrying with it a heavy weighted nymph or even lead shot on the point and droppers of a smaller size and weight at intervals above. This rig was then bounced along the river bed and when at the end of the very short trot the weighted nymph was drawn up towards the surface to induce a fish to take on the lift. This method may work well on rivers like the Welsh Dee, as it was described in one article, but on most chalk streams wading was not normally allowed and all fishing was done from the riverbank. As for standing in the river very close to the fish and dangling a weighted nymph as described I thought would be very unproductive on the gin-clear Itchen as the wary wild brown trout and even the grayling would just not tolerate such intimacy.

Anyone with any experience of the chalk streams found that, on most beats, wading was not allowed because it disturbed the river bed and did colour the water for some distance downstream thus disturbing the fishing there. With heavy growths of weed this Czech method can become very difficult to execute. Having watched this method demonstrated on a spate river there was little doubt in my mind that, while this method does catch fish, for me it was a very boring method of artificial bait fishing that had little or nothing to do with fly-fishing. It was merely a form of coarse fishing for game fish that bore no relation whatsoever to conventional fly-fishing. I think many regular chalk stream anglers agreed with my view on this although I accept that these thoughts may not please others.

All the new materials and improvements in tackle have allowed more versatility to be available to the angler of today which has and does at times alter the ways in which some anglers view their sport and in the ways by which they fish.

This ongoing evolution formed its own standard of ethics or sportsmanship and it is surely down to the individual angler to form his own approach. Democracy rules in most fishing clubs and associations so it is down to the dedicated club anglers themselves to ensure a suitable standard of fishing ethics are maintained around them.

These and other methods of fishing were not to be despised as long as they did not harm fish or fish habitat and were within the laws as set down by the fishery and the Salmon and Freshwater Fishery Acts. It was down to the fishery owners and fishery managers to decide what equipment and fishing methods were permitted on their particular waters. Our own individual angling ethics embraced the rules and regulations set down by the owners and fishery managers of the waters we have the privilege to fish.

Although Halford and Skues did not always see eye to eye over some things and Halford in my view was rather too dogmatic in instilling his purist views whereas Skues who we must remember used the dry fly for most of the time, but was also quite happy to fish his nymph to subsurface feeding fish. If we take a look at Skues' patterns of nymphs we find they were all representative of the natural insects and in no stretch of the imagination could they be called lures or attractors. Some fishermen now euphemistically call some patterns of lures and attractors nymphs just because they are fished below the surface.

To define our personal chalk stream fly-fishing ethics we could do worse than carefully study the works and fishing philosophies of those two fly-fishing doyens mentioned and select from them the happy balance.

I still prefer to catch my trout on a dry fly, although I do use the nymph quite happily when needs must, I know darned well that I would catch more fish if I did not persist for so long with the dry fly but that is the way I like it.

Two other subjects that stirred up the emotions of fisherman more than anything else were the subjects of catch-and-release and the use of barbless hooks. Although these two subjects are more to do with the management of a fishery rather than in the methods of angling they are complementary.

Catch-and-release has been used by fishery managers with the logic that the fish will live longer and will grow bigger particularly in stocked waters where natural regeneration cannot occur through lack of spawning or such like as in still water ponds and lakes and reservoirs. To be successful in such situations it could be shown to work but only if the fishing pressure was extremely light. This was a situation that rarely occurred in the commercial put-and-take fisheries where high fishing pressure is the order of the day. Even though catch-and-release was used in such circumstances on stocked fish I felt very strongly that this policy was fundamentally wrong and could very well give the impression to opponents that anglers were just playing with a fish that was purposely put in the water to regularly catch-and-release at will. In practice this did not happen as the fish, once caught a couple of times, learnt from its experiences and became almost uncatchable and also went off the feed to such an extent that it would lose condition and die of starvation – not good for the business of selling quality fishing time. The factors of hooking mortality or sub-lethal hooking stress became important considerations where the fishing pressures were high.

Catch-and-release using barbless hooks could be used properly where there was a genuine wild population of trout and the objective was to protect and enhance that population until such times as it recovered to a state where a controlled harvest could be instituted. The use of catch-and-release was used very successfully to allow a wild population of spring salmon to recover. In such circumstances it was shown that the mortality rate was low and re-catch rate was also low.

The use of barbless hooks has not been shown to significantly reduce the mortality when compared to barbed hooks but the use of such hooks did reduce the handling time of the fish that increased their chance of survival after release. Hooking stress did not cause mortality in fish that were healthy and lived in a good environment but hooking stress, added to a fish already under stress from adverse environmental conditions or pollutants, could cause premature mortality or greater susceptibility to predators, diseases or parasites.

As I progressed into the fascinating sport of fly-fishing, my stock of artificial flies increased sequentially over the years. My collection not only grew in numbers but also in the diversity of patterns, whether devised and tied by myself or purchased at the local tackle shop. No matter how tatty some of these flies have become over the years, either by use, age or simply nostalgia, I still find it hard to weed them out and consign them to the dustbin. As a result I have many redundant fly boxes crammed full of flies that I open rarely let alone take to the river.

The same applies to the rest of my fly-fishing tackle. Of the many trout rods I have accumulated over the years I find that I now regularly use only two of them. One for dry-fly fishing and the other for the heavier duties for still water trout and or sea trout. The rest gather dust under the stairs where there are split-cane rods, glass fibre rods and early models of carbon fibre all of which were deemed to be state of the art at their time of introduction. Throughout my fishing life I have had a love for cane rods, because not only was split-cane the only material used for fly rod making when I started fly-fishing but it is the love and respect one develops for them. Each rod is an individual work of art that has been delicately and lovingly hand-crafted by a dedicated craftsman. For many like myself this has been for me a joyous life long love affair with split cane rods the physical beauties and seductive charms of which have captivated me all my fishing life. This is a feeling that only a fly-fisherman can even begin to explain, particularly if one is predominantly a dry-fly fisher who caught his first wild trout on a cane rod.

It is either through laziness or experience, drawn from 50 years of dry-fly fishing, that has taught me that to be comfortable when fly-fishing is paramount. Equally important is the selection of suitable colours and shades of the clothing worn. Having decided upon the right clothes to wear the next thing for me is to ensure I carry as little equipment as possible. I cannot help but smile privately to myself when I observe some of today's so called chalk stream 'experts' fly-fishing. Not only are they usually weighed down with a mass of useless equipment dangling from every corner of their clothing but also some demonstrate a naïve immunity or a decided lack of understanding as to the colour and shades of the clothing they should wear.

These important aspects of fly-fishing I learnt in my early formative years when I had the great privilege and opportunities as a young riverkeeper to observe, listen and learn whilst sat at the feet of those doyens of fly-fishing Frank Sawyer, Dermot Wilson and 'Ollie' Kite. Not only was it observing the demonstrations of their streamside field craft when stalking rising trout but mentally noting also the way they were dressed before entering into the stalk. The success rate of any hunter relies so much on adept field craft in the matter of the approach, and the ability to merge body outline discreetly into the natural surrounding environment, thus enabling the fisher to get closer to his prey to deliver the *coup de gras* delivery cast.

On one occasion 'Ollie' Kite came to fish on my river. We were sat together one lunchtime outside of the fishing hut sharing a glass or two of his famous home-made rocket fuel that he called dandelion wine. He said that it was not until he had watched some black and white film of himself fly-fishing for trout that he realised that the shirt he was wearing made him stand out like a sore thumb on the riverbank. Being one of his army shirts it was originally a standard army issue khaki colour which, when new, blended well into the general background, but after years of wear he had not noticed that with the constant wear, washing and ironing the original colour and shade had been bleached out and it had now taken on a very light creamy beige colour which stood out quite vividly even on black and white film.

Today so many fly-fishers dress in these modern bright coloured shirts, gaudy baseball caps and multi-pocketed waistcoats some of which are even made of bright shades of coloured materials. When on a riverbank and dressed in such garb, many of these fishermen stand out like flashing warning beacons on a motorway as any slightest movement they make can be readily seen a mile away. This brightly coloured uniform has almost become a standard twenty-first century game angling dress code, aptly illustrated on some of the glossy covers and in pages of game fishing magazines. The clothing fashion seems to have been influenced by the American scene. Anglers appear dressed in light, ventilated, cool fabrics of a vibrant colour; no doubt very comfortable in hot weather when worn for attending the CLA Game Fair and fishing shows around the country, or for attracting attention while delivering casting demonstrations. They may also be fine for the sweltering heat and bright tropical sunlight when wading the bone fish flats of Belize or tarpon fishing from a boat off Key West for which use I suggest these clothes were originally designed. However I am not quite sure these bright colours are conducive to successful stalking of wild trout in a more traditional UK river. Is it any wonder any self-respecting trout in their vicinity retires rapidly from the scene?

Before being taken to task I would admit that in days gone by even those doyens of fly-fishing of yesteryear such as those mentioned above also conformed to a certain dress code that was regarded as standard required fishing kit at the time. However in those days it was one of sober neutral coloured shirts and pullovers, tweed hats, and tweed jackets over topped with waxed Barbour jackets if it was wet, and brown or dark green corduroy trousers stuffed into wellies or thigh waders. In my earliest days on the Itchen neckties were expected to be worn by all fisherman, including me, if I was going to act as ghillie for the day. Thank goodness the strict adherence to this rigid dress code was relaxed with the advent of the swinging sixties. In the past the major difference for anglers was the unwritten rule that the clothes worn were to be of a universal colour mixture of dull green, olive and brown all of which readily merged into the natural background colours of the riverside environment, whatever the style.

One has only to ask any expert pigeon shooter or game keeper what his killing success rate would be if he wore one of today's brightly coloured baseball hats and shirt when sat in a pigeon hide expecting to attract wary wild wood pigeons onto his decoys. His obvious answer would apply equally to anyone stalking wild trout in a river.

Nowadays, whenever I fish my home chalk stream or any river that holds trout, I make sure to fish with the absolute minimum amount of tackle according to the conditions of the day. I have refined my tackle requirements down to absolute basics. Other than the rod, reel and line, all my requirements for a day's trout fishing or come to that for the entire season can be stowed quite easily in the two breast pockets of my dark-green fishing shirt and one trouser pocket.

So often I have seen anglers fishing up a chalk stream and carrying with them two or three rods made up, ranging sometimes from a one weight through to maybe a six weight. Many now even wear chest waders when they are not necessary, plus the obligatory multi-pocketed waistcoat, over which is worn a waist bag and even a bulging knapsack on the back all of which are usually crammed full with items and gadgets many of which I am sure have not seen the light of day for years and when viewed from a distance they resemble a cross between on over-laden mountain yak and an over-decorated Christmas tree finished off with a host of extra items of kit that cannot be stored in the waistcoat because all forty-eight pockets are already so full they have to suspend all this extra tinsel from every conceivable corner of their clothing. OK, maybe all the kit is required if the angler has hiked over twenty miles up to some isolated highland loch and intends to camp out or has trekked for miles up a wilderness river system in New Zealand, however is it really necessary to carry all this gear when actually fly-fishing on our more popular trout rivers in UK? Some only need a set of fairy lights and a piece of mistletoe or holly in the hat and the comparison would be complete. I admit I may be cynical now, but I have learnt to say nothing and merely smile inwardly to myself as I am so often reminded after catching sight of my own reflection in a car window, who am I to make any sartorial comment?

~~~~~

For interest my minimalist trout fishing kit would consist of the following basic items:-

Sage 9ft 5wt SLT 590-4 (four piece)

A thirty-year-old Hardy "Lightweight" reel loaded with a Snowbee DT 5wt floater with a 13ft tapered Umpqua leader attached.

A spare Umpqua 13ft tapered leader down to 7x

A 25 metre spool of fluorocarbon tippet material 7x

A 25 metre spool of fluorocarbon tippet material 5x

A small cheap clear plastic six sectioned fly box for my selection of flies and nymphs. Capacity of which circa 100 assorted dry flies, emergers and nymphs.

A small 10gm plastic container of 'Abolene' which is my preferred floatant.

Lastly, my trusty twenty-year-old Swiss Army angler's knife which is the complete fisherman's tool box that has scissors and a disgorger plus all the other tools including tweezers, can-opener, and obligatory corkscrew, which rests in my left-hand trouser pocket attached to my belt by a stout cord.

I wear an aged, baggy 1920s style brown tweed cap that has a good peak, although I hate baseball caps and wouldn't be seen dead in one I do have to admit their long peaks are excellent in bright conditions.

Besides wearing wellies or thigh waders for kneeling and bank crawling when its wet, I may carry a lightweight hooded nylon waterproof if rain threatens, which doubles up as a small ground sheet if the banks are wet and a sit down fag break rest is needed, and after use can be folded away to nothing and stuffed easily into the back trouser pocket like a pair of golfing gloves. I am more than happy to use this basic selection of kit wherever and whenever I fish for trout in the UK be it in moving or still water. If it happens to be cold then I wear a suitable olive-coloured fleece.

With all this neatly stowed about my body there is still plenty of room left for my fags lighter and handkerchief an odd bar of chocolate and even, heaven forbid my mobile phone. Complete comfort and freedom of movement is the object as I do detest to be constrained by any excess equipment around my body.

A good pair of Polaroid glasses are obligatory. As for a landing net I prefer not to use one and only take a small folding one which is clipped to my belt when fishing a river that has high banks when played out fish cannot be drawn safely into the hand for release or despatch.

Probably few will agree with my philosophies or even with my selection of kit, but they both suit me in the way I wish and enjoy to fly-fish and I have the utmost respect for those who wish to differ. I am certainly not competitive when it comes to fishing and although I enjoy deceiving trout and possibly would catch more of them if I did become more competitive with other anglers but to me inter-angler competition is not the aim of the game in my book. Fly-fishing to me is a solitary sport and, if indeed there is any competition, the challenge comes from dealing with the conditions that Nature sets before me and the competition is just between me and that elusive trout. It saddens me to witness and listen to some anglers who have the need at all costs to be seen to be top rod and to have captured the most and or the biggest fish. This is of course an unfortunate natural human trait that is more apparent in some than others.

Although I have caught my fair share of fish over the years even so some of my most memorable days spent fly-fishing have been blank when it comes to numbers of trout caught. I have spent many wonderful days in some of the most beautiful wild natural surroundings on earth where my attention has been captivated for every minute of the day with not only the stunning scenery around me but in observing some of the most incredible native flora and fauna. Not only on my home chalkstreams of Hampshire but also on remote highland burns and lochs of Scotland, in the wildernesses of Montana, Wyoming and the rugged wilds of Northern Ontario, Labrador, New Brunswick and Quebec. I have been very privileged to visit and experience and appreciate the natural beauties of such wonderful wild places and consign my private records of them to my memory banks for instant recall in my later years and they will all derive from just being a fly-fisherman.

~ 7 ~
A Cast of Characters

ne day, having spotted from afar the bend in the delicate cane rod, I suspected that a fisherman had hooked a large wild brown trout. From the position on the bank where the fisherman was playing the fish I even had a very good idea which particular trout was hooked. Knowing the angler well I knew that he would wish to be left alone to play and land this good trout. After a few tense minutes the trout was drawn gently into the bank and the fisherman stepped into the water, gently slipped his hand down the line and gingerly extracted the barbless hook from the jaws of the trout. By the time I arrived the angler had placed his rod on the riverbank and was kneeling down in the water with the trout gently cradling it too and fro. In silence we both admired the heavily spotted, deep bellied brown trout as it recovered its strength in the caring hands of the angler.

"Would you like me to weigh the fish – I have a pair of pocket scales so we can slip her into the net and weigh both together and then release her unharmed?" I enquired.

The angler did not raise his head but just slowly shook it from side to side.

"I happen to have a tape measure in my pocket, would you like me to measure your fish?" I volunteered, remembering that American anglers measure their fish rather than weigh them.

Again the angler did not raise his head but merely shook it from side to side.

"Would you like me to photograph it for you as I see you have your camera strung around your neck, it won't take a second and you'll be able to show it to your friends back home?" I added.

Again the slow shake of the head and with that the fish, now sufficiently recovered, with one powerful bound darted out into the depths of the cold River Itchen.

The angler watched the disappearing fish and slowly straightening up turned to me and explained in a slow Kentucky drawl, "Thank you for your suggestions but I now have this picture in my mind of how big that fish is and I will carry that with me throughout the year and during the hot, humid days of summer when working in my office in New York. I'll remember too this wonderful river and its

Valley and this exact spot in it, the cool breeze and the smell of the newly mown bank grass, the sigh of the willows behind us and the pale blue Hampshire sky but most of all I'll remember this trout. I don't want this lovely picture cluttered up with the statistics of weight or length or even a photograph as none would ever compare with the one I carry up here," said the angler, gently tapping the side of his forehead with his forefinger.

As I wandered off up the riverbank I realised that there were some dreams that money could never buy.

~~~~~

We had a regular visitor who came to fish as a guest of one of the tenants. John was one of those fishermen who had such boundless enthusiasm for the whole sport of fly-fishing and so much so in fact I am convinced he would have willingly dry-fly fished a small puddle in the car park for a whole day and still say when he left that he had had the most wonderful day's fishing, and he would have meant it!

One warm sunny day in late spring John was fishing the far side of the middle beat where along this particular stretch of the bank there were several low footbridges that passed over the small inlets that seeped spring water into the river. John was standing on one of these narrow two plank bridges when he spotted a rising trout just upstream and mid-stream from where he was standing and so proceeded to cast his fly in its direction. At the time I was attending to another fisherman on the opposite bank but was keeping half an eye on John's progress, when suddenly the trout rose to his fly and took a firm hold. John, in his excitement, had lifted heartily into the trout and as he did so also took a step backwards, a trait that many inexperienced and experienced anglers exhibit. The bridge was only a narrow affair so John gracefully fell backwards into the muddy ditch behind him.

Like any true fisherman at no time did John let go of his rod and I can see him now with his rod held up in the classical position for playing a trout. From where I was standing there was only the rod and a pair of hands visible, one hand holding the rod and the other winding in on the reel the rest of his body was immersed in the black mud. A second or two later a mud covered head appeared just above the level of the bridge and a black figure tried to heave itself out of the mud whilst still doing everything correctly with the rod and keeping the right pressure on the fish. The mud was thick, deep and black so with two hands fully occupied playing the fish he was unable to get out of the predicament in which he found himself. All I could make out from across the river was a set of beaming white teeth a black face and a pair of panda-rimmed eyes. A hysterical laugh emanated from this grotesque apparition wallowing

Fishing guests from South America.

in the mire, which reminded me of a prehistoric dinosaur heaving itself out of some primeval bog. John continued to play the fish in perfect fashion until I had time to run down to the next bridge and cross over and run up the other side and extract his landing net that was still somehow attached to his belt and thankfully net the fish safely. I dispatched the fish solely because it had caused such merriment to all the onlookers. Eventually I managed to pull John free from the mud and as he stood on the riverbank his laughter was so infectious we both just sat down and cried with laughter.

The story does not end there. John had arrived on the river driving his brand new Range Rover and as he had a long journey ahead of him back to Essex he was rather reluctant to mess up the pristine leather interior of his new pride and joy. I suggested that he came up to my cottage, had a shower and borrowed some clean clothes in which to drive home. This he did. On arriving at the cottage, Paula spotted us coming up the path and rushed out to find out what had happened. As we told her we attached the hose to the kitchen tap through the kitchen window to hose off the surplus mud from the tall, pungent, oozing pile that was John. The retelling of the story then started Paula off into an uncontrollable fit of laughter and, as it was very catching, all three of us ended up once again in a helpless state. My only wish was that I could have taken some photographs to record the incident for posterity.

To this day every time I walk over that little bridge I am reminded of that hilarious incident and the vivid memory of a pair of hands and a set of white teeth and a pair of white-ringed eyes peering out of a morass with rod still held in the classical position.

~~~~~

Another tenant who fished with us regularly at that time rang me early one morning from the local maternity home where his wife had presented him with a bouncing baby daughter. Naturally he was full of the joys of fatherhood and was determined to celebrate and was keen for someone to share his joy. We arranged to meet on the river at about midday and he duly arrived with a superb bottle of Batard Montrachet White Burgundy, which was ceremoniously opened, and the baby's head duly wetted. We did manage to fish together for a short while until it was decided that we should go for a spot of lunch at the local. I have always tried to keep my tenants happy and accede to their wishes so off we went and this time it was not the usual pint of Courage best bitter at the bar, it had to be champagne, so out came a bottle of Dom Perignon 1980 – I remember the date on the bottle(s) to this day.

It was a very enjoyable lunch break and the baby's head was well and truly wetted once again and we did eventually make it back to the riverside at around four in the afternoon, both of us by then feeling no pain whatsoever. We actually managed to fish again and even caught some trout but this time it had to be a real team effort as by this time neither of us were particularly steady on our feet so the one on the riverside took the rod and wielded it in the direction of the river while the other acted as a counter balance, or prop, and in that way we very slowly fished our way up the river both leaning towards and against each other as if joined at the shoulders like a walking A-frame. How we ever did not end up in the river was a miracle. Many years after we both still reminisce about that crazy fun day. It was instances like that and the many others that made my life on the river so much fun and so very memorable.

There is no harm in the maxim that states: 'Put the fun back into work'. Not every day on the river was like that of course, but life was far too short for any of us to be miserable and or deadly serious every minute of every day.

~~~~~

About the same time another great character comes to mind very readily and although he only fished alternate weekends he was a superb fisherman.

The Friday, Saturday and Sunday of his weekend were always intense and concentrated dry-fly fishing and the keeper had to be very much on parade. It very soon came clear to me that he was one of the most deep-thinking fly-fishers that I had encountered up to then. Here I thought was again another great chance to learn from experiences of someone who had fished the Itchen all his life and who had also a wealth of fishing and river knowledge.

We would sit for hours by the river just talking fish and fishing and fishery management and at times soon I would be presented with a book to read on some fishing subject we had been discussing the previous weekend. These books had been taken from his extensive library of some 500 fishing books many of which were first editions. One book he lent me was by a Colonel Harding on the subject of what the trout sees from underneath the water. We had talked and discussed this vexing subject for a couple of months and this was long before Messrs Goddard and Clarke produced their great tome upon a similar subject discussing how well do trout see surface floating insects from below.

The early eighties at Martyr Worthy was a very busy time as the tenants we had then were really making use of the river with few weeks passing when there were not visitors and other fishermen being entertained. For almost ten years from 1977 onwards I was left to more or less run the river with little contact or direction from the owners. No news being good news I presumed that all was well and I should carry on as before, which I did. As long as the tenants were happy and had no complaints and the river was well kept up together that was all that was required. At times I felt that I was completely on my own.

Fortunately during those years there were no major decisions that had to be made or any disaster with which I was not able to cope. When tenants moved on I managed to find suitable replacements usually from the guests of tenants who had fished the river over the years. Many of these people became firm friends and have remained so over the years. As time passed all the tenants would tell me when they were not coming to fish or when they were going away on holiday and each without exception always invited me to use their fishing whenever I wished whilst they were away. I felt so very privileged that they trusted me in this way. Therefore, I was at times able to invite one or two close friends to fish, and the tenants always knew that at no time was there ever any charge made for this wonderful opportunity. Besides there being a rule that tenants were not allowed to sublet their fishing and I would never ever have dreamt of taking money for fishing that had so kindly been given to me. This continued right up to the end of my time on the river and I will be eternally grateful to those tenants who so willingly let me use their waters at such times. These pleasures were gratefully received and never abused.

~~~~~~

One of the great pleasures of those early days at Martyr Worthy was getting to know the tenants some of whom had fished the river for many seasons and one man in particular I remember had fished the Itchen for 43 consecutive seasons, not all at Martyr Worthy, but always somewhere between Winchester and Tichborne. His knowledge and fishing expertise was exceptional and for a young keeper 'the old Commander' was another fount of 'trouty' knowledge that just had to be tapped. He was the very epitome of all I had imagined a dry-fly fisherman should look like – pipe in mouth, dressed in a check shirt, club tie, brown herringbone Harris tweed jacket, corduroy trousers and a very old battered Barbour jacket, black Dunlop bull's-eye wellingtons and tweed pork pie hat with his ancient patched Hardy fishing bag strung over one shoulder and his landing net on a lanyard across the other carrying in one hand his prized Hardy JJH Triumph cane rod in its brown bag tied neatly with a bow at the top and the well-weathered wicker picnic basket with its broken leather strap in his other hand.

I was able to learn from the Commander so much about not only my river but also the wily ways of the wild trout that abounded within its waters. The old Commander probably did not realise it but he did teach me a great deal and over the years we became very good friends.

Whenever the Commander was due to fish I would make sure to be close at hand when he arrived on the car park. As we walked together slowly down to the footbridge from where the first recce of the water would always be undertaken to ascertain which way the wind was blowing and if and what fly was hatching which determined where we would start to fish that day. The whole conversation would revolve around what had happened on the river since he was last down to fish, who had caught what and where, and on what fly and all the many other questions a fly-fisher normally asks when he first arrives at the river.

I have many times in latter years described to young fly-fishers and young riverkeepers in particular the ways of the Commander in an effort to transmit to them that wonderful feeling of expectation yet supreme calmness which exuded from him whenever he came to fish. This to me perfectly exemplifies all that is good in fly-fishing.

Once we had arrived at the fishing hut and stacked away all his gear from there on time mattered not a jot as he leisurely unpacked his rod and meticulously lined up the rod joints and attached his Hardy Perfect reel and threaded the line up the rod rings. All this was done usually sat on a bench outside the hut, which allowed him also to watch what was happening on the river just upstream of the hut. The Commander was an avid pipe smoker and as with every pipe smoker there is an ingrained ritual to be played out each time before a pipe is filled and lit, and the Commander was no exception to this rule. I can still see and hear him now sitting there with his trusty Hardy cane rod threaded up without a leader attached crooked in his arm as he dismantled his trusty briar and gave it a thorough reaming out with his ancient pipe smoker's penknife and giving it a hearty blow through before he ceremoniously reassembled the pipe and filled its ample bowl with his own particular brand of pipe tobacco. The lighting up of the pipe could take quite some time before full ignition had been achieved but all the time the Commander's eyes had hardly left the water as he spotted trout rising and accurately mentally marked their position using various natural markers along the bank such as a particular flower or tuft of grass. Whilst marking down the rising fish he was also identifying what insects were hatching and which ones the trout were taking.

The next operation was to select the right leader for attachment to the fly line, so out came an old leather wallet that was once used to store damp cat gut casts which now contained a good selection of knotted tapered nylon leaders of various lengths and strengths. The chosen leader would be gently unwound and given a gentle stretch so as to get rid of any memory that nylon sometimes can have. A figure of eight knot attached the fly line to the leader, as braided nylon loops were unheard of in those days. Now to the big decision, what fly? Out would come two very old Hardy fly boxes that were crammed with dry flies of all sizes and shapes and colours mainly all tied by that doyen of fly tyers of that era, Peter Dean of Sussex. As the Commander took out a pattern he would first hold it up to the sky to get an idea of its silhouette and then hold it out low and against the river so he could compare the artificial to the natural fly that was drifting down on the surface of the river. Eventually he would tie the chosen fly to the tippet, or cast as we called it in those bygone times.

The final act was to apply the floatant to the fly and as Musilin was about the only preparation available then a gentle little finger wipe was sufficient to make the fly float and water resistant.

Some mornings this pre-fishing ritual would take an hour or more and no matter how many fish were rising the old Commander never hurried or appeared to be over eager to start the battle. In the usual course of events by the time he was ready the trout were really going to town and feeding well and rising regularly. Having mentally marked each trout, he relit his pipe once more, slowly slid off the bench and gently crawled upon his knees up the riverbank using the

(*left to right*) Mr Stroud, The Commander, Paula and Captain 'Roddy' Casement celebrating The Commander's birthday.

well-grown fringe that I had allowed to grow along the riverbank as cover. On hands and knees the old Commander could just see through the fringe top as he crawled along until the nearest marked trout was within range of a deftly presented dry fly.

The 9ft 6in Hardy Triumph cane rod the Commander used had the traditional slow dry-fly action yet it had sufficient crispness which together in the right hands could accurately present a size 18 dry iron blue dun like thistledown at 15 to 20 yards. Such distances were usually unnecessary with the Commander as his observation, preparation and, most importantly, his field craft usually enabled him to present his first cast to a trout from about 12 or 15 yards. With just one or two false casts made to one side to get the right distance so as not to disturb the target trout the Commander would then place his fly perfectly first time just sufficiently upstream so the drifting fly came down over the trout just like a natural and without a hint of drag. Drag being one, if not the major, hazard that dry-fly fisherman have to contend with particularly on the Upper Itchen where the water is gin clear and has a multitude of different current speeds across the river surface.

One day, when I mentioned the Itchen being 'clear as gin' the Commander retorted, 'Yes, clear as gin and twice as bloody expensive'.

So many times I witnessed this wonderful display by the old Commander of how to fish the Martyr Worthy beat for wild trout on a clear bright spring day.

Many times, after a couple of hours, I returned to see how he had fared only to find that he had only fished up less than 50 yards of the river. Yet after inquiry as to the sport he had had during the morning it was nothing for him to have taken a good brace to take home and had caught and released eight or ten other wild trout of various sizes. That to me is just what the River Itchen used to be like.

Not only was the Commander such a good dry-fly fisher but he also had the most wonderful sense of humour which at times really tickled me pink.

Towards the end of his fishing career the Commander had to organise someone to drive him to and fro the river as his eyesight was not good enough for him to drive his car from mid-Sussex. Although he fished on for quite a few more years and still caught many trout although he could hardly see, being the man he was and an ex-naval commander he said he was now fishing by radar.

One morning the Commander arrived with his driver who was a retired Royal Navy Captain. These two made a great pair and at times acted like school kids continually playing practical jokes upon one another.

I caught up with them that particular morning at the middle beat hut just as they were about to start fishing. The coin had already been tossed to determine who fished the south bank and who fished the north bank. The Captain was making his way to the footbridge to cross over to fish up the south bank; the Commander was on his favourite bench stoking up his pipe. As I arrived he asked me what I was doing that day, as I had my little spinning rod under my arm. I said that I had spotted a couple of jack pike down in the bottom beat pool and as there was nobody fishing the beat that day I thought that I might try and wheedle them out. So wishing me good hunting off I went.

After a while I managed to catch and kill one of the pike and as I returned back via the middle beat the Commander spotted that I had caught a pike, came over looked at it and asked me what I was going to do with it. I said that sometimes I chopped them up and fed them to the dogs or just buried them. The Commander asked me if he could have it so I handed it to him and he then with a twinkle in his eye bade me to follow him back to the fishing hut where all their fishing bags were hanging up and the remnants of the picnic lunch were still on the table.

The Commander took down the Captain's fishing bag and gently tipped out the entire contents on to the table. Then he gently placed the dead pike at the bottom of the bag and proceeded to neatly replace the contents of the bag. As he hung it back up on the wall he turned to me, winked and told me not to say a word.

It was not until a couple weeks later when I caught up with the Commander again was I able to ask what happened. Well, you can just imagine the Captain returning home and hanging his fishing bag up in the cupboard under the stairs as one does and it did not take many days for Mrs Captain to notice a strange smell pervading the lower part of the house. The rest I leave to your imagination! The Commander and the Captain both roared with laughter when I next met up with them and enquired about what happened to my pike.

One day, as I was passing by the beat old Commander was supposed to be fishing, I noticed him sat on one of the other seats along the river bent forward intently studying the ground around his feet. On approaching I noticed that he was dangling a piece of string onto the ground and on even closer observation I saw there was quite a weight attached to the end of the string.

The old Commander's eyesight had been waning for several years and if and when he had dropped a fly as he was tying it on to his leader it would fall into the thick grass at his feet so for him with poor eyesight it was then almost impossible to find it again. With his active and practical mind he thought he would remedy this problem by purchasing a large horseshoe magnet which he attached to a piece of string and kept in his fishing jacket at all times. Whenever he dropped a fly he would unravel the string and dangle the magnet in the grass around his feet and most times retrieve not only his lost fly but also many others from other poor-sighted fishermen, this ploy thus saving him the cost of purchasing replacements. This became such an interesting occupation for him so whenever the fishing was quiet he would systematically move from one seat to the next and spend most of the day finding flies that other fisherman had lost. It was surprising what types of fly he found and some of them left a great deal to be desired when it came to thinking Martyr Worthy was purely a dry-fly fishing beat.

It was one of the saddest days on the river when the Commander finally decided to give up his rod with us. On his last day I secretly arranged for several of his special fishing friends to arrive at lunchtime. I asked my wife to bake a big fruit cake and we bought a nice bottle of dry sherry, which I knew he liked, and we had a surprise party at the top beat hut. I still have a treasured photograph recording that lovely but sad day. The Commander was then in his late eighties and I did see him once more when one of his friends brought him across to see me a year or so later. He was by then quite frail and almost completely blind and I had to take his arm to guide him down to the footbridge where we stood for some time saying nothing just listening to the river. Fortunately, right on cue, a trout rose quite near to hand. He heard it, turned 20 degrees to port and pointed towards the sound source. He was spot on with his direction and estimate as to the distance the fish was from him. I am sure if he had had a rod in his hand he would have covered that trout perfectly.

It was the meeting with such wonderful people like the Commander that made my riverkeeper's life such a rewarding one. Who wants overtime pay when one has such magnificent memories as that to cherish?

I recall the last day the old Commander came to fish he had just celebrated his 82nd birthday and, as it was a warm spring morning, he decided to go fishing on his own rented beat on the River Itchen at Martyr Worthy. He had fished the Itchen for some 60 seasons and knew almost every pebble of the river bed and every inch of the riverbanks, but time, the pressures of business and wartime service had taken their toll on his health and he now had difficulty in moving about, his vision was failing and even on this perfect early June morning his breathing was laboured.

I welcomed him to the river and while we discussed the tactics for the day he assembled the classic Hardy cane rod with which he had fished for the past two and half decades with such deadly accuracy and at times with devastating success as many a wild Itchen brown trout would testify if it could.

Some sixth sense told me to stay with the Commander on that morning, as it seemed that he should not really be left alone on the river. So together we walked quietly to the riverbank, selecting the appropriate fly for that morning, a size 18 iron blue dun, as we went. This was to be a study in ghillying in the time honoured way, as within seconds of arriving at the water's edge I spotted a good trout rising gently to the odd iron blue dun as they sailed down between the tresses of swaying ranunculus. I instructed the Commander to aerialise 10 yards of line. Habits of 60 years of fly-fishing had not been lost and, with all his disabilities, the old man was soon gently flexing his rod and the line sailed slowly too and fro. To me this was just poetry in motion.

"Now upstream 10 yards and six feet out from the bank," I instructed him. "Now again, but two feet more to the right. That's perfect, let it come, he's coming up – now!"

The Commander with perfect timing lifted and tightened into the trout and the reel then screamed as the fish took off for the far bank. After several strong runs and a couple of aerobatic leaps the trout was soon under control and gently drawn over the landing net. Somehow the tiny size 18 hook held and perhaps the old veteran trembled more from excitement than infirmity as I lifted the landing net.

As we stood looking and admiring the heavily spotted wild two-pound brown trout the Commander said, "Put it back, that trout deserves to live to fight another day".

Without a word I knelt down and gently removed the hook and held the fish in

'Take five' at the top beat hut.

the cool water head upstream until it had recovered its strength and had darted off into the deeps of the river none the worse for its battle but maybe a mite wiser.

The Commander with his fading eyesight squinted at the fly on the end of his line and asked, "What fly was it?"

"An iron blue dun, size 18," I confirmed.

With that the Commander took out his scissors and carefully snipped off the fly and gingerly attached it to the lapel of his Harris tweed jacket. Again he squinted at the end of the leader and asked, "What cast did you put on?"

"A 9 foot knotted tapered 6x," I replied.

Once again the old man took his scissors and snipped off the leader and neatly rolled it up in tight loops and placed it into his leather wallet. Picking up his rod again he slowly reeled in all his fly line onto the reel and turned to me and said, "Ron, that will be my very last trout ... ever ... thank you."

Now, who can say how much that trout was worth?

There have been many fascinating experiences over the years meeting and fishing with some very interesting and well-known people. Many of which were and still are well-known household names and come from the many walks of the public, political, industrial, sporting, military and artistic world. There can be few occupations like a riverkeeper that offers so many opportunities of meeting and studying such a wide variety of people. So often it will be found that the public perception of the persona of many of these prominent people changes markedly after meeting and fishing with them away from the public eye. Fly-fishing gives one an excellent insight into the real character of such people, many of whom in their every day environment portray a totally different persona.

Having been an average, yet keen, club cricketer it was a great privilege to have discussed at great length the ups and downs of England's test match performance against Australia with a current county cricket captain who was a regular guest of one of the tenants. There are also vivid memories of telling the assembled members at the bar of Winchester rugby club that I had recently spent a whole day fishing with one, if not the best, Welsh international fly-half in history!

One charming visitor was the then current Black Rod in the Houses of Parliament. That was a wonderful memorable day spent in his company and I was captivated by some of the accounts of his experiences whilst carrying out the duties of his historic position within the palace of Westminster. His accounts held me spellbound for most of the day spent in his company and opened my eyes to much of the priceless heritage and traditions upon which this country of ours has evolved.

Away from the riverbank at a game fair some years ago I vividly remember being introduced to a prominent member of the royal household who happened to be a very keen fly-fisher and fly tyer. Having sported a luxuriant growth of mutton chop whiskers for forty years or more I was immediately quizzed on the potential of my whiskers for tying up some hair wing salmon flies for use on Royal Deeside.

Less memorable were some guests during the financial boom and bust years of the 1980s in the city markets where fortunes were made and lost by wheelers and dealers on the stock market long before the dot com and hedge fund era. Fishing with some of these wheelers and dealers did become quite hard work at times especially when fortunes had been recently lost on some precarious investment. Black Thursday, 1988, still stands out in my mind when things in the city went topsy-turvy after which several once familiar faces were never seen again on the river.

It is quite surprising to some that several well-known rock stars fly-fish. One in particularly became a regular rod on the Martyr Worthy water for many years and subsequently became a good friend. Sat in one of the fishing huts over a tin of beer listening to his reminiscence of his early years in the 1960s and 1970s of booze, drugs and wild living was quite frightening yet it is a mark of his character that he has put all that behind him and now lives a relatively quiet country life with his wife and family.

One particular season we seemed to have a surfeit of admirals of the Navy, due mainly to the fact that one of our regular rods being an admiral who during the season would invite his friends to fish and these friends were usually other admirals. One particular morning I met the admiral and his guests in the car park just as another rod arrived who happened to be a naval commander so that day we had a full complement of Navy people fishing. As we walked down to the river the commander jokingly ordered me to go ahead and stand on the footbridge and pipe the admirals aboard! I duly obliged as I had my dog whistles on a cord around my neck and used one of them in obeisance of the command! Not knowing the correct pipe I made one up much to the amusement of the assembled company who all saluted in traditional naval style as they marched off down the riverbank and the senior admiral looking back and saying to me, 'Very good, carry on bo'sun ... full ahead both'.

~~~~~~

During the late 1990s a television production company were given permission to use a part of the river to film a few minutes footage for the well-known TV program *Kavanagh QC* in which that well-known actor the late and much missed John Thaw portrayed the part of Kavanagh. It took two days to capture the required two minutes of filming. The top fields were packed with trucks and lorries as a small transient self-sustaining village sprung up overnight. Wardrobe units, lorries loaded with props, Actors' caravans and fully equipped mobile kitchens, which fed a crew of about fifty people three superb meals each day. To estimate the costs of the whole operation just to film two minutes was difficult to judge but it is little wonder our TV licenses are so expensive. The village was transformed for a day with one of the cottages beside the river suddenly turned into a quaint riverside pub that even dispensed real beer. However, the one and only barrel supplied by the props department didn't last very long once the film crew had a chance to taste the local ale during lunch breaks.

Between shots I noticed John Thaw standing on the footbridge looking studiously into the river. On enquiring whether I could help him he said that where he lived there was a small stream flowing through his land and he has been fascinated with all the various water plants that grow in and around his little stream. Unfortunately he said that he had not the time to find out the names of all the plants but he did so much appreciate their natural beauty. Before being called for the next shot I spent a very pleasant few minutes identifying for him all the different plants that were in view from the river bridge.

Another shot was of one of the actors stood in the river fly-fishing and the shot was to be John Thaw standing on the footbridge talking to this fly-fisherman. I had been contracted for the day by the film company to ensure that this fly-fisherman looked the part. He had to be dressed correctly with all the right fishing clothes including hat, waders, rod, reel and line with flies attached. I was instructed to spend an hour or so teaching the actor, who had never held a fishing rod in his hand before, how to cast with a fly-fishing rod. Not an easy task. Finally, the film director was satisfied with the actor's newly acquired casting skills even if the instructor was not.

The wide diversity of the people who came to fish the river regularly was amply illustrated by one of the tenants of the fishery who lived in New York and regularly came over to fish the Itchen. His occupation until he retired was as Conservator of American Art at the Metropolitan Museum in New York This gentlemen would visit with his wife several times during the course of the season and we soon became very good friends particularly after he had been introduced to the residential hospitality of the Wykeham Arms in Winchester where they stayed and the delights of the good lunchtime food and quality wine at the Chestnut Horse. In fact during one of their visits to UK they both came all the way up to Scotland to visit my wife and I after I had retired just to assure themselves that we were both happy in our new home. People are so kind.

Of the many guests and notable visitors I had the great pleasure and privilege of meeting and fishing with over the years one couple particularly stand out above the others.

Several years ago I received a phone call early one morning from one of the fishing tenants asking if he could invite a very special person to fish the Itchen. This immediately seemed a strange request to me as tenants are at all times allowed to invite guests to the river and for them to share the fishing. It transpired later that this special person had tentatively asked whether it would be possible to fish the River Itchen on or as near as possible to the waters that eminent Edwardian statesman Lord Grey of Falloden fished when he was Edward Grey the British Foreign Secretary in the early years of the twentieth century prior to the First World War.

Once agreed, three days were set aside for this special visitor and I was to be available for all these three days but the actual day of arrival and the visitor's name would not be made known to me until the minute he actually pulled into the car park. This, I learned later, was purely for security reasons. The plot thickened when I was instructed to keep all this completely to myself and to tell absolutely no one else. This immediately put me in quandary although I admit now I did mention it to Paula and explained to her that it must be kept strictly to ourselves. I had been asked where I would be taking the special visitor to lunch. The Chestnut Horse was suggested, just a short walk across a field, so I was asked to book a table for six people for each of the three appointed days.

When the arranged day arrived I dutifully manned the car park at the appointed time on the first morning but alas no one turned up. A cold shiver ran through me as it suddenly dawned on me that this could be a clever wind-up by some of my practical joking friends, Messrs Gary Coxon & John Reddin

On the second day a posh car arrived on the car park and two very large and important looking people alighted and in an American accent one enquired if I was Mr Holloway. It was only then I was informed who my special guest was to be. It was none other than the recent President of the USA, Jimmy Carter. After a quick mobile phone call a dark-windowed car glided silently onto the car park and out stepped Mr President with his charming wife, Rosalind. After the introductions we walked down to river and made base camp at the top beat hut. It was to be the beginning of a very enjoyable day.

The President insisted he carried his own fishing gear and at the fishing hut I offered to put up his rod and tackle up for some dry-fly fishing. As I did so I noticed that his tackle was not exactly top quality but a well-used efficient middle of the range set of tackle that had been obviously carefully selected by the owner. I thought to myself that this man has fished before and so it was to be proved as the day went on.

The security men accompanying the President were brilliant and although they never let the President out of their sight for a second during his visit they remained discreetly at a distance from us as we fished up the river pausing for some time as we sat together on each bench seat for a long chat. We talked about the river, fishing, Edward Grey, conservation, and the threats of global warming and discussed his many questions he asked about the farming in the Itchen Valley. The President was very knowledgeable about farming matters and mentioned that he has three farms of his own in Georgia. Although he said that he is called the peanut king in the media he in fact grows more cotton than peanuts. Two subjects I studiously avoided were politics and the Middle East crisis both of which I was not qualified to discuss and secondly to do so would have spoilt a beautiful late spring morning on the banks of the Itchen. I think John Humphrys of the BBC would have been proud of me. Not many riverkeepers have the chance to discuss things of mutual interest and put the world to rights on conservation matters with an ex-president of the United States.

President Carter and his wife, Rosalind, on a fishing trip to the Itchen.
'Moc' Morgan (*left*), who arranged the visit, was my, and President Carter's, friend.

The President told me that although he fished a great deal when he found the time he had not experienced such challenging fine and far off dry-fly fishing as he had experienced that morning on the Itchen. He worked very hard on his fishing and eventually managed to catch and return a good wild brown trout of about one and half pounds on a well-presented elk hair sedge fly which made his day and brought a huge sigh of relief from me.

Although the British security agent in the party assured me that the two American bodyguards were armed I did not notice any obvious unnatural body bulges that might have hidden some awesome piece of hardware. They were very laid back and said to me that, so far, it was the most relaxing day of their whole UK trip and wished the President went fishing more often.

It was decided to walk over the field to the pub for lunch and the President and his wife stopped many times to take photographs of the pretty thatched cottages in the village of Easton. On entering the pub at about one o'clock our arrival coincided with the weekly gathering of the retired captains of industry and merchant banking who now lived in the Valley and met at that time each week to sink a few gin and tonics and discuss the financial and industrial problems of the nation and the world. I will never forget the stunned looks on their faces as I introduced my fishing companion to them all. It was quite a memorable lunchtime in the Chestnut Horse all of which the President and his wife enjoyed tremendously. I introduced the President to all the locals who happened to drop in and he made them all feel at ease as he chatted to them all. I also introduced them to traditional English crusty bread a strong cheddar cheese and pickled onions and good old-fashioned real ale in pint glasses. Although he loved the ale and bread and cheese he found the onions rather too hot for his palette.

Returning to the river after lunch Rosalind fished in the afternoon and indeed out-fished her husband as she caught three good-sized grayling on the dry fly in a couple of hours. Of the two I would suggest she was the better dry-fly fisher of the two but I hesitated to say so at the time.

It was one of those memorable days in the life of a riverkeeper that I will certainly not forget. To mark his visit to the Itchen I managed to obtain a copy of Edward Grey's wonderful book, *Fly-fishing*, for the President which I later sent on to him in USA. He very kindly wrote in his own hand and thanked me for his day on the Itchen and enclosed a signed copy of his own personal 'Sporting Journal'.

~~~~~

Over time the river continued on much the same, the trout were just as plentiful, but alas the fisherman seemed to change. Maybe it was my perception or perhaps it was just me getting older. I may eventually come to terms with logo-emblazoned tee shirts and baseball caps, multi-pocketed waistcoats crammed full of gadgets, combat trousers and expensive designer polarized sunglasses, nought weight carbon fibre fishing rods, large arbour reels, copolymers and expensive zip-up leather lined wellies. How the occupants of the riverbank have changed. That's all part of progress.

Mentioning strange gadgets on the riverbank brings to mind an old dowager Duchess who at times was invited to fish by one of the tenants. Her Grace never appeared on the river to fish without her 10ft long tree-pruning clipper. I soon came to realise the sense in this as she was not the best of casters of the dry-fly and invariable would find the top branches of any tree that happened to be in the way of her very energetic back cast. Most of her day was spent clipping off branches in an effort to retrieve her fly. I said to her host I wished she would come and visit more often as she would soon save me a great deal of time tree pruning in the winter.

~~~~~

One of the fishermen who was a tenant with me in those early times was the legendary Dermot Wilson. Unfortunately Dermot is no longer with us but I found him so very interesting to talk with and whenever he was on the river I was more than happy just to listen to all he had to say on trout fishing, tackle and our wonderful chalk streams.

At that time Dermot was running a unique mail order fishing tackle business from Nether Wallop Mill. With his experience in the world of advertising with J. Walter Thompson he built a superb fishing tackle business that was unique at the time. He and his staff also offered within it a service that was unmatched and I do believe it was mandatory that all his staff understood that all business was to be conducted with a sense of humour, which was an attitude of ground-breaking proportions in the fishing tackle industry in the 1960s and 1970s.

As a young riverkeeper Dermot encouraged and helped me so much in my new found profession by talking to me about the early keepers he had known and particularly discussing river problems of previous years that he had experienced and how they were resolved. His love of the chalk streams and of the Itchen in particular shone through whenever he was on the river. Just to listen to him talking about his beloved Itchen to one of his many guests from North America was enough. I am convinced that by his enthusiasm alone he converted many of these guests to become regular summer migrant visitors to the chalk streams of Hampshire.

Sadly, I remember the last time I saw Dermot before he died. I had managed to persuade him to come and fish the top beat which he had told me on so many occasions was his most favourite piece of chalk stream water. This I can well believe as he willed it that his ashes were to be scattered along the banks of the Itchen on the top beat at Martyr Worthy and so they were. He was a great fisherman and a true friend who is greatly missed.

Another great character of the Hampshire chalk streams that cannot be overlooked at this time was the one and only Col. 'Scrappy' Hay founder of the famous Rod Box tackle shop in Winchester (now at Kingsworthy) and father of Ian who is now runs the shop. 'Scrappy' lived up to his Army nickname because if ever anyone stepped out of line just watch out, stand to attention and block up your ears. However, he really appreciated all the hard work the riverkeepers did on our rivers and would regularly support them when the need arose. He was the first riparian owner to support the keepers' request to adjust the July weed cutting dates to a more sensible length of time. He was very much respected by all the keepers.

For many years he would make a grand tour of all the resident riverkeepers and deliver a 'thank you' bottle or two to each keeper on Christmas Eve. As his all day tour would usually end at Martyr Worthy needless to say the Colonel's face would be bright red by that time of day and his driver, Tim, was not much better. By the time they had ensconced themselves on my settee in front of a roaring log fire and had tucked in to our ritual offering of at least two very large home-made sloe gins and a large slice of Paula's fresh made fruit cake I think the pair of them were more than ready for home. I wondered at times if they would ever make it back to their car, let alone get home safely.

Those were great times in which to have been a riverkeeper with such characters and with such kindness and appreciation being shown by the likes of 'Scrappy' Hay. Again, dearly missed by all the riverkeepers along the Test and Itchen – they don't make 'em like that these days.

It was by getting to know all these people that I was able to learn things that helped me to broaden my experience and knowledge as a riverkeeper. Some employers expected a keeper to be just an artisan who kept the river, cut the weed cut the grass and kept his mouth shut and as far as the anglers were concerned and all the many other contacts made during the seasons on the riverbank were, and should be, of little consequence.

I soon found that many of the people I met had certain snippets of experience and knowledge that was very useful to me. With Pat Fox next door and with all the members of the Hampshire River Keepers' Association, plus the many experienced fly-fishermen I met, my knowledge grew rapidly. The continuous study and observation of brown trout and the many other animals and insects was of great help to me as I eagerly learnt what the river was all about and what made it tick.

The reputation of a river or a particular stretch of a river is built mainly by the understanding and fishing ability of the people who fish it so it is those people alone who create the reputation of a fishery. It was the people who fished the part of the river that I was responsible for who were the creators of the worldwide reputation that this part the Itchen gained during the 1980s and early 1990s. This reputation led to a regular stream of visitors from around the world, people who came to fish as the guests of the tenants.

There were many uninvited visitors who would just turn up and stand on the public footbridge to look at a river that had gained a reputation as being a great example of what a true chalk stream should be like. It was strange but during those great years the quality of the river and the fishing was at its very best. Maybe this was just because the people who fished it were not only expert fisherman but also loved the river, a feeling that I shared with them. Beauty is in the eye of the beholder they say.

One visitor who had been invited by one of the tenants to fish as his guest flew by Concorde from America just for one day's fishing on the Itchen. The guest was met in the car park, escorted to his allotted beat and all his goods and chattels settled into the beat hut. This visitor was so excited and thrilled at being on such a piece of water that he had read so much about that he spent most of the day just walking up and down the riverbank beat oooing and aaahing at the trout as they rose. He did not even assemble his rod until after lunch and as he had to be back at the airport at 8pm he spent all of 30 minutes actually fishing. We have a name for such people as that; we call them 'When-I's' as when they have returned to their home base they can safely say to their fishing friends. 'When I fished the Upper Itchen' or 'When I fished the Test...' I found that many of the fishermen who visited from North America were really excellent dry-fly fishers and it was an absolute joy to be in their company and watch them work out the nuances and intricacies of fishing the dry fly on the Itchen. It was such a pleasure to be in the company of such people who appreciated fully the wonders of the Itchen trout and its Valley.

It just happened at that time some of the tenants had friends and contacts from around the world and who travelled a great deal not only in their work but also in their play. We therefore had a regular stream of interesting guest visitors to the river each year many of which have subsequently become close friends of mine. One particular friend has often telephoned me from his stuffy office in downtown New York just to enquire what fly was hatching at the time on the Itchen. He said that our chats about the river kept him sane during the hot months in the city and the phone call would enable him to picture the Itchen as I described the fly activity and how the trout were behaving on that day. Others correspond and discuss all things fishy and tell me all about the interesting places they have visited or are planning to visit and fish. The fly-fishing world is very small when one thinks about it.

The two common threads that link all these reminiscences are fly-fishing and the River Itchen. It is interesting to observe that whenever two fly-fishers meet for the first time, irrespective of who or what they are and especially along a chalk stream riverbank with fly rods in hand, any remaining social class structures that still exist in this country today just seem to melt away. This maybe is what makes fly-fishing such a wonderful sport that is enjoyed by such a wide spectrum of the human race.

It gave me great pleasure to share the beauties of such a wonderful river with people who really appreciated the natural beauty and the fly-fishing that it offers.

Learning to Use a Fly-Fishing Rod

These three beautifully drawn cartoon strips by Bernard Venables were originally published some sixty or more years ago in the Friday edition of the Daily Mirror. They depict, and succinctly describe, the basic principles of how to use a fly-fishing rod. These basic principles are all just as relevant today as they were all those years ago, although split-cane rods and plaited silk lines were used then.

Today, rods are now made from high-tech carbon fibre and fly lines from modern sophisticated plastics which illustrates how far fishing tackle manufacture has progressed over the intervening years, nevertheless the basic fundamental mechanics in the use of these modern fly rods in conjunction with today's fly lines have not changed at all.

It would not take very long for a angler who follows the simple directions closely, given so clearly by Mr Crabtree to Peter in the illustrations, to become sufficiently proficient to go out and enjoy some wonderful fly-fishing. There is certainly no mystique about fly-fishing or in the use of fly-fishing rods as some people may think, just follow the directions and with a little practice the abilities will soon grow and so opens up a whole new delightful aspect of fishing.

A beginner will benefit from some good advice from a recognised, qualified professional game angling instructor who can advise on the best value purchase of the relevant and suitable tackle and provide a few casting lessons. This will certainly pay off in the long run as it is far better to learn all the good habits first! Local, qualified instructors can be found by contacting The Association of Advanced Professional Game Angling Instructors (AAPGAI) ~ www.aapgai.co.uk.

~

One of the most enjoyable aspects of the sport of dry-fly fishing for wild brown trout learning to think like a wild trout and by doing so learning through quiet contemplation and observation more about the various moods of the river, the weather, the natural environment and the diverse amount of insects that trout eat and the ever-changing reactions of the wild trout to these things in their own natural habitat. As in any activity that requires a certain amount of tactile abilities dry-fly fishing becomes even more enjoyable if the equipment can be used with a degree of expertise. To derive enjoyment it is not necessary to be world-class champion caster

delivering a dry-fly great distances because most dry-fly casting is done in close proximity to the fish. Astute field craft and stealth and delicate presentation of the dry fly, plus prolonged powers of concentration, are the essential abilities that a successful dry-fly fisherman needs in abundance and those abilities only come from just going fishing!

~

It is necessary to be in tune with the river and be taught by the fish through good observation.

A natural brown trout is a wild animal with a very strong, natural, built-in sense of survival so it is necessary to be on their wavelength if the trout is to be convinced that the dry fly presented is a tasty meal that is safe to eat.

A day's dry-fly fishing can be so absorbing and most times enjoyed in beautiful natural surroundings. Day-to-day problems of life's hectic world, that weigh heavy on the mind, become very small beer by the end of a day spent beside a river with a dry-fly rod in hand — even if the trout have not been co-operative!

~ 8 ~

Have Rod, Will Travel

little incident that occurred in the summer of 1978 that was eventually to affect the rest of my riverkeeping life quite considerably was a short letter published in the *Trout & Salmon* magazine letters to the editor page.

The letter was a heartfelt plea that asked if anyone could or would allow the writer to see a true chalk stream and who was willing to explain and talk about how chalk streams are managed and keepered. This cry for help appealed to me as I could at the time equate with the feelings of the writer in his apparent love of rivers and the history of the Hampshire chalk streams that had led to his quest to try and find out more about them. As there was no phone number given only an address somewhere in Devon, I wrote a brief note and posted it off, inviting the writer to give me a call.

By return I received a phone call from Chris Marshall, an expatriate Yorkshireman, who had emigrated to Canada some years previously and was now in the midst of a sabbatical from teaching English in Canada. Chris was living in rented property with his family at Sidmouth in Devon while he prepared and wrote his thesis for his doctorate in English and was planning to return to Ontario when this was completed.

Chris said he would like to come up from Devon for a few days to see me and if possible look at and talk about my river. I agreed to meet him and it seemed almost as soon as I had replaced the receiver there was a knock on my back door and there stood Chris. I had booked him in overnight at the White Swan pub in Alresford but after the first day of his visit we swiftly became friends and so Paula and I invited him to stay with us to save him money as the Swan accommodation was a little steep for a mature student as Chris was then.

During his brief stay Chris grilled me on the how, when and why of the river and riverkeeping. It came to light that Chris had just been elected 'conservation and restoration' leader of his fishing club that leased water on Cold Creek, which is a spring fed tributary of the River Trent system in Southern Ontario that drains into the north shore of Lake Ontario. Chris was eager to discuss his plans for his home water and we brainstormed over many photographs and slides of his home water that showed very well some of the problems under which the creek was labouring. Based on the information I managed to glean from the pictures and the discussions we had together Chris carefully wrote down the best advice I could offer. I must admit he hung onto every word and each day would go through the notes he had written up in bed the night before, to clarify each detail one by one. Here, I thought, was a man who is dedicated to his river and is determined to do his best to rectify the man-made problems that had so seriously degraded the trout habitat in his home stream in Canada.

Chris asked me, during his last walk around my water just before he returned to Devon to complete his thesis, whether I would be prepared to visit Canada and look at Cold Creek the following year. By that time he would be back in Ontario teaching English in Trenton High School and would have consulted his fellow fishing club members to ask if they would consider inviting a limey riverkeeper from England to advise them how to improve their stream. I did not take much time to answer his question, I said, yes, of course, believing in my heart of hearts that would be the last I heard on the subject once Chris had left England. Oh! Ye of little faith. I should have known better. From then on I received a regular update from Chris explaining all the plans for my visit.

When I eventually stepped off the jumbo jet at Toronto Airport the following summer there started a completely new aspect to my life. During the preceding year of planning, the Cold Creek Club had organised several seminars, set up meetings with other clubs, meetings with the Ministry of Natural Resources (MNR), arranged on stream workshops, and a host of other social events. I was in for a very busy time. News had even spread as far away as Pennsylvania in USA that a riverkeeper from Hampshire, England was in Ontario advising and helping to restore the trout habitat on spring-fed streams. So out of the blue I was invited to go down to Pennsylvania to have a look at their streams in the Cumberland Valley area.

During my stay in Canada Chris had insisted that I stayed with him and his wife, Liz. After discussing my invite to Pennsylvania Chris volunteered to drive me down to Carlisle near Harrisburg in the Cumberland Valley, a journey of 500 miles down Highway 801. The limestone streams of this area are famous in the history of fly-fishing in America, the LeTort, Boiling Springs, the Yellow Breeches are all revered dry-fly fishing destinations for generations of American fly-fishers. Through the grape vine of Trout Unlimited I was invited to meet America's only riverkeeper, Charlie Fox, who had done so much trout habitat enhancement and restoration work completely voluntary and at his own expense on the Letort River. August in Cumberland Valley in Pennsylvania is not the place for any one to be if heat and humidity is a problem. As soon as I had met

Charlie early one morning he was eager for me to have a look at the Letort and it was not long until I was poured into a pair of chest waders and we were off along the banks of the stream.

We battled through dense undergrowth with Charlie sending rattlesnakes and the odd copperhead snake scuttling off with a stick and me in clammy chest waders. The one abiding memory of that visit was the constant 36°C (96°F) heat and 90% humidity for days at a stretch during which time we looked at all the habitat work Charlie had done over the previous years. I do not think that I had ever been in such awful humid conditions or had ever felt so unfit even though I played rugby in my younger days, still played cricket and was doing a very active job. It was such a relief at times to jump into the car and wind up the windows and get the air conditioning running at full blast. How people could permanently live in conditions like that amazed me.

Charlie Fox and his distinguished fishing compatriots were the instigators of the trout catch-and-release philosophy in USA and were actively encouraging all fly-fishers in Pennsylvania to do the same. This fishing ethic has now spread worldwide and is not only now just about trout but the wild Atlantic salmon populations throughout the northern hemisphere are now benefiting from catch-and-release.

I sat with Charlie in his back yard in Carlisle with Vince Marinaro, Don Ebright, Dave Williams, and that great character 'Lefty' Krey plus several others whose names I am unable to recall. We discussed, over many cold beers, catch-and-release, trout habitat and its restoration and all the things anglers and riverkeepers talk about the world over. I was fascinated to talk with Vince Marinaro and listen to not only his thoughts on the protection of brown trout in the Le Tort spring creek but also his views and thoughts on what the trout sees from below the surface of the river. Unfortunately, Vince sadly passed away not long after I had left Pennsylvania.

Before I returned to Ontario to carry on my work with Chris I was invited by the Fish Commissioner of Pennsylvania, Mr Ralph Abele, to meet his chief fisheries biologist, Del Graff, to discuss fishery management and catch-and-release while we made a grand tour of the major fisheries in Cumberland Valley area ending up at the huge Bellmont State Hatchery. Here I saw the largest hatchery that I had ever seen with a complex of at least 100 concrete raceways all over a quarter of a mile long beside a dozen huge fry rearing sheds and brood stock ponds. This facility produced several million trout every year to stock the rivers in the State. Many of the raceways held golden rainbow trout that are the colour of goldfish but a bit paler. I asked why they produced these golden

Directing restoration work on Cold Creek, Ontario, Canada, 1981.

rainbows and, believe it or not, the answer was that the fishermen of Pennsylvania like the bright colour because they can see the trout easily in the rivers. It could only happen in America.

During my stay in Pennsylvania, Chris and his club committee had been busy arranging a two-day river restoration workshop out on Cold Creek. All and sundry in the fishing world of Ontario had been invited to be shown how some of my methods that I used on the chalk streams of Hampshire could also be adapted for use on the spring-fed limestone streams of Ontario. About 150 people turned up for the two days, which started on the first evening with an introductory talk by Chris followed by my descriptive slide show of my River Itchen in Hampshire showing some of my riverkeeping methods. This went well although there were some questions from some very stern looking fisheries biologists sat in the front row of the audience from the Ontario Ministry of Natural Resources department of fisheries.

Dr Doug Dodge who led this contingent asked me several pertinent questions about my work in UK, but the one I do remember well was, 'What was the productivity of wild trout in the River Itchen?' Luckily, just before I left England, there had been some studies done on the Itchen which produced a guideline figure that answered the question. I reeled off a series of figures of several kilos per hectare production of wild trout in the Itchen and Doug and his friends immediately put their heads together and scribbled away on scraps of paper. Eventually they looked up, all with shaking heads. They did not believe me, but were far too polite to say so. This was a good start I thought.

It was not until two years later when Doug was in England where he was attending a fisheries conference in York that he visited me on the Itchen and spent a day or so looking at my water did he then admit to me that my production figures could have been correct as he marvelled at the obvious fertility and quality of the habitat in and around the River Itchen.

On Cold Creek the next day I conducted a practical demonstration at a severely eroded stretch of riverbank of the Creek where I used windfall trees and logs to build a protective wall to prevent any more erosion which was then backfilled with rocks, stones, brushwood and soil. The completed structure was designed to encourage natural regeneration of native wild plants that in turn would further help to stabilise the degraded riverbank. Halfway through this demonstration I met Doug Dodge again. After listening to me describing how, why and what I was doing it was not long before he was in his chest waders and was standing in the river beside me helping to drive retaining posts and placing tree trunks to build the wall. It was from that moment in time in the stream and on the banks of Cold Creek that not only was a great friendship made but the birth of a minor revolution in Canada on how habitat restoration could be achieved with little expense when natural materials were used like windfalls of which there were millions and millions lying rotting all over Ontario.

I became increasingly involved with the Ministry of Natural Resources in Ontario, Canada and was privileged to visit that wonderful country on several occasions during the early 1980s.

With my growing experience in maintaining, protecting and restoring wild trout habitat on the River Itchen in England, Doug Dodge thought that I could be of some assistance to his staff who were endeavouring to restore the heavily degraded trout streams of southern Ontario. I was invited several times to tour, talk and discuss trout habitat restoration on their problem rivers and headwaters. At the same time Doug would ask me to talk to his young field biologists and describe to them how I looked at a river to determine what restoration work was needed and the methods that could be used.

My travels took me up to Owen Sound on Lake Huron to the North and out to the Niagara Falls and beyond in the south. I saw some wonderful rivers and was fortunate to fish one or two of them along the way. The diversity of game fish and other species in Ontario was tremendous and there was hardly a month of the year when a fly-fisherman could not, other than when bad weather got in the way, cast a fly rod.

It soon became very clear that the same principles of river and fisheries restoration and protection applied equally well in Ontario as they do in Hampshire. It was all a matter of degree and a cognisance of the differing climate conditions. The severity of winter and affects, such as snow melt, all had to be taken into consideration and, green though I was, I soon learnt to understand the differences. However, many of my techniques and ideas that worked so well on the River Itchen, when adapted correctly, worked very well in Canada, once these significant differences were taken into consideration.

During many of our tours around Ontario looking at various rivers Doug would, as we travelled the highways and byways, give me wonderful historic background lesson on the whole of Ontario. From the activities of the early settlers and the native Canadian Indians, culminating in all the land use changes that have occurred since those early times that have altered the whole landscape of the Province. It was inevitable that many of the rivers would also have changed. Deforestation was, by far, the major contributor to this along with the clearing and working of the land for agriculture purposes. In many instances in southern Ontario cold water rivers became warm water rivers and as water temperatures rose so the cold water loving species either moved upstream to find cool water or died out completely.

It was these types of problem that Doug had to address as the annual stocking of catchable trout had just been curtailed by the Provincial Government as costs of producing several million trout each season became prohibitive. Fortunately it had been agreed that the money saved by closing the hatcheries was to be spent on the restoration of cold water fisheries habitat. Somehow when Government anywhere saves this amount of money, and it was many millions of dollars, it hardly, if ever, gets spent entirely on what it was intended. However there was at that time a great movement throughout the Province of Ontario, led by Doug Dodge and his dedicated staff, towards cold water aquatic habitat restoration to provide more self-sustaining stocks of fish.

It was during one of my visits to Ontario that I was introduced to the writings of Aldo Leopold and the philosophy of holistic catchment management. From here on my whole philosophy of river management took on a totally new aspect as I gradually learnt more about it. This was in the early 1980s and at that time such a philosophy was almost unheard of in the UK although UK Government agencies were in charge of our rivers. We sat on Doug's back porch deck drinking

Demonstrating the use of natural materials for fixing protection
for undermined bankside trees in Cold Creek, Ontario, Canada, 1981.

a cool beer one evening, having just returned from one of our tours, discussing this relatively new management philosophy.

From that time on Doug sent me copies of all the interesting papers and articles on the subject that had either been written by him or by other recognised experts in the field. So began an ever-growing pile of paper on my desk. On one of Doug's visits to my house in the Itchen Valley I showed him my office and he remarked that my filing system was very similar to his 'pile it up on the corner of the desk and when the pile falls over start another one'.

Doug's interpretation of holistic catchment management was explained as: *Holism: a tendency in nature, by ordered grouping, to form wholes that are more than the sum of their parts*, although Aldo Leopold never quite said it that way. It was certain that the phrase 'holistic catchment management' captured everything he expounded.

The holism idea was part of a stunning medical breakthrough by Hans Seelye, in the late 1950s or early 1960s, who was a psychologist working on stress in humans. He predicted that a stress applied to one part of a person's system could affect more than the area of the direct hit, and change other parts of the system for better or worse. From this Ken Loftus, who was a leading fisheries biologist within the Ministry of Natural Resources in Ontario, considered applying this concept to the large lakes across the northern hemisphere, and in doing so discovered that stress on aquatic systems applied to one spot on a lake would make resultant ripples throughout the entire lake. Furthermore it must be remembered that the Great Lakes were then being detrimentally affected as much by what happened on the land within the drainage system, or catchment, as by direct 'hits' on the water. As a result of this idea gaining support, the Canadian-United States International Joint Commission (IJC) spent three years and several million US dollars writing a report called 'Pollution from Land Use Activities'. Thus was born a philosophy that spawned many ecologically focused documents that led to not only the Great Lakes Water Quality Agreement, but to many other important decisions relating to catchment management not only in Canada and the USA but in the UK and worldwide.

Ken Loftus was not alone with this hypothesis, but he was the first to say it out loud. Very soon after others 'came out' and proclaimed the same philosophy for other major systems, including wildlife areas, such as oceans. I believe the late Jacques Cousteau wholeheartedly embraced the concept.

It took the Large River Symposium, held in Toronto in the late 1980s, to put this idea firmly on the map to by bringing together scientists from around the world and encouraging them to look at large rivers holistically and on a catchment scale.

This philosophy took many more years to become accepted, let alone established, in the UK, although one John Gardiner, of the then Thames Water Authority, did write some excellent papers on the subject their contents appeared to go unnoticed by the policy makers and John soon departed to sunnier climes.

I joined the southern branch of the Institute of Fisheries Management (IFM) where I became caught up within this new philosophy and the more I learnt from the flow of information supplied by Doug in Canada the more I felt that I should perhaps start to promote it in this country. I asked the IFM to allow me to give them a short presentation on the subject of holistic catchment management.

For the whole of one very wet January evening at the Hampshire College of Agriculture at Sparsholt I proceeded to bore the pants off some not very interested IFM branch members, many of whom have now come around to thinking more holistically about river system problems than they did on that damp night. It took 15 years for the philosophy to be fully accepted in UK and more importantly, used in the planning and implementation of riverine restoration.

In Hampshire I even had the temerity to suggest to the oligarchic Test and Itchen Association that they might promote and encourage the local National Rivers Authority to consider embracing this philosophy in their proposed river management plans. I was told in no uncertain terms by the hierarchy of the Association that this philosophy was totally impossible and quite unrealistic. I may be wrong but I had a distinct feeling at that time that these people did not take too kindly to being told by a riverkeeper that holistic catchment management would be the way forward in the future. In retrospect I do not think they appreciated what holistic catchment management meant anyway.

Twenty-two years later things have changed. I only wish that those same people were still about today because as and when the EU Water Framework Directive from Brussels is implemented in Hampshire they will see that the whole river system, as the Itchen is, will have to be viewed by law as one entire aquatic ecosystem, managed holistically as one single ecological unit. That is just what holistic catchment management is all about.

Those word sound bites of the eighties like 'holistic catchment management' and 'sustainable economic development' plagued the manifestos of many policy making committees in the UK yet I feel that the latter could and should be complemented by the addition of the word 'environmentally' so it reads 'Environmentally sustainable economic development' which puts a totally different complexion on the meaning of the original.

Following my early visits, the Ministry of Natural Resources subsequently produced a stream restoration manual for the guidance of fishing clubs who were considering doing some restoration work on their own streams and many of my techniques were illustrated and recommended in that manual. It was not until I retired last year that Doug finally told me that from that first meeting on Cold Creek and the subsequent visits I made to Canada that a three million dollar program of river restoration was started in Ontario mainly based on my chalk stream methods that I demonstrated on Cold Creek. I don't take full credit for that, as all I did was to act as the messenger, as all the knowledge and expertise I gained and which I had adapted to the Canadian scene came from all the people back home like Frank Sawyer and Pat Fox and other riverkeepers of my era.

There were many very enjoyable aspects of my many visits with Doug and the MNR. One enjoyable incident that I shall never forget and that was our trips to

Port Dover on Lake Erie which became a regular event, mainly because I do like good fish and chips. There was an old sail-making loft on the lakeside in Port Dover on Lake Erie where there were rows of old wooden scrubbed tables with wooden bench seats and old fishing nets hanging from the ceiling and a bar that dispensed draft cold beer in half gallon earthenware pitchers. The main food on the limited menu was perch and chips. Fillet of perch, the same species of perch that we had in UK I believe, was sensational battered and deep-fried and along with a glass or two of cool beer – what else does one want for lunch? The only problem I had at the time was that Canadians drink beer out of tiny little ten-ounce glasses and I, coming from England, required a pint glass because, as I said to the locals, half pints do not go to heaven. I complained bitterly about this but to no avail.

All the perch were netted out of Lake Erie and as we ate trawlers were coming in and out of the harbour, bigger than those that once worked out of Fleetwood in the UK. Doug told me that the perch quota for that season had been set for the perch fishery in Erie at 10,000 tons. Most of this catch went for canning and was then exported to Europe. Ever since that day, every perch I caught in UK reminded me of the delicious deep fried perch and chips at Port Dover. I was tempted many times to kill a few out of the Itchen and deep fry them just to see if they tasted the same as those in Lake Erie.

During those halcyon years of the 1980s I was very fortunate to be invited on several occasions to accompany friends, who fished as tenants on 'my' river, to fish for salmon and trout in some of the most famous fisheries in the UK and even abroad. If these trips did not clash with the weed cutting dates, as my duty was to look after the river first and foremost, and my long suffering wife, Paula, did not object I could usually get away by using my holiday entitlement. In fact during all the thirty years of keepering at Martyr Worthy I only missed one whole weed cutting period and that was in my final year when I severely tore the cruciate ligament in my left knee while weed cutting and could hardly walk let alone undertake a heavy weed cut. Other than that week I can only remember having to get help on two other occasions, one when an infected wisdom tooth had to come out under anaesthetic and the other time when a dose of bronchitis laid me low.

One memorable week was spent staying at Borribol Lodge on the famed River Helmsdale in Scotland where I managed to grass my largest Atlantic salmon to date. Another week in another year was spent on the Brora just down the coast from the Helmsdale and the numbers of fresh run grilse were a sight to behold. In retrospect I must be one of the most fortunate of riverkeepers to fish not only those two wonderful rivers but also all the others in this country and abroad.

This era was highlighted by a trip to the Miramachi in New Brunswick in Canada as a guest of Hoagy B Carmichael where I had some of the most spectacular sport catching and releasing large Atlantic salmon and grilse on this very wild river with just moose, beaver, bald eagles and ospreys as company.

There was one generous invitation that unfortunately had to be turned down and that was to fish for Atlantic salmon and some large wild brown trout in Iceland, unfortunately the dates for this trip did clash with the heavy July weed cutting dates on the Itchen. People have been so kind and generous to me over the years.

Among my experiences of fishing in foreign countries the dry-fly expedition onto the famed spring creeks of Cumberland Valley in Pennsylvania through which the Le Tort, Yellow Breeches and Boiling Springs flow are experiences not to be forgotten. These Cumberland Valley streams are the nearest things to a chalk stream there is in North America. I thought the Itchen could be difficult to fish at times but the Yellow Breeches at Allenbury must be one of the most difficult dry fishing sessions I have had in my fishing life. The tremendous hatch of white wings almost defeated the 'man from Itchen'. I had little in my fly box to match this fly that was the size of a blue-winged olive but the wings and body were white. Eventually some trout succumbed to my offering of a small lightly dressed Lunn's Particular when the spinners started to fall in the early evening. It was hard work but so enjoyably challenging.

One of the most beautiful fishing places is Ireland; a fly-fisherman's paradise, as the Emerald Isle is blessed with so many rivers and loughs that hold wild trout and salmon as well as a wide variety of coarse fish and of course draft Guinness. Where else in the world was it possible for a fisherman to catch a good big wild trout on one cast, a large salmon on the next and a large pike on the following cast? There was great coarse fishing to be had, as well as the great sport of catching pollock, bass, and mackerel on a fly off the rocky coast of Connemara in Galway Bay before tackling extraordinary quantities of the 'black stuff' in the evenings, it did taste different in Ireland I am convinced. All experienced in one trip to Ireland and at the same time meeting some really wonderful people who, almost without exception, had a great sense of humour and a boundless talent for making you welcome.

To be more specific there were many rivers to fish but the Erriff, Moy, Delphi and the Blackwater for the salmon and the reviving Ballynahinch system and Lough Currane for the sea trout plus Loughs Mask, Sheelin and Corrib must be high on any visiting fisherman's list to fish. For an angler who loves just to wander with a fly rod in the hand then Ireland was the place to go as there were

The use of natural rock and cobbles on Cold Creek, Ontario, to re-establish river banks and create habitat diversity within the river channel, Canada, 1981.

so many streams to fish for trout that were available just for the asking at most times. In fishing terms it is difficult to stop talking about Ireland as there was also the mayfly time on Loughs Corrib, Mask and Sheelin and others loughs of equal quality. There was one eternal memory that will stay with me about the Emerald Isle and that was the miles and miles of hedgerows in the west of Ireland that are made up of wild fuchsias which, when in bloom, are just one amazing sight to behold.

In the late 1990s I was invited to present a paper at an international conference on Wild Trout at Montana State University in Bozeman. USA. This trip to Montana was an exciting and exhilaratingly affair. I worked hard on my presentation that was entitled, 'Man-made Rivers Can Work'. It was a pocket history of man's influences over the past 3000 years on the River Itchen. It set out to show that on such a changed aquatic ecosystem as the Itchen is today that with care and good management the habitat for the natural production of wild trout can be maintained and improved.

My presentation was well received and even some of the hard-nosed fisheries scientists gathered there complimented me on the common sense content of my paper, which did come as some relief after all my fears during the preparation and traumatic 24 hour journey to Montana which entailed delayed flights and lost baggage.

The real highlight of this visit to USA was that during the conference I did meet up with a couple of fisheries biologists who worked in the great Yellowstone Park. As I had given myself a few days after the conference to have a look around these very kind people offered to show me the park and the fishing sites of note. I managed to fish for superb big wild brown trout on the Madison River, Slough Creek, the Gallatin (of *A River Runs Through It* fame) and many other creeks. Not only was the scenery stunning these locals were able to keep me away from all the crowded tourist places like the Old Faithful geyser and, knowing all the back tracks, with their four-wheel drive they were able to show me not only some of their work they do but also some of the wonderful wildlife of the Park. It turned out to be a memorable trip and just before I left Bozeman I was taken out to the O'Hair ranch on Armstrong's Creek which is a well-known trout creek that runs into the great Yellowstone River to see some restoration work that had been done to repair the damage that had been done to this unique fishing creek by some tremendous floods the year before. I flew home across the Atlantic thinking to myself how refreshing it was to be in the company of such like-minded people when it came to wild trout and wild trout problems. I certainly learnt a great deal from that visit and would very much like to return to explore further the beauties of Yellowstone and that includes the trout fishing of course.

Since that trip I have talked to several people from the UK who have also visited Yellowstone to fish and to a man they have indicated that they were so disappointed in the fishing. As I explained to them that a fishing trip to the Yellowstone requires a great deal of forward planning, not only with the logistics of getting there but also organising the fishing when you arrive. It is like any destination fishing trip in the UK to new and unknown waters it is essential to get hold of some good and reliable local assistance before the trip is fixed. It is so easy to be in the right place at the wrong time, it is so easy to go to the wrong waters at the wrong time. It is essential to get hold of some qualified professional guidance and advice. There are several well-respected and reliable fishing outfitters in and around Yellowstone who can help so why spoil a good and already expensive trip by not paying a few dollars more for the right help and advice.

All successful fishing trips anywhere in the world are about being in the right place on the right waters at the right time.

~ 9 ~
Aliens!
Escapees & Introductions

After my first trip to Canada and the USA I was asked by Alex Berendt, who organised an annual Fishery Management Conference at his famous Two Lakes Fishery near Romsey, to give a presentation at one of his fishery management conferences.

Alex was a redoubtable character who, before the Second World War, had worked as a carp farmer in eastern Germany. He became a German prisoner of war in England and stayed on after the war was over. He was able to rent and finally buy a couple of old fish-ponds at Ampfield near Romsey and from those early days he enlarged the ponds and excavated four more on the site. At that time carp farming had very little attraction to the English population so Alex decided to stock his ponds with trout and from those early initial stockings of brown trout he changed to stocking rainbow trout and so the legendary Two Lakes trout fishery came into being.

The experiences of constructing these lakes and the management of the trout and the marketing of the fishing was soon to become the blueprint for many other like-minded people in UK who saw a demand for quality trout fishing of a standard that the ordinary fisherman could afford. So the trout put-and-take industry was born in UK. Alex then founded his annual fisheries management conference, held initially in a large tent beside one of his trout ponds. These meetings were so successful and well-attended that Alex was soon able to build a large wooden lodge that could be used as a function room, conference room or lecture hall.

The 1970s saw the beginning of the boom in the establishment of put-and-take trout fisheries in UK and at one time there were many entrepreneurs who perhaps saw this type of fishing as a licence to print money.

Alex was constantly being asked for advice on the setting up of such fisheries that he decided to hold a annual conference where experts would present lectures on many of the aspects of construction and management of such fisheries, also at the same time pointing out all the pitfalls and minefields that have to negotiated along the way. The conference grew in reputation and it was not long until world-renowned fisheries experts were clamouring to present papers at the now prestigious Two Lakes Conference.

This truly international reputation Alex made for this annual event was clearly shown with scientists from America, Canada, Netherlands, Sweden, Norway, Belgium, Israel and the UK who rubbed shoulders with one another at the wonderful lunchtime buffets that Alex's wife, Catherine, used to provide. Over the years this annual meeting of the minds of the top people worldwide in fisheries management was an opportunity and, whatever happened, I made sure that I did not miss attending any of them. I was able to learn so much by talking and listening to these leaders within the science and I made some lifelong friendships.

At about that time the trout farming industry had begun to take off in earnest in UK with trout farms springing up all over the place wherever there was flowing water. The chalk streams of Hampshire were therefore prime targets for budding trout farmers as the constant flows of quality spring water of the Test and Itchen offered almost ideal conditions for intensive trout farming. Very quickly several huge trout farms were constructed on the rivers and thus began a series of unfortunate events that at times caused some very serious damage to our rivers.

I have often compared the trout farming industry to the broiler chicken industry, which burst onto the scene in the 1960s when almost every farmer built a broiler shed. As time went by these single units became unprofitable as the market became flooded by over-production from some newer and bigger producers who could mass produce more economically so the little farm enterprise of one broiler shed had to close. So the evolution continued where it was down to may be two or three major nationwide producers who satisfied the entire market requirements. So it was in the trout farming industry but not before many ill-sited, poorly constructed, and badly managed fish farms were thankfully forced to close. It was only the modern well-sited, properly managed and controlled sites that were able to scrape a living out of trout farming. The demand for live trout for the stocking of all the new put-and-take fisheries and a growing demand for trout as a farmed food instigated the boom.

As the new industry of inland trout fish farming was comparatively new any laws and regulations to control the location, construction and management of these enterprises were almost non-existent or, at best, very weak. At that time there were little or no controls where a farm could be sited or how much water it could take from the river and use even though it was returned to the river.

The quality of the returned water was in many cases heavily polluted with fish excrement and at times the receiving waters would be bright green with malachite green and the river swamped with escapee rainbow trout.

It was not long before the effects of these farms were being witnessed and felt by the owners of some of the desirable river trout fisheries. Untreated effluent discharges from many tons of growing trout; the abstraction of too much water, mass escapes of at times many thousands of small and large rainbow trout into waters that held only wild brown trout were the main problems.

Alex Berendt, aware that I was very concerned about the effects fish farming was having on the chalk streams, asked me if I would be willing to present a lecture to his conference on that subject. We discussed at some length a suitable title for my presentation and finally came up with 'The Effects of Commercial Trout Farms on the Chalk Streams as seen through the Eyes of a Riverkeeper'. This very evocative title appealed to me as I had a great interest in the subject. The objective of my presentation would be to discuss the potential of this fisheries management tool being adopted in UK.

I started to prepare my paper with the objective of presenting clearly all of the problems that these intensive trout farms caused and the possible detrimental effects the operation of them was having on our precious trout steams. I drew on my experiences on the Itchen and from other riverkeepers and fishery owners from around the country. I made sure to get to know the fish farmers as well to understand their point of view. I soon found in my researches that some fish farmers were very co-operative but on the whole the majority were, I found, arrogant to the point that they would not even discuss the matter with me and some even banned me from entering their fish farms. This attitude only made me even more intent on gathering facts and figures to show that some of the farms were indeed having a detrimental effect on our chalk streams.

My researches took a great deal of my time, as I knew that there would be some of the most qualified and experienced fishery managers in the world in the audience. I, a lowly riverkeeper, had to get all my facts right for a start. I sweated for days and days on the preparation of the paper. I had never attempted anything so important before and nine months of blood, sweat and tears passed before I asked Alex for his thoughts on my paper prior to the conference day. As the conference date approached I was getting more nervous by the day and at times even wondered why I was doing it, thinking that I would be more content keeping solely to riverkeeping.

If it had not been for the support and encouragement that I received from Alex and his wife, Catherine, I do not think I would have completed and presented the paper.

The fateful day arrived and I was second up on the opening session. I sat there looking at the audience of hardened UK and European fish farmers and fishery owners, and some from further afield, assembled in the front two rows. It did seem, indeed, a formidable audience, all keen as mustard, as are most delegates on the opening day of a three-day conference. I cannot remember how long it took nor hardly remember what I said, but fortunately I had prepared and practised for weeks and although I read my paper I did know it off by heart. I had also been through the contents of it with Alex a week previously and, as he was happy with all I had to say, I was confident that at least I wouldn't make fool of myself although I might get lynched by the audience. I am sure I detected a mischievous twinkle in Alex's eye.

I remember vividly the response from the middle to the back of the hall which erupted in appreciative applause and 'Hear! Hear!' when I finished, the first two rows received my presentation in stony silence. I was pleased that my first public presentation of this nature was well received from around the hall. Although I received some flak from some fish farmers, I knew that I had at least struck a chord with a certain element of the fishing community and felt it was all worthwhile. Fortunately the timetable was such that any question and answers were to be taken at the end of the session so I could at least escape outside for some fresh air and a fag. All I did was to 'tell it as it was' in those early days of trout farming.

On my return the expected barrage from the fish farmers was comparatively and surprisingly polite. I thought that I had got away quite lightly as I enjoyed my buffet lunch with some friends until a very up-tight man approached me and told me that I would be hearing in due course from his solicitor. He smiled and went on his way and I continued my lunch and thought nothing of it.

The presentation did raise considerable discussion and, although I did not fall out with anyone, Alex complimented me on the content and in the way I handled the responses from the floor. It was quite a shattering experience for me but, in retrospect, one I shall never forget. From that point in time I was categorised as being anti-fish farming and some fish farmers even today 25 years on still have that view.

A week later I received a recorded delivery letter from an Isle of Man fish farmer stating that he was going to sue me for all I had over part of my presentation as I had mentioned the Isle of Man within my discussion of possible routes for the year round importation of rainbow eggs from other parts of the world giving better continuity to the fish farming business.

I ignored the first letter. A few days later I received another by recorded delivery, this time with the Isle of Man government stamp and crest upon it. This time I was now a mite worried, as I knew that I did not have any money and I certainly could not afford to employ a good lawyer and besides I was confident that I was right. How naïve I was in those days.

I pondered my plight for a few days when it occurred to me that a high court judge lived in the village and also owned a stretch of river just off our bottom boundary and for whom I had done some riverbank work and weed cutting at odd times. I decided to approach him. Nothing ventured, nothing gained I thought. An appointment was made for the following evening at 5.30pm.

I duly knocked on the door and was ushered into his study with its wall-to-wall books, fishing tackle and a huge roll top desk in the bay window. I was ordered to pour two very large scotches from the huge drinks cabinet and told to sit down, and from over the top of his spectacles the judge asked me how he could help. I briefly told the story to date and he then asked me to read my paper word for word as I had presented it at the conference.

As I read it the judge continued to write a letter, answer the telephone and each time he would just grunt and say sharply 'carry on, carry on'. I was worried that he may miss some salient points but I have since realised that judges have this wonderful capacity to appear to be not listening when in fact they are taking in every single word. When I finally finished he took a scrap of paper and wrote out a couple of sentences that he said I was to scribble on the back of an old coal bill in pencil and enclose it in a second-hand brown paper envelope and address it to the Isle of Man government and post it without a stamp. I thought he was joking but he said to do it and let him know what response I received.

I followed his instructions to a T. Lo and behold, another recorded letter arrived. This time the envelope was steaming.

I took it to the judge and he read it and, with a grim face, wrote out a further two sentences and told me to send it in a similar manner to the first. This I duly did.

Back came another recorded delivery letter and again I passed it on to the judge. He told me this time to come and see him on the following Sunday evening.

When I arrived he met me at the front door and said I was to meet a house guest who was also a judge but who also happened to be one of the country's leading experts on libel and slander and that over dinner the previous evening the two of them had discussed my problem at length. I was introduced to the expert judge who then explained in depth the meaning of the words in a final reply to the complainant. After an hour of law talk I was guided to a desk and told to write down a few very short dictated sentences, written this time in copperplate writing on my best headed notepaper, addressed in a quality envelope and posted with a first class stamp to the Isle of Man government. The two judges said that they would guarantee that I would not hear another word. Twenty-five years on I still have not.

As I left the judge's house on that memorable night I remember the judges parting words, 'If we had been in chambers those letters would have cost you at least £300 each so Ron would you cut the weed in my river next week'.

I did happen to know the Clerk to the Court at Winchester Crown Court and he told me a story about the same judge.

He recalled quite clearly one spring day some years before when the judge was sitting on a case that, at about noon, the judge interrupted proceedings and declared an early lunchtime adjournment instructing the court to reconvene at 3pm that afternoon. Apparently, he quickly disrobed, jumped into his car and drove off at breakneck speed to his own part of the River Itchen. I know this to be fact as I had often seen the same judge fishing in green wellies with a Barbour jacket over his pin-striped suit. On that particular day there was indeed a terrific hatch of iron blue. The judge knew, as he sat in court looking out of the window, that the conditions were right for a hatch of this fly. Wet and windy.

The era of the Two Lakes conferences was a great time for me and many others from around the world – a wonderful opportunity to learn and for that opportunity I have to thank Alex Berendt most of all. Without Alex's vision and appreciation of the need for a teaching forum of such a nature that he produced in those Two Lakes years the science of fisheries management would much the poorer today. I am still an avid learner and even though I am retired I still enjoy attending informative conferences or reading the proceedings if I am unable to participate.

I do hope one day someone will write a book about Alex and document his huge contribution to fish farming and fisheries management. Indeed his wonderful sense of humour, aspects of which need recording and Alex certainly deserves much credit.

There were at the time some very wealthy landowners who saw in trout farming for the table a very lucrative source of income that could be raised from their rivers. Unfortunately, during the 1970s, many fish farms were built on the chalk streams with minimal planning and operating controls. Before long three major and two smaller trout farms were constructed on the headwaters of the River Itchen and I lost count of the farms constructed on the Test catchment. It was not long before some of the predicted disasters that I had highlighted came to fruition.

Of the many troubles, escapees from trout farms on the Itchen were the worst nightmare with which we had to contend, although water quality in some farm effluents was at times very poor. The worst escapee episode was of some 30,000 six-inch rainbows from a farm in the headwaters of the River Itchen. It is difficult for anyone to imagine what it was like to have a wild brown trout fishery suddenly swamped with that many fish swimming around our fishery and other sporting fisheries on the Upper Itchen. The resident brown trout suffered, as did the anglers' sport. Along with the revenue from fishing rentals that was the only income for some of the riparian owners. It was the arrogant attitudes of some of these fish farmers that upset me because they did not appear to care a damn about the effects and loss of income to fishery owners that their inefficiency in fish farm management had caused. It was a notable feature that when we were fishing these fish out of the river no offer of assistance from the fish farmers was received at any time.

With the help of the National River Authority we were able to electro-fish out some 20,000, which we buried, leaving some 10,000. These fish absolutely ruined a whole year's sport fishing on the Upper Itchen. For months a dry fly would be snaffled by a little rainbow as soon as it was cast on the surface. To catch a wild brown trout that season was almost impossible. It took some persuading to convince my tenants that the coming winter would solve the problem. Escapee rainbows thankfully tend to drift downstream and none spawn effectively even if they become resident. Very few of these wretched things over-wintered and the ones that did were attacked mercilessly by keepers and their friends.

What also astounded me was the attitude of many of the riparian owners at the time as all they appeared to do was to 'tut tut' to the Test and Itchen Association (T&I) knowing full well that they were supporting the fish farming operations of one or two of their wealthy members. This is how I saw the situation and I felt that I could not tolerate all the apparent high powered inertia shown by the T&I so I contacted the Anglers' Cooperative Association (ACA) who dealt with pollution events mainly, in fact they claimed that they had never lost a case when it came to gaining compensation. I explained the situation relating to escapee rainbows and suggested that I deemed these fish to be a form of pollution. The

ACC tended to agree with my point of view and said they would look into it. They did come to the river and studied the situation intensely and after deliberation stated that there was pollution by escapee rainbow but the problem was that as there were four rainbow farms on the river system and each farm disputed the fact that these fish were from their particular farm. It was therefore difficult or impossible in fact to prove which escapee fish came from which farm. This impasse was then left for a while until a situation arose where an escape had occurred elsewhere where there was only one fish farm on a system. Luck was with us as a major escape occurred on the Upper Kennet a few months later where there was just one fish farm above a fishery that suffered from a major escape of farmed fish.

The court case was finally heard even though the fish farm had subsequently gone into liquidation prior to the case being heard. Never the less the ACA took the insurers of the fish farm to court and won the case for compensation and costs. This milestone case set the precedent for the future. The implications of this case reverberated around the fish farming industry and set in motion some major changes. Now fish farms are licensed, far better sited, far better designed, far better constructed and are, in most cases, very well managed. If the fish farmers had applied all these parameters to their operation from the very start none of this anguish would have taken place and many of our rivers would not have to have suffered from so many fish farm abuses.

I came to witness and appreciate again the oligarchical attitude of the Test and Itchen Association was taking over all the complaints they received from not only the riverkeepers but also from some of the non-fish farming riparian owners. It was my view at the time that this oligarchy was basically influenced by wealthy landowners who wanted to build fish farms so the complaints got nowhere. Even in my position as a keeper I continued my battle and from there on I was deemed as anti-fish farm. I cared not a jot what these wealthy people thought of me, as I knew full well in my mind that what I was fighting for was for the good of the river and the self-sustaining wild trout that lived within it.

The arrogance shown by some of these fish farmers was, at the time, mind blowing and although it has taken many years for legislation to catch up and for the fish farming industry to get its act together, in the meantime the demand for trout flesh in the super markets levelled out and increases in annual production reduced to a fraction of historical figures.

If I was part of the cause of these changes I feel I might have contributed something towards this outcome.

~~~~~

Environment Agency fisheries staff electro-fish a carrier stream for escapee rainbow trout.

During my war of attrition with the authorities I foresaw, and was concerned about, the effects of excess levels of phosphorus on a river system. My researches revealed that it was a basic element that had a considerable part to play in water quality and I believed that it was not taken into account by the then Southern Water Authority.

One factor was that an excess of phosphorus would trigger the growth of unwanted algal blooms. I pressed the Water Authority to monitor the effluent discharges from fish farms indicating to them that this could be the source of the algal blooms that grew with some ferocity in the river each spring. I had ascertained that there was in fact a quite high natural background level of phosphorus in the Itchen so any artificial addition from the untreated sewage effluent from a fish farm could well accentuate the algal problems. I kept on to the Authority for months at a time to get some indication whether they were monitoring the phosphorus levels of all the fish farms and the sewage out falls from the municipal sewage works.

It was not until 15 years later that I happened to meet the retired water quality officer who was in charge in those early days. Over a very friendly drink in the pub we talked over old times and reminisced over the lively discussions he and I had all those years ago. He freely admitted that at the time they the Southern Water Authority did not know about the effects of phosphorus. Before we departed he did say that in retrospect he did admire me for sticking to my guns as much has since been proven and phosphorus is now recognised as a major pollutant in fish farm effluent.

For anyone who has worked on the Itchen or Test it would be remembered that each spring the river bed and river weed would regularly become covered with a brown algae. This covering would start in early March and finally disappear during late April or early May. This varied from year to year, as did the strength of the growth. I first noticed this during my first year on the river and was naturally quite worried about it so I asked around and Pat Fox said that it happened most years and as far as he and his father before him could remember such was the case each spring. I ceased to worry when I discussed it with Frank Sawyer and he too said the same thing, he reckoned it was just a natural yearly phenomenon and assured me that it was nothing to worry about.

Young keepers and inexperienced owners who see this bloom do show some concern but time will tell them that it will disappear as rapidly as it came. I had the feeling that the cause could be a combination of water levels at the time, speed of flow, temperature, sunlight and background levels of phosphorus.

What with the river periodically turning bright green from a fish farm over-dosing with malachite green for fungus diseases the other major hiccup was when the whole river bed from one fish farm downstream for about a mile suddenly became covered with sewerage fungus, which indicated that there was a major phosphorus problem with the inefficient settling arrangements the fish farm had installed.

For several years I took up the cudgels and wherever I could I would extol the virtues of the need to protect our rivers from these degrading effects of wrongly sited, ill-constructed and poorly managed trout farms. I know I was not very popular but I sincerely believed, and continue to believe, that intensive fish farming can only be detrimental to a river system. Although I earned a reputation for being antagonistic towards trout farm owners my attitude was formed from my being in the forefront of witnessing the effects that some of these fish farms were having on our rivers. However, from the very beginning I regarded trout farming as an excellent form of fish production for food purposes, if controlled well.

With the growing concerns about the apparent decline in the volumes of fisherman's insects in our chalk streams led to a recent intensive study by the Environment Agency and other partners which it is hoped will reveal whether fish farm effluent is one of the contributing factors. I am still not convinced today that adequate precautions are taken in keeping the phosphorous content in trout farm effluent down to acceptable levels.

Twenty-five years on, the fish farms that are still in operation on our rivers are not quite the threat now as they were then. Although legislation and controls are now in place to protect our rivers I am still convinced that all our rivers throughout the country would be far better off if there were no fish farms at all on inland waters.

Today, all fish farms on our rivers have to be licensed and are tightly restricted as to the amount of water they can abstract, use and the quality of the return. They are therefore constrained as to the amount of fish flesh a farm can produce. Once full production is achieved further growth is impossible. As profits diminish due to over-production and poor marketing the inland trout farming industry is struggling to survive in some areas and this is illustrated in the number of farms that have now gone out of business. Fortunately, the demand for live or dead trout for food has levelled out and I deduce the demand is slowly diminishing.

For fear of being called a hypocrite regarding my views on the effects of trout farms I did, for several years, rear brown trout at Martyr Worthy but on a vastly different scale to a commercial rainbow farm in two small stew ponds from eggs and milt that I had taken from genuine wild stock from the Upper Itchen. The few hundred fish I produced were then sold live for stocking parts of the chalk streams that wanted quality trout for sporting purposes.

I asked my employer if I could clean out an old unused watercress bed that was fed with a good and constant spring just to rear up some quality brown trout that I could sell live for stocking to subsidise my meagre wage. The objective of the exercise was many fold: to see if I could do it; to obtain some much wanted extra income; to learn more about wild brown trout and their reproductive cycle. My employer agreed as long as it did not take too much of my time.

The first job after cleaning out the debris of many years accumulation of silt and vegetation was to make the little pond fish proof against incomers and escapees. This being done the next job was to acquire some wild brown trout eggs from which the whole process could start.

I borrowed a long seine net from a friend and when the time was right and the wild trout were up on the shallows in the river actually in the act of spawning. With help I managed to surround the shallows with the net and pull it to the riverbank and from the mature hen and cock fish I managed to select four pairs of clean healthy mature fish. These were placed into a large ten foot square tank that I had let into another spring ditch that had a good spring flowing through it. The rest of the trout caught were released and within a few hours were seen to be back onto their redds no worse for wear for the unscheduled interruption to their spawning activities.

The four selected pairs were covered over with a thick net to protect them from the unwanted attentions of predators and also to keep them calm in their strange surroundings. After they had settled for a couple of days I took them out and stripped the eggs out of the hens and fertilised the eggs with the milt from the cock fish. This being the first time for me I asked Frank Sawyer to come over and guide me through the whole process and between us I was able to lay down two trays of fertilized eggs in a small plastic fry trough in the spring ditch above the rearing pond. These trays were also well protected from birds and, more importantly, from the bright light.

I managed to rear some 6000 yearling brown trout from these eggs. I sold 5000 to a fish rearing unit on the River Test who wanted some fresh stock to grow on to stock their fishery. The remaining 1000 I reared on to two year old and sold to fisheries lower down the Itchen who wanted quality Itchen-bred brown trout also to stock the river.

As time went by I ended up finally with a trailer on the back of my Subaru with a carrying tank for the transporting of live fish with oxygen cylinders and an emergency air pump that ran off the car engine. I was a complete fish rearing unit but on a minuscule scale. Each year, after the initial guidance from Frank, I was able to undertake every aspect of the rearing from egg through to mature trout completely on my own. It was great fun and a very rewarding little escapade into trout farming and it taught me a great deal about brown trout.

From these meagre beginnings I managed to expand to where I would each season sell 2000 two-year-old hand-graded full-finned quality Itchen brown trout. I had to enlarge the holding capacity to cater for the various age groups of trout and to have space to rear on half a dozen quality brood hen fish. I did not bother to hold any cock fish as I could very quickly run the net around the shallows each spawning time and take a few cock fish out for their milt and return them directly back to the river. At no time were any of the trout I reared planted out into the river at Martyr Worthy as the river was already well stocked with wild trout although I dare say a few fry did slip out of the grading net at times but nothing in great numbers.

Although I did not make a fortune it did pay for the running of the car and allowed for a few luxuries at Christmas time. I maintained that, although these trout I bred and reared artificially, they were as near as one could get to wild fish in that they were only one generation away from the genuine wild fish in the river and to aid this I always used wild cock fish from the river each year.

I was also very happy at the time to allow students from Southampton University to use the facility for research purposes. One girl student did her PhD thesis on external parasitology on wild and reared brown trout using my wild river fish and the reared fish in her work. Although it cost me several trout killed for research purposes I was very interested to watch and learn from the student as she went about her diligent research work.

The brown trout is a remarkable species of fish and I believe we still have a great deal to learn about them. This may come about when the scientists really get into studying and identifying all of the discreet strains of brown trout that still remain in many of our waters in the UK using modern DNA techniques.

Studies now being conducted on the Ferox trout of some of the remote Highland lochs of Scotland are starting to reveal some remarkable information on this strain of brown trout. As the species is further researched so more information will come to light that will assist us to understand more about this fish and so help us to help it survive and return to many waters that have lost their native stocks through man's influences.

As for the resident brown trout of the Itchen I have uncertain views as to their purity, as over time various introductions have taken place and these continue to this day. Light introductions will have little effect, as Nature in its 'survival of the fittest' will decree what is good for the Itchen strain and what is not. It will not be until some lengthy genetic studies are undertaken on the resident stocks that we will be able to really say how 'pure' the Itchen browns are.

I only wish that today's genetic research, with all the new and accurate genetic techniques, were available to me at the time, as I would have hosted some in-depth genetic studies of the brown trout populations of the Upper Itchen. I hope this research will be done before I die as I would be fascinated to find out the genetic background of the wild trout populations of the entire Itchen system.

Nature, and the brown trout's ability to adapt, is the crux and will decree the future quality of the wild trout of the Itchen. Any brown trout is a pure brown trout, it is only the identification of its genetic history that indicates its suitability to the water in which it lives. It is like bringing in some trout from a pristine stock of trout that have lived uninterrupted by any introductions from a highland Scottish loch system and introducing them into the waters of the Itchen and expect them to thrive well. If they did survive to breed then the likelihood of them breeding with their own strain would be very remote and if they crossed with a resident Itchen trout then the offspring may have a chance of survival if the Itchen genes were dominant, allowing the offspring to have a better chance of adapting physically and genetically to Itchen conditions.

During my lifetime spent as a riverkeeper much of that time has been spent in identifying and becoming familiar with many of the various species of flora and fauna that inhabit the rivers and river valleys. This occupation becomes second nature to a riverkeeper. Few species in Nature do not have their allotted place within the big picture of life. At times some creatures and plants and insects find their way into places where Nature did not originally intend them to be. This situation usually occurs when man is involved, when creatures or plants are moved from one place to another. Nature itself decides at times to encourage such movement from one habitat to another. Any new plant, animal or insect arrival, be it introduced by man or a natural arrival, is immediately identified by scientists as an alien species if it has not been recorded before in Britain. Not being trained as a scientist in any sphere of natural history I do have to take to task some scientists who appear to me to suffer from tunnel vision when identifying and discussing the merits of some species of the flora and fauna of Britain as being designated indigenous or alien.

When does an introduced species become eligible to be called wild? What indeed are the differences between 'introduced' and 'indigenous', 'wild' and 'native'? When does 'introduced' become 'indigenous' and 'wild' become 'native'?

I have no wish to enter into the ongoing debate on the genetic integrity of brown trout, which are a species of fish common to many rivers and waters of Britain and have certainly been evident in these waters since the retreat of the last ice age. However, man in his wisdom has over the centuries exploited this species to his advantage by capturing mature native brood stock and rearing their offspring in enclosed waters and used the resulting captive offspring to eat or seed back into rivers and lakes for aesthetic, biological or commercial fishing reasons. The key question is what are the differences if any, between these artificially reared fish and the native fish that are still abundant in our waters? Although a fish has been reared by the hand of man is it any different to its native brothers and sisters? I believe not, although I accept on release its behaviour patterns may be somewhat different to its native brothers and sisters and that it may not even survive very well in the wild environment due mainly to the nature of its upbringing in unnatural surroundings and being fed artificially. If it does survive after release to breed naturally with a released compatriot or with a native cousin the resulting offspring will not be radically different in any way to the offspring of a natural native pairing. The offspring of a pairing of stocked fish reared in captivity and then released to breed naturally can still legitimately be described as genuine wild trout. These offspring cannot be termed native as humans have interfered with its breeding albeit in a previous generation. It is suggested also that with the modern genetic knowledge available today that any genetic comparisons made between these 'wild trout' and the resident 'natives' would indicate that little significant genetic change will have taken place due to man's interference. From the time of release the subsequent offspring of these introduced fish, Darwin's theory of survival of the fittest kicks in along with the fish's capacity to adapt successfully to the ecological conditions of the water in which it is born.

Experiences noted from some older generations of chalk stream anglers indicated that there were noticeable physical differences between native River Test trout, native Itchen trout and native Kennet trout. In the 1960s I caught a traditional green-back brown trout on the Kennet and compared it with a native trout from the Upper Itchen. There were noticeable physical differences, the shape and colour and markings of brown trout differed markedly between the many discrete populations that lived in so many diverse ecological conditions throughout the British Isles. This came about primarily through many uninterrupted generations of natural breeding of like-with-like in isolated situations.

I would dispute strongly that native trout fight more vigorously than wild trout or generally are they any more difficult to catch. Determining the fighting potential of a trout or specific strain of trout is usually more reliant on a combination of either water temperature and or quality, food availability, general habitat conditions and the cumulative stress levels within a fish at the time, than on the integrity of its breeding history or genetic make up. However, in Nature there are exceptions to the rule.

Unfortunately many of the historical noted physical characteristics of some recognised strains of native brown trout experienced and observed by anglers years ago have now almost been completely lost, as numerous annual introductions will have probably diluted many of these physical phenomena. If perchance a river system was allowed to return to a natural self-sustaining population of trout no doubt over many generations of natural reproduction within the river these specific physical characteristics may well slowly reappear once more.

The whole aspect of introduced species has since been of interest to me and I have made some interesting discoveries on the subject. One question that begs to be asked and should be asked and answered is 'What is a British wild flower?'

Considering the question of what is indigenous and what is introduced I recall quite vividly discussing with a visiting angler, who happened to be a qualified botanist, the various wild flowers that were evident along the river margins. One particular species that was in its full flower at the time was the yellow musk, as we riverkeepers call it, yet identified by the expert as *Mimulus luteum*. This plant is abundant along the river margins of the Itchen at Martyr Worthy and has long been one of my favourite species of wild flower. This plant was common along the whole river system as it was on the neighbouring River Test and indeed on many rivers throughout Britain and was even seen as far afield as the outer isles of Scotland.

Unfortunately the expert botanist said, 'Ahh! Yes, but the *Mimulus leuteum* is not native to this country it is an introduced species'. Introduced by whom and when, I asked. Unfortunately the botanist was unable to answer that question. Since then I understand that the earliest written records that mention yellow musk appeared in Edward Newman's botanical magazine, *The Phytologist*, in 1815.

It seemed to me that the same rule applied not only to plants but also to animals and insects, whether a species was introduced accidentally or deliberately by humans. Surely any species of plant or animal, once thoroughly established, in and on our soil or waters and maintaining a self-sustaining existence in the wild should be recognised as a resident British species. This is irrespective of it being deemed detrimental or beneficial to the general ecological health of the countryside, either aquatic or terrestrial.

The common rabbit has been here for 2000 years or more yet is still termed as an introduction, as are many of our well-known species, the brown rat, the black beetle, the pheasant, capercaillie, the red-legged partridge, the fallow deer, the garden snail, the stinging nettle, and many other species. All of which have arrived with or without man's help. Some of the latter day horrors included the North American mink, the grey squirrel, the ruddy duck, Japanese mitten crab, Japanese knotweed, Himalayan balsam and giant hogweed. It is an ongoing process evolving since time immemorial.

In my experience observing the way a new species whether introduced or not, adapts to the ecosystem and find their niche in the web of life and prosper has taught me a great deal about some species. For example, when the grayling were introduced by man into the Upper Itchen in the mid 1980s the numbers initially exploded for several years and it seemed that the river was packed with grayling and no other species. In fact the excessive numbers of grayling ruined the dry-fly fishing for wild trout for several seasons and still does in places. As time passed the grayling slowly adapted to the conditions by making room for itself within the ecosystem and established a natural self-sustaining population within the balance of fish biomass within the river. The presence of the grayling significantly reduced the productivity of the native brown trout as inevitably something had to give way to allow for this new species of fish to proliferate.

As predicted at the time, the introduction to the Itchen of a new alien species, as the grayling was, had a detrimental effect on the river and on the traditional angling experiences for wild brown trout for which the Upper Itchen had been noted for the past two hundred years. It was at that stage that the grayling population of the Upper Itchen should have been identified biologically as a self-sustaining wild species of fish because that was what they have unfortunately become.

The foolhardiness of these artificial introductions should stand as a prime irretrievable example of what not to do regarding alien introductions into any aquatic ecosystem. Similarly this principle should apply to all alien plants, animals and insects. I find it sad that some angling organisations and scientists welcome, and even condone, the introduction of alien species into our rivers while the river owners, fishery managers and keepers rightly treat any alien introductions with total disdain and try to eliminate them. Many species have been introduced over the centuries into this country and this will continue to be the case but it is surely biological folly to actively promote and condone their proliferation.

We must strive to do more to protect and enhance the environment for all the flora and fauna that Nature supplies and let Nature alone determine and select which species within it thrives the best. Over-simplistic this concept may be but once the concept of holistic river catchment management is adopted, whereby within the aquatic ecosystem everything is interconnected, then these simple principles become more applicable.

During the last ice age there were very few resident species of flora and fauna populating these islands and not until the ice retreated did the exposed barren land become populated with new fauna and flora. Nature determined what species would thrive and so over time the diversity of life expanded over these lands. It was not until man arrived and brought with him exotic animals and plants did this diversity expand even more. All the species that now inhabit these isles have either been brought in by Nature or by man so where do we draw the line between native, wild and introduced?

~~~~~

An incident that occurred in the late 1980s the action of which has in my view had one of the most serious ecological effects on the Upper Itchen River and its fishing – the arrival of the grayling. In my opinion this event changed the whole fly-fishing experience quite dramatically. It all happened when, for some unknown reason other than outright thoughtlessness and irresponsibility on the part of the then National Rivers Authority (NRA) fisheries personnel, four hundred live grayling were introduced into Alresford Pond. This pond lies in the headwaters of the Itchen system on a tributary of the river called the River Alre. The stocking of these unwanted species of fish was carried out by the NRA without any prior consultation whatsoever with any of the fishery owners of the Itchen or the Test and Itchen Association. Furthermore the most galling part of it all it was carried out without even an official, section 30, fish movement order.

The grayling had been electro-fished out by request of the owner of a trout fishery on the middle reaches of the Itchen and rather than destroy them the NRA decided on the spur of the moment to introduce them into Alresford Pond. To understand the crass stupidity of this action it must be clearly understood that, since the last ice-age, grayling had never, ever lived in the upper reaches of the River Itchen. Grayling had however been introduced to the middle and lower reaches of the Itchen back in the middle 1800s and although they readily adapted to the conditions there and rapidly became self-sustaining their spread did not effect the upper reaches of the river above Kingsworthy.

For 150 years the 'grayling line', as it became to known, could be identified quite clearly at Abbots Worthy just above Winchester where the river flowed down the valley in three main streams and an imaginary line drawn across the valley which, for some unknown reason, defined the upper limit boundary of the upstream movement of the grayling. Fishery biologists and riverkeepers over the years have been aware of these phenomena but could never give a clear biological or physical explanation as to why it occurred. There were no major physical obstructions in the form of mill weirs or impassable hatch gate systems to prevent the upper reaches of the river becoming colonised by the grayling. So a fish rise observed in any of the fisheries above this point was truly a trout rise.

When the news of this introduction of grayling into Alresford Pond filtered down the Valley, which only took a day or so, my personal verbal reaction was unprintable. Unfortunately, the hierarchy of the Test and Itchen Association of that time were totally unconcerned by this and they disregarded my protestations completely possibly because they had been duped by the NRA fisheries officer into believing that this introduction would not have any detrimental effects upon the river whatsoever. How naïve some people can be. In his defence all the fishery officer of the NRA did say was that the grayling were introduced for the newly formed Alresford Angling Club who had recently taken a lease on the lake and in his opinion these fish would benefit the anglers but not affect the river downstream. An admirable objective certainly but it was an action taken with little consideration for the consequences. It will never be known whether this officer at that time was aware that the River Alre, a tributary of the Itchen ran through the lake. So it was inevitable that these newly introduced fish would soon find a way out and that way out would be downstream.

It took several years for the grayling to fully colonise the river downstream, as each year grayling appeared and were taken by anglers at points further and further down the river each season, until this movement eventually linked up with the resident population at Kingsworthy some six miles from Alresford Pond.

It became indisputable that the presence of grayling changed the whole fly-fishing character of the upper river as the entire dry-fly fishing experience altered inexorably for the worse in my opinion. A fact later verified by the fishery owners and the anglers who tenanted these waters during the changes.

Observations showed that the grayling proliferated very rapidly and they appeared to have very strong powers of adaptability. The numbers in each river stretch grew to extraordinary proportions and very soon huge shoals of grayling began to plague the shallows and gravel runs pushing the resident brown trout to one side by sheer weight of numbers. Shoals of several hundred grayling, containing some fish of three pounds plus in weight, were not uncommon and soon became a feature on many of the reaches of the river from Alresford down to Kingsworthy. I caught 34 grayling on a dry fly in one short afternoon session during a hatch of medium olives and did not have to move my backside from the convenient bench that was situated beside a good gravel run. The worrying thing of all this was that I did not see one trout rise in or around the whole area containing what must have been several hundred grayling. In a normal course of events prior to the grayling arriving this particular gravel run would have held several good feeding wild brown trout of a range of year classes.

Unfortunately, as fly hatches diminished and the grayling population continued to grow, even more pressure was exerted on the historic resident native fish populations. Historic fishery management policies, that had prevailed for almost three hundred years on the upper reaches of this river, allowed the native fish population to naturally maintain its own species diversity and biomass levels at naturally controlled, constant levels. If there were space in the fish biomass of the river Nature would have filled it before.

This huge explosion within the newly introduced grayling population made its mark and took its toll. My observations showed that the new grayling population had risen to occupy about 65% of the total fish biomass in my beats. Therefore, I concluded, there must have been a rescheduling of the composition percentages of the native fish biomass of the river as the river would be naturally incapable of sustaining this massive increase in weight of fish while still maintaining the historic levels of the resident native fish. Something had to give. All the other native fish species, except perhaps the pike, reduced in biomass weight to make way for the weight of grayling. This being the case then 64% of the original native fish biomass was lost and common sense told me the native resident species reduced most was the brown trout. This may not be scientific evidence yet to date no scientists have disagreed!

A river can only grow and sustain a certain weight of fish flesh per hectare and that amount is controlled firstly by water quality, by the amount and availability of food, by space, by spawning facilities and by cover within the river. How that total weight was divided up between the resident and native fish species was the question. Unfortunately, for the Itchen the grayling were there and thrived, the damage was done and we had to live with it for ever more. No known legal forms of fish removal techniques could remove the grayling entirely from the river, besides the process would have been very expensive.

The damage was done and the owners, keepers and anglers had to adapt. I felt fortunate to have known and been able to have fished the Upper Itchen before the grayling so radically and irretrievably changed the quality of the fishing experience on the upper river. Every angler of that era was the last to experience the Itchen at its natural best.

At the time I undertook some long in-depth correspondence with the Grayling Society and although they were aware of the situation they sadly did not seem to care a jot as the only crumb of comfort the then Chairman of the Society could offer was the comment 'Oh! Well it will give more opportunities for grayling fishers to go fishing after the trout season had finished.' Little did he realise that it would have been uneconomic for us to open the fishery to grayling fishers in the autumn and early winter at, say, £20 per day as not only would the soft riverbanks suffer but also the trawling of gold heads across spawning trout would not be a very good idea. The arrival of the grayling has subsequently brought little or no appreciable economic or even ecological benefits to the Upper Itchen. The reverse was true as in places fishing rents had to be reduced as fishermen who remembered what the fishing quality was like before grayling complained about the reduced quality of the trout fishing sport on the river due to these vermin. They were not so willing to pay the high rents for a reduced quality fishing experience and who could blame them. Although the Grayling Society does great work in other spheres on behalf of this species it is little wonder I allowed my annual subscription to the Society to lapse.

~~~~~~

I noticed one grayling and wild brown trout interaction while observing mature grayling spawning one spring day in mid-April. Although grayling do not dig a redd like trout they do appear to vigorously polish the gravel on their chosen spawning site with their vigorous pre-spawning activity. The grayling I observed that day had chosen an area where some trout had spawned earlier on in the January. These trout redds at that time of the year would have held in the gravel the alevins of the trout which would have hatched in mid-March and which were still safely locked in the gravel while they were absorbing their yolk sac prior to swimming up through the gravel to emerge in mid to late April as perfect little swim up wild trout fry. Unfortunately, although the spawning grayling did not dig the gravel, their polishing and very hearty spawning activities completely flattened those five trout redds. So what the chances of survival of the trout fry were in these circumstances was anyone's guess.

This story was an ideal example of the damage that can be done to the environment and to our resident native species by the thoughtless and unwarranted introduction of any non-native species of fish. Man has still to learn or take heed of any lessons gained from the introduction of the grey squirrel to this country from North America and from the damage and effects that the greys have incurred on the resident red squirrel and its pine cone habitat to date. Very slowly, the consenting agencies to these actions became aware of the threats and effects that any introduced creature could and did have on our fragile countryside. Over the centuries there have been many introductions of foreign species of plant, insect and animals, including fish, so even now we all must learn from and be even more aware of the ecological tragedies that have occurred in the past and are liable to happen again in the future if we continue to allow these man-made introductions and movement of non-native species to continue unchecked. This philosophy goes for not only grayling but also any other fish species. I shudder at times and a cold feeling runs up and down my spine whenever a report is read on the progress of the insidious spread of the zander or pike-perch within the UK. Some foolish people who purposely, but illegally, move this species about and introduce them into new habitats are exacerbating the misguided introduction of this highly predatory species from the continent. In such cases it is quite feasible that this voracious predator could demolish the resident populations of other resident species of native fish in those receiving waters and possibly create an unsustainable monoculture of one species – the zander.

I did not dislike the grayling as a sporting species, I enjoyed fishing for them in places where they were native and I admired them greatly not only as a beautiful looking species in their own right but also for the great sporting challenge they offered particularly on the dry-fly. Not for nothing are they rightly called, 'the queen of sporting fish'. They are absolutely fine in their natural waters but they should be left there and not introduced into any other waters that have not historically held or supported native grayling populations.

~ 10 ~
Predators and Poachers

he basic objectives of gamekeepers and riverkeepers are somewhat similar except that the end product species is different. The gamekeeper seeks to protect and enhance habitat for his pheasants or partridges and to wage war on the many natural predators that can and do play havoc with the survival percentages of the wild or reared birds under his care. Similarly the riverkeeper is constantly looking to protect and enhance the aquatic habitat of the trout within his care while keeping an eye out for signs of activity by any one of the several predator species that can and do predate on the trout.

Besides the two-legged wellie-wearing predator, who hails from the nearby town or village, perhaps the pike would be the most consistent predator of any trout stream of the chalk valleys with cormorants, feral mink and grey herons all did their bit to keep me on my toes and give me a few sleepless nights. If they were allowed to all predate unimpeded the total combined damage inflicted on an unprotected fishery can be quite devastating.

There are several other creatures that could and did regard trout as food. There was the otter, which fortunately made a strong comeback to the chalk stream valleys after almost becoming extinct. Fifty years ago the otter was regarded as an enemy by many riverkeepers of the day only because there were so many of them. When I was a boy I remember talking to an old keeper on the Test and listening to his stories of the otter drives the riverkeepers organised between the two Great Wars up and down the Test Valley where twenty or more gamekeepers and riverkeepers would, with the aid of dogs, systematically drive sedge bed after sedge bed out towards a row of standing guns just to reduce the numbers of otter. Fortunately, today riverkeepers know and realise and understand that the chalk stream otter feeds predominantly on eels and only takes a few trout from the river.

All the riverkeepers I knew, loved and jealously protected the otter and quite happily expected to lose the odd trout to 'ottey' even if it was just for the chance of knowing they were about. I did wonder that if the otter population grew by any extent whether control measures would be necessary to restore a balance. Otters could once more become a pest if their numbers were allowed to increase beyond a sensible level. That situation, if it ever arose, would be many years off although there were growing complaints from some trout farmers who were beginning to have problems with marauding otters getting into their trout ponds. I did regret that some of the do-gooders, who, I must admit, at times contributed a great deal for the good of some of our threatened species, did tend to become over-protective. In doing so they lost sight of the fact that all our wildlife species, if they are to survive in a healthy state in this intensive man-managed environment, need their populations to be kept in balance. Whether it is lack of food, habitat or, heaven forbid, the shotgun or Nature herself that becomes the controlling factor in the density of the otter population time will tell.

In the past, good gamekeepers and riverkeepers were able to control certain predator species keeping their numbers to such levels that they were of little problem, but without exterminating them. A careful balance was maintained. There was then little legislation as there is today where an over-protective society and an artificial over-managed environment has created and encouraged some species to rapidly multiply uncontrollably as a result of the loss of natural predators creating devastating imbalances between species. Man has intentionally, and or inadvertently at times, removed the natural predators of some species leading to a population explosion. For example, fewer full-time gamekeepers in Hampshire has effectively created a population explosion of magpies that in turn may have reduced the populations of many of our much cherished song birds.

Another good example is the numbers of grey heron that were once sensitively controlled by riverkeepers when numbers grew and it could be shown that they were over-predating on a fishery. I do not know a keeper who would wish for the last heron to be dispatched or even for the last cormorant come to that. In the old days the keepers were able to keep the numbers in balance within the needs of the ecosystem around them without any interference from uninformed government legislation.

Predation by herons was not usually a major problem, once a pair took up a feeding territory. Although, at one time, we did have some serious problems with large numbers of herons that had been attracted into the area by predating on the spawning shallows and unprotected stew ponds of a trout farm further upstream.

I am a firm believer in Darwin's theory of 'the survival of the fittest' and all that it entails. I also believe that most of our native species of creatures in this country have very strong powers of adaptation to our ever changing man-made and increasingly artificial environment. As and when man-influenced imbalances do inevitably occur within these species then man should be allowed to assist in the redressing some of these imbalances for the overall health and welfare of the animals themselves. Nature has its way in redressing imbalances but unfortunately some of her methods would not I believe be very acceptable to many people.

To a chalk stream riverkeeper the pike has been recognised as one of the top predators. Many a great battle was waged over the years between *Esox lucius* and me. Mr Crabtree, alias Bernard Venables in his wonderful book *Mr Crabtree goes Fishing,* dubbed the pike as 'The Lord of the Stream' and so right he was. 'Esox', as I call him, is one of Nature's most successful freshwater killing machines and an arrogant noble brute to boot. No other species of aquatic predator, other than the trout, has ever evinced so much attention or created so much concern among chalk stream anglers, fishery owners and some riverkeepers as has the pike. Pike have been an integral part of the food chain in our chalk stream rivers at least since the last ice age and I hope they will be for a long time into the future. They have just as much right to be in and live in our streams as do the trout, eel, stoneloach, minnow or bullhead. If the pike were allowed to multiply completely uncontrolled the trout population would have been the first species to suffer. It was a case of managing a balance in an ecosystem.

My job as manager was to assist in redressing imbalances, as and when necessary and as on most chalk streams. I often thought that it would be an interesting exercise for a scientist to contemplate what the species diversity and individual species biomass would be if the river was left totally untouched for a hundred or so years. My supposition was that the species diversity would alter very little and that the individual species biomass of some species would alter quite radically. Darwin's 'survival of the fittest' theory was kicking in.

In the history of the Houghton Club on the River Test, at the time James Lunn took over as riverkeeper in the 1880s, the predominant species of fish resident in the Houghton waters was indeed pike. Intensive keepering on these hallowed waters by subsequent generations of the Lunn family changed this situation quite substantially. If however those waters were left unkeepered I am sure it would not take many seasons for the fish populations to return again to a pike dominated aquatic ecosystem. This illustrated to me so clearly just how very artificial many of our chalk streams really are today.

So many times over the years a fisherman has told me that they have spotted a huge pike in the river that was lying in the deeps of a pool or hiding under a tress of ranunculus. My initial reaction was to ask how big it was, and if this huge

Students from Sparsholt College have a good day's pike fishing.

fish appeared to be seven pounds or more I did not worry for such a pike was more likely to feed on smaller pike than to bother themselves chasing healthy young trout about the river.

I found that the bigger the pike the more it fed on other large fish in the river. If the average size of trout in the river were about a pound in weight then the big pike would mostly be feeding on other slightly smaller pike than itself, as there were rarely any other big species of fish in the Upper Itchen. The little jack pike, ranging from one ounce through to four or five pounds, inflicted the most damage as it was at this size range that they fed heavily on trout fry, fingerlings and yearlings which, if not checked, made tremendous and damaging inroads in the survival rates of a year class of wild and native trout.

Whenever I saw a large pike in the river, which were predominantly female, I tended to leave her for some time to help me clear out the stock of jack pike before I would think of removing her. The river around a big pike's territory usually created a blank area within which resident trout were reluctant to take up their vulnerable surface feeding lies giving the appearance of an area of river that held few rising trout. If I ever noticed such an area of river when there was a good hatch on, or other areas of the river where no fish were rising, I would usually find a pike had taken up residence close to hand.

Knowing that big pike, weighing ten pounds or more, were more likely to be

The 'Jaws' of the Itchen.

Riverkeeper's 'gibbet' for pike heads.

females was very useful to me. If I spotted a female pike moving upstream to seek out suitable spawning areas in spring I could, with certain dexterity, systematically remove the numerous smaller male pike that were drawn upstream, attracted to this big female for breeding purposes. The best cull of this type I ever achieved was when I was able to remove eight small males before I was able to finally remove the egg-laden female just before she was due to shed her eggs.

Pike in chalk streams are relatively territorial out of spawning time. I found also if after spawning the area is devoid of pike the chances of finding any new incomers taking up residence was quite rare. The time to cull the stocks of pike was between 1 February and 30 April. Although territorial, I discovered that pike would move considerable distances to find suitable spawning facilities. I soon learnt where pike were to be found and the areas that held pike did not change from year to year. It was usual practice for many years on some trout fisheries to annually electro-fish the fishery for the sole purpose of reducing the numbers of pike from within the fishery. Some owners thought this was good fishery management. On fisheries where records were kept of this practice some very interesting facts did emerge. On one fishery on the river some way downstream of my water, it was found that the average annual cull of pike by electro-fishing was regularly around twenty-one pike per year and that the average size range of pike removed remained almost constant. When the practice of annual electro-fishing was ceased it was found subsequently that the number of pike observed in the water reduced but the average size of pike that were resident increased.

Any observant resident keeper knew how to catch pike so regular electro-fishing was considered a waste of time and money, particularly if contractors were retained to operate the electro-fishing gear. I eventually took the view that the use of electro-fishing gear, solely for fishery maintenance reasons, should be banned. Electro-fishing gear was only necessary for use by experienced, licensed, qualified fisheries biologists for scientific monitoring reasons.

The pike population had to kept under control and this was achieved with a bit of cunning. In the season of 1981 I decided to have a purge on the pike population. With a group of keen young riverkeeping students from the college at Sparsholt we removed 18 pike from the river at Martyr Worthy in one day.

At that time the river also held an exceptional amount of genuine wild trout and I felt that it had almost become over-stocked with them, as the then average size was just under one pound. The natural head of pike in the river at that time had grown in proportion to the population explosion of the trout but it appeared to have had little effect on the huge population of wild trout and the grayling had not yet arrived at that time. Pike and brown trout have been the predominant two large species of fish in the headwaters of the chalk streams for 10,000 years or more so have survived and evolved together. As long as the pike population was keepered well then both species did and needed to thrive equally. Like them or loath them the pike did have an essential part to play in the aquatic ecosystem of a chalk stream. It would be a sorry day if ever the last pike were ever removed from the river. Again it was all a matter of man maintaining a balance between species in a heavily managed man-made artificial environment.

I attributed natural trout population explosion to a series of exceptional spawning survival years when conditions for the young of the year survival was way above the norm. There were in fact too many 6-10 inch trout in the river. It is little wonder the pike population went up. This was Nature trying hard to redress the growing imbalances. To help remedy this situation we instructed all our fishermen to kill all the trout they caught including all undersized trout, so for several seasons we had catch returns that made odd reading. It took several seasons for things to level out and return to normal whereby the catch size returned to between a pound to a pound and a half on average.

For many years grayling had been persecuted by some owners and managers of trout fisheries who wanted to reduce or even try to remove a resident or introduced population of grayling and, in some places, electro-fishing was used to control them. One fishery, fortunately not on the Itchen, which was considered by the owner to have far too many grayling living and breeding in their one short stretch of river, would annually electro-fish and dispose of about 1500 grayling. This practice went on for many years until it was suggested that if the annual practice of electro-fishing was curtailed then the grayling numbers would reduce naturally. Eventually, after much persuasion, the electro-fishing was stopped. Lo and behold, when a survey was undertaken to assess the effects of non electro-fishing a couple of years later it was found that the grayling population had in fact reduced drastically in numbers quite naturally. There were good representatives of each year class of grayling, the average size and weight had risen, the actual numbers of grayling present in the waters had reduced and yet the total biomass was still the same. The economic benefit of this change was that the fishery could offer excellent dry-fly grayling fishing for decent sized fish in the back end of the year after the trout season had ended. Prior to this all that could be fished for in the grayling season was vast shoals of small young of the year and one-plus grayling.

Although electro-fishing equipment was a very useful fishery management tool to experienced fishery biologists I was certainly not in favour of individuals or fishing clubs being allowed to use this equipment unsupervised on any waters even if they did have an operator's licence. There is so much unknown and or potential damage that in my opinion could be done to fish, insects and insect larvae by the innocent or inadvertent misuse, or näive use, of what must be considered a deadly dangerous set of equipment. It was best left to the professionally trained staff from the Environment Agency and if electro-fishing was deemed to be required on a fishery it should only have been used for scientific monitoring of species and not as a lazy man's way to manage a fishery by removing any healthy but unwanted species of fish as was the case on many beats in the past. Recent investigations on the use of electro-fishing to control a species of fish have revealed that the practice is inefficient.

Feral mink became a serious problem in many areas of the UK and for the Itchen the problem started suddenly with a major escape from a mink fur farm, the result of a deliberate release. Almost overnight the Upper Itchen Valley was swamped. The best the Environment Agency could do was to purchase as many cage traps as they could and distribute them to the keepers. I took three cage traps and commenced trapping the mink.

Mink were the simplest animals to catch when the right spot was found to set the cage trap. No baiting was needed; all that was required was to find a well-used track alongside or beneath a low river bridge or an overgrown ditch that gave the illusion of a dark and interesting tunnel for the mink to investigate, as they are the most inquisitive of creatures. Whenever a female mink was trapped I soon learnt to leave it for a few hours or overnight before I dispatched it, as she would draw in some grass, make a bed and curl up and go to sleep quite happily. The female fouled the bed of grass in the trap and so took on the very pungent mink type odour – an odour once experienced never forgotten. This grass was left in the trap after the mink had been dispatched which would then attract male mink into the trap. This ruse worked very well for me and over a period of 18 months I killed just over 80 mink in three traps.

Today there are still a few mink about and we will always have them from now on. It is a matter of constantly keeping a trap line going and keeping on top of the population. Unfortunately and sadly, there are now few, if any, full-time riverkeepers in the Upper Itchen Valley so regular trapping is now a thing of the past. Running a trap line is a twenty-four hour operation and by law traps have to be visited regularly twice in every twenty-four hours.

The common cormorant was another regular visitor. Pat Fox and I would both spot this bird most evenings quite regularly. The bird would take trout and other fish out of the river and we would certainly have taken it out if the opportunity arose when we had a twelve-bore shotgun under our arm. We were not too concerned at that time though as that one solitary bird had as much right to be there as any other and as far as we were concerned it was not inflicting too much damage.

Over the years the situation changed dramatically as the populations of the inland living cormorant has exploded. This fish-eating predator became permanent residents on many inland waters, with flocks of several hundred being counted in their permanent roosts up and down the chalk stream valleys. This situation is created by the fact that the seas around our shores have been fished out by man and so these birds were forced to seek food in the more prolific man-managed inland waters many of which were heavily stocked with delicious trout.

To illustrate the damage these birds were inflicting on the River Test, a cormorant roost was identified within the Valley and the Environment Agency placed a large sheet of polythene over the ground under the roost where it was left for a few days. The sheet collected all the droppings from the roosting cormorants and after a while the sheet was taken up and all the droppings sifted. The evidence of damage soon became obvious as within these droppings several hundred salmon smolt tags were recovered. These were mini-tags originally implanted into reared salmon smolts prior to their release to the river that would allow the scientists to trace the origination of the smolt or identify a returning grilse or salmon once it had spent its time at sea.

Although the relative agencies did issue licences to certain fishery managers to cull some of the cormorants, this effort had little or no affect in reducing the vast numbers of these birds although it might have temporarily relieved the frustrations of some fishery managers. This situation was again another ideal example of the imbalances that occur in Nature, created mainly by man's activities elsewhere in the ecosystem. Nature will eventually redress these man-made imbalances but she takes her time and in the course of achieving it some strange and unexpected effects can be felt by other species. It was shown that the shooting of cormorants had minimal effect in reducing the overall population numbers and it only served to move the problem on to another site.

The last predator that needs a mention is the two-legged wellie-wearing variety. Wherever trout were kept and tended, either wild in the river or in rearing ponds, they inevitably received visits from the poachers.

In the 1960s and 1970s poaching was quite common on the Itchen as salmon and trout could fetch a reasonable return for the professional poacher, provided mainly from some of the less reputable hotels in the Valley, for at that time there were fair numbers of salmon running the river. I soon knew when there were salmon in the upper river as I would soon spot known poachers' cars parked in odd places and dodgy characters could be observed peering over the road bridge at the bottom of my beat.

When I started on the river I remember clearly my employer saying quite clearly to me that regarding poachers he would rather have a live coward than a dead hero. What he meant was that if I came across poachers in numbers on my water that I was to back off and call the police rather than being brave and tackle a whole gang of professional poachers on my own. I was not concerned about getting into a punch up as I had had some very useful training on self-defence in the Army but, nevertheless, I got his drift. At that time there were two active gangs that worked the rivers in Hampshire and the jungle drums would soon let me know when they were active.

There happened a chance meeting in my local pub one evening when one of the known poachers came in with his wife for a drink. I called them over and offered them a drink, which they accepted with alacrity and a quizzical smile. During our conversation I casually asked him where he had been poaching and he said, without a batting an eyelid, that he had taken a brace of nice trout from the Test that very morning plus a very large pike that he killed and laid on the doorstep of the riverkeeper's cottage just to wind him up and to indicate that he had been about the river long before the keeper had got out of bed. I went on to ask him if he liked pike fishing and he said he did. I asked him if he would like to fish out some pike on my water to which he readily agreed. We made a date for him to come to my cottage the following Sunday morning.

He arrived at the appointed time and we went off to the river where I showed him the boundaries and where the pike holes were, as if he needed showing, and left him to it, thinking nothing ventured nothing gained from my ploy.

He arrived back at the cottage a couple of hours later with four pike on a string and, after asking where he had caught them, we went for a pint at the pub. I said to him that he would be welcome to come and fish for pike whenever he wanted as long as he let me know when he was coming and that he left the trout alone. As an extra bonus I suggested he could also bring his son and his ferrets and ferret some rabbits out of the bank alongside my paddock. He shook my hand and said it was a deal and that he would now ensure that none of the other poachers would put one foot on his new-found patch.

From that day on I didn't have any bother from either of the two gangs of well-known poachers. Not like one very belligerent keeper downstream who continued to try and make a macho point in taking on the poachers head on. For all the times he was beaten up and had to have time off to recuperate he did not learn. My tame poacher said that all the other poachers just did it to wind him up. From then on all I had to contend with over the years were from some keen young fisherman from the next village who had nowhere to fish and the odd visitor who could not read the private fishing signs and the annual visiting travellers who stayed in the Valley for a few days each spring.

Today there is little or no money to be made out of poaching the chalk streams now that farmed salmon is so cheap in the supermarkets. The days of the full-time professional poacher on the chalk rivers are long gone as very few salmon now enter the rivers and the monetary value is so small. Most of the poaching today is done by people who do it for the sheer thrill of it or as a challenge to see how much they can wind up the local riverkeeper. Some drug addicts have been caught taking gravid salmon off their redds below Winchester but this practice was soon nipped in the bud by the Environment Agency bailiffs. The only poaching that is affecting the chalk streams now happens at sea where home based and foreign trawlers are hoovering up vast quantities of exiting salmon smolts and salmon that are homeward bound to our rivers after spending at least a winter at sea. These are the poachers that now need sorting out.

I recall an incident many years ago when my next door neighbour's two boys were about twelve or thirteen I caught one of them, red-handed dip netting one of my rearing ponds and had two good sized trout already in a bag. I scolded him severely and sent him off home to tell his parents what had happened knowing full well they would punish the lad in their own way.

At teatime, an hour or so later, I heard a knock on the door of my cottage and on answering it there stood the young lad holding a jamjar full of assorted coins and his mother standing right behind him. The boy was instructed to apologise for taking the fish, which he did sheepishly and at the same time he thrust the jamjar full of coins into my hand to pay for the trout he had taken. This jar contained all his holiday money he had saved since Christmas. I was rather reluctant to take it but his mother was mouthing, 'Take it! Take it!' I kept a stern face and explained to the lad the error of his ways and warned him that Mr Hiscock, the village policeman, would be called if he was ever caught taking trout again. Suitably chastised the lad was then sent off to bed. The following morning, after the boys had gone off to school, I took the jar of money back to his parents.

Twenty years on the lad has children of his own and he still to this day cannot understand how, when they were young and even older, I always knew when they had been about the river. They usually left evidence of a recognisable footprint or something dropped.

Over all the years as a keeper at Martyr Worthy the fishery suffered from very little serious poaching. The odd multi-hooked long line baited with worms left overnight tethered underwater from a bridge stanchion perhaps, but nothing really serious. Just as a pheasant keeper puts so many birds to a wood so he allows for some predation either by natural or man-made causes.

Certificate

'HOLLOWAY ITCHEN 900'

8½' splitcane trout fly rod, specially built and finished to a design created and extensively tested by Mr. Ron Holloway, one of the leading River Keepers and fishing authorities in the Chalk Stream country of Southern England. Ron Holloway felt the need to recreate the traditional quality splitcane trout rod to be used when fishing the Chalk Streams and as no such rod was available on the market, he set about to design his own. Master Rod Builders Farlow/Sharpe were consulted and agreed to produce the limited edition of these fine rods, and Harold Sharpe, himself, has been supervising the production. The samples have been altered very little, which goes to show that Ron Holloway's original conceptions were correct from the start.

This superb fishing rod is for Chalk Streams enthusiasts who require a rod capable of delivering a delicate presentation combined with adequated distance casting power.

It is fitting that Izaac Walton is buried in Winchester Cathedral, that overlooks the hallowed waters of the Itchen where the ideas for this fine rod were conceived during 1980, which was also the 900th Anniversary of Winchester Cathedral. In honour of this Ron Holloway has decided to name the rod 'The Holloway Itchen 900'.

Limited edition of 100 rods only.

Number 001.

Signed *R. J. Holloway* .

R. J. Holloway

Harold Sharpe

Harold Sharpe

During the late 1970s and early 1980s, when glass fibre was the most popular material from which dry-fly rods were made and carbon fibre was just making an appearance, new quality cane rods became more difficult to find as the revolutionary man-made materials become more fashionable. Having been brought up to use cane fly rods I was naturally reluctant to discard their use as for me they were just perfect for the dry-fly fishing to which I had become accustomed on the chalk streams of Hampshire.

There were of course some excellent dry-fly rods rods made of glass fibre and I still use one particular one for teaching purposes as it has the almost perfect dry-fly action, the 'Bruce & Walker', 'Orthodox' 8ft 6inch 5 weight that cost all of £15 new! Nowadays carbon fibre technology has advanced to such a degree that there are now some superb actioned dry-fly rods made from this incredible material. My favourite for chalk stream dry-fly fishing is the Sage XLT 9ft 6in 5 weight which is so much lighter and yet has a wonderful through action so reminiscent of a cane rod of similar length.

Dedicated to the use of cane rods as I was at the time, I decided to design a suitable cane rod for my fishing on the Itchen. For this project I enlisted the help of Harold Sharpe of 'Sharpes of Aberdeen' who was recognised as one of the best cane rod builders in UK at the time. Harold and I worked together on the design and action of the rod for some considerable time and many prototypes were discarded until such time I achieved all the characteristics within a dry-fly rod that suited me. A numbered limited edition each with its own certificate of origin was produced and named the 'Holloway Itchen 900'. I still possess and use number 001 and my wife Paula has and uses 002. Some rods were sold in UK but the rest were sold in Canada and the USA where cane rods were then still very popular. It was interesting to note that I spotted one of these rods in a tackle sale in London some years ago and I gather it sold on for £400.

Although I would be the first to admit carbon fibre has revolutionised the use of double-handed rods in salmon fishing I am firmly convinced that cane still has its place on the chalk streams or wherever traditional dry-fly fishing is popular.

~ 11 ~
River Management
Considerations

s the 1980s faded into the 1990s so the rivers of UK began to suffer from a series of serious drought years when rainfall averages dropped dramatically. Some rivers were seriously damaged and fish life in some took a downturn in productivity. Even the chalk streams with all their buffering capacity from the vast amounts of water stored in the huge natural aquifers began to show signs of stress. During this worrying period the chalk streams managed to hold up and few if any fish in the rivers died although all around the valleys in southern England many of the still water lakes and ponds were seriously affected with low water levels, high water temperatures and very low oxygen levels causing many fish to be lost. It was only in the headwaters of the chalk rivers where water temperatures were kept down by the input of the permanent spring discharges of cool water were the river's occupants able to thrive almost unaffected.

The poor fly-fisherman however had a hard time of it as any surface activity mainly occurred late in the evening and any attempt to fish during the bright searing heat of the day was generally unproductive to say the least besides being very uncomfortable and quite thirst making. The doom merchants, who only seem to emerge whenever there is a major natural catastrophe imminent, started to blame climate change, exhaust gasses and all the other perceived man-made actions that were or about to wipe out our rivers. I am the first to say that I cannot agree that those series of drought years did not have some prolonged effect on the rivers. They certainly did and it has taken Nature some years to heal the damage. Unfortunately, many fishermen and fishery managers have very short memories and or knowledge of all that has happened historically on the chalk streams.

History teaches us that over the centuries similar events have occurred on several occasions in the past and the rivers still survived and very soon, in biological time, regained their strength and healed themselves without man's help. One has only to read Halford and Skues or Waller-Hills to realise the Test and Itchen lived through equally difficult natural events time and again over the past two hundred years.

Bank cutting, 1996.

Weed cutting, 1996.

Worn out.

Cut weed drifting downstream
by Easton bridge during a
summer cut.

Returning home,
a job well done.

Patterns of starwort in the middle beat after a weed cut ~ no ranunculus visible!

Spot the trout and grayling! (The solitary trout, *top left*, swims ahead of the shoal of grayling.)

The riverside paths and fringe that have to be maintained.

The top beat in the summer, 2006.

Marilyn Bechely, the artist, by the middle beat hut surveying the cut weed patterns.

Bridges, such as the top beat footbridge, have to be repaired and kept safe.

A view of the middle beat in summer, 2006.

A view of the middle beat in winter, 1997.

Winter snow on the Itchen, 1987.

Early autumn light on the Itchen, 1998.

River Itchen winter scenes, 1986.

Unfortunately there is not a river in the British Isles that has not at some time been interfered with by human hands so in natural emergencies similar to the drought years it is man's historic and present actions on the river and its catchment that have to be looked at very closely to see if any of those actions are directly contributing to, or exacerbating, the problems that Nature periodically inflicts upon them.

Abstraction is one human action that comes to mind, as so many of our rivers are now used as potable water supplies for local communities. In the normal course of events water taken from a river for such purposes had a marginal affect on the river. It was only when the rainfall reduced, the springs that fed the river failed and the ground water levels fell that the river became distressed as diminishing amounts of water flowed down its channel that abstraction became a real bone of contention.

Once again if only the doom and gloomers thought about how Nature works and tried to understand what the basic necessities were that a river catchment required to maintain a healthy aquatic environment and the incredible natural healing powers that a river possessed would our rivers have had a chance to survive in the condition Nature requires. It was my unhappy experience at times to witness some of man's actions that were totally alien to the natural good of a river. Although the burgeoning river and soft bio-engineering sciences were sometimes helping to restore many of our wounded rivers I did at times wish these well-lettered scientific people had taken more time to appreciate what Nature achieved in its own way and in its own time, when given the chance, and what could be achieved if restoration efforts were in tune with Nature.

One of the more noticeable effects of the droughts of the 1990s on and in the chalk streams was the effect they had on the aquatic plant life. That prized plant the ranunculus was one of the first to suffer and for several years struggled to survive in good health and strength as it did prior to the droughts. On some stretches of river the plant appeared to die out completely and in other places its growth was very weak to say the least. Again the doom and gloomers came off their fence once again and had a field day saying that the loss of the ranunculus was all down to pollution and that the plant would never ever return.

The ranunculus did suffer badly during the droughts, which was to be expected and it has taken several years of good water flows for it to recover to its healthy pre-drought state. Although the worst of the drought years occurred in the early and middle 1990s the actual ground water levels and river flows did not return to the ten year average for some years after and it was not until 1998 and 1999 onwards that the annual flows returned to, or exceeded, the normal pre-drought ten year average. By the turn of the twenty-first century most stretches that suffered the most from reduced ranunculus growths regained their prized plant and so smiles once more returned to the faces of some of the fishery managers, riverkeepers and owners. While ranunculus is a superb plant in a chalk stream, there are other aquatic plants that, although they may not look so attractive, will carry out the same function and the river and trout would be just as healthy without it. One thing I learnt was that the growth patterns of all of the aquatic plant life varieties in a stream were far from constant and variations in the annual growth and density of species did change from year to year and from month to month. All of which was controlled by the subtle ever-changing climatic conditions which control water volumes.

Another perception that became very popular during the drought years was that the rivers had suddenly become too wide and so needed to be narrowed. The uninitiated in chalk stream history and characteristics would have tended to agree with that statement if the water flows of the early nineties were anything to go by. On most stretches there was hardly enough flow or volume of water to fill the river channel and the overall speed of the flow had dropped away significantly giving the impression of an over-wide channel that was slowing down the flow. It was commonly believed that to compensate for this, a programme of channel narrowing had to be embarked upon.

Whenever there has been need to repair riverbanks on the Itchen, I reduced the channel width a trifle where observations had indicated clearly to me that the river had eroded the bank and slightly over-widened the channel. In places narrowing became a phobia to some owners and some bank reinstatements went to the extreme and narrowed the channel by as much as 25% in places which for a while was fine in the continued low water conditions. It was not until full flows returned, followed by some large flood events, that the extent of this folly showed up. This was illustrated quite clearly in the floods of winter 2000/1 by some unusual movement and re-profiling of large quantities of river bed materials and some serious inundation of surrounding land and this all was caused by over-energising the river channel by the excessive channel narrowing.

The river was continually striving to achieve a natural state of dynamic equilibrium, a natural ongoing action within every river in the world. Any given stretch of river endeavours to create a shape for its channel creating conditions whereby the flow will transport sediments into the stretch at the top and allowing for the same amount of sediment to flow out of the stretch at the bottom. This held for eroding streams like the Upper Itchen and its sediments, mainly sorted gravels. Unfortunately, when man interfered and altered the shape of the channel the river tried hard to return the channel back to its historic shape to achieve its dynamic equilibrium. I experimented with the use of dye-marked stones placed onto the bed of the river and over time tracked their movement down the riverbed. It was very surprising how far a stone moves, even in normal flows.

In lowland rivers similar to the Itchen if and when the fifty-year flood event takes place of course considerable riverbed re-profiling will take place and some major changes in channel shape will take place. It is absolute folly in my opinion for man to get into the river and physically rearrange these substrates back to what they were prior to the flood event. This natural event is the river working naturally and telling us where it wants to be and as long as the new channel has not damaged the natural or original banks then the new channel profile should be left untouched, and the trout will not mind.

On the Upper Itchen the substrates of the river were mobile, and even in the normal course of events the bed of the river changed its shape and depths subtly year by year. Gradually gravel shallows deepened and deeper channels filled in, the river bed profile changed constantly. Overall the trout habitat features did not change too much although they may have moved about a bit!

In the natural river channel instances of shallow runs are known as 'riffles' and deeper areas are called 'pools'. Every river, whether man-made or not, will strive to form its own pool to riffle structure and ratio. If the natural process is interrupted the river will always try to return itself to the natural pool to riffle ratio dictated by the gradient and flow regimes of the river, producing a 7:1 pool to riffle sequence down that channel, creating one shallow riffle to every seven channel widths. For example, if the river is 15 metres (50 feet) wide then there will be a shallower run every 107 metres (350 feet) of channel. It is a marvel of Nature.

The River Itchen channels carried copious quantities of clean spring water of constant temperature and chemical make up that flowed over quality gravel substrates that together encouraged the growth of prodigious amounts of river weeds (macrophytes) which in turn provided cover and food for a healthy range of plankton, insects and animals that supported several species of fish, including trout. With man's help these healthy building blocks man and Nature have produced one of the country's most famous and productive trout fisheries.

One of the benefits of good aquatic plant management, in a chalk stream particularly, was that, by judicious weed cutting methods, the height of the water in many given chalk stream channels could be controlled quite precisely. The channel gradient was quite critical in this exercise and it worked better on the higher gradients of the Upper Itchen than it did on the lower gradients of the river downstream.

During one of those bad drought years, even when the flow volume of the river at Martyr Worthy fell to 63% of the ten-year normal summer flow, the river appeared to any observer to be almost bank full. This illusion was created by cutting the weed in a bar effect so that the water levels were held up giving the impression of a series of mini waterfalls created by these weed weirs all along the river. This worked fine for all those awful years of low water flows. During those drought years we at Martyr Worthy embarked upon some serious channel narrowing and further bank stabilization was planned using the hurricane damaged trees that had been stored together with some purchased telegraph poles.

After some in depth discussion by the owner and the Environment Agency, English Nature and a company that produced a plastic or geotextile membrane that retained soil and fine materials in water, it was decided that this plastic should be used along the river's edge to retain the soil and backfill to create a more stable bankside margin. In practice this geotextile material works very well and a firm but artificial bank was achieved. I thought this was unfortunate for the river. I was not happy with its use as the material created an unnatural flat upright edge from the riverbed to the surface for the whole length of its use and the Itchen was not an industrial canal. Very much against my wishes, 75% of the top beat at Martyr Worthy was treated this way. It looked fine to the observer when fully vegetated on the surface and to all intents and purposes it did a good engineering job and made a firm bank to walk along but unfortunately it reduced the available swim-up fry and young of the year cover along the margins of the whole stretch by 75% by eliminating the rough natural river margin that provided much needed cover and protection for trout of any age group. To maintain and protect and enhance the populations of self-sustaining stocks of brown trout, particularly within the chalk streams, required constant and regular maintenance, enhancement or the restoration of suitable spawning gravels and also the protection, enhancement and restoration of all the vital habitat that swim up fry required at this most vulnerable stage in the life of a wild trout in our chalk streams where the highest mortalities occur.

A further instance of over mismanagement is where gravels are regularly and diligently water-jetted or raked to cleanse them of accumulations of silt to aid spawning unfortunately at times little or no consideration is given to providing, protecting or ensuring that there is sufficient suitable swim up fry cover available just downstream of these treated spawning areas.

Little wonder natural trout regeneration is not what it used to be.

It was coincidentally at this time also that some of the fishing tenants moved away to live in other parts of the world and so there were further rod changes on the river and although the new rods were delightful people, somehow much of the fun and exuberance seemed to have been lost and although the fishing quality was maintained the river was becoming less and less fished with the same enthusiasm of yesteryear. Having thrived on the excitement of the fishermen and having shared in their enthusiasm for the river and the fish there was a now a certain sense of loss. Some of the tenants had work to attend to in far away places and so the fishing pressure was further reduced to the odd fisherman turning up for an hour or two at a weekend. There was one dreadful period when, during the whole month of May when the river was at its very best and seething with rising trout each day and the fly hatches a sight to behold, only two half days were fished during the all the weekdays of the month and only two weekends were fished by the owners.

Maybe I was old fashioned by caring so much but it soon became a daunting and ever-saddening business for me, after spending weeks preparing the river, weed cutting, cutting the grass around the huts and keeping all the footpaths open and clear and spick and span then for no fishermen to turn up at all to enjoy and appreciate it. The river needed to be fished, as there were by this time some large fish that needed to be removed, but some of the tenants were now totally hooked on total catch-and-release so returned all the large and small trout. I tried hard to convince the fishermen that some trout needed to be taken out regularly to keep the up quality of the trout and the fishing for them to a high and challenging standard.

The prime trout were the two and three-year olds and any trout older, although they may be in good bodily condition, were not usually all that good to eat if compared to a one or two year old wild trout. Any larger trout of over four years old would usually start to lose condition and eventually die and could be taken out when pike culling with a spinner.

In these man-made aquatic ecosystems that are our chalk streams it was essential for management to maintain the right delicate balance and health within the populations of fish in any given stretch of water. This was assisted by encouraging the fishermen to utilise catch-and-release but only in the right way, to take only a few of the young small trout and to remove the large old trout that, if left for another season, would only deteriorate in condition or may be become over cannibalistic.

There have been two major natural events that occurred during my time on the River Itchen both of which left their mark on the Valley. Dutch elm disease became rampant in the Itchen Valley from about 1972 onwards and its effects over a period of a few years changed the whole skyline as the huge mature elms lost their foliage and within months became bare skeletons silhouetted against the skyline. The disease finally swept through our part of the Valley and during the course of a couple of years over two hundred tons of elm wood was removed from our property alone. It was a devastating time. Elm was a wonderful wood for use in water as it took a long time to rot. There was so much elm available the local saw mills just could not take any more so many more tons were just burnt on site. The price of a cube of cut elm went as low as 15 pence a cube at one time and some estates could not even give it away. We certainly did not go short of firewood for several years although I did manage to persuade a sawyer to cut a load of planks and a good selection of piles that I could use for bridge work around the river.

There was a stand of huge elm trees between my cottage and the river that created a shady forest glade protecting our chicken run and my work shed. I remember when these trees were finally felled that the butt of one of the largest trees, when removed by a huge Volvo tractor, was purported to weigh 15 tons or more according to the driver. When all the trees were removed the whole area suddenly became a barren landscape and it took some years for even any willow or elder regeneration to take place. It was interesting to note a mass of fresh elm shoots appeared annually from some of the old elm stumps, which within a year or so grew rapidly to a height of about twenty feet only then to be struck down with another dose of the dreaded disease. It was interesting to note that all the time the new growth retained a smooth bark the virus-carrying beetles were unable to get into the soft underbark to lay their eggs. As soon as the new growth reached the stage when the bark started to crack then it allowed access to the beetles and the death of the tree soon followed.

Within a few years the old skyline was soon forgotten and even locals who had lived all their lives in the Valley could hardly remember where the huge elm trees once grew.

The second natural event of note was the great hurricane of 16 October 1987. I do not think Mr Fish will ever live down that fateful statement he made prior to his evening weather forecast on television the night before when he said he had received a call from a lady who had heard that there was a hurricane coming. Mr Fish assured the whole nation that this was not the case although there might be a gale coming in from the Atlantic and, as it was time for the autumn equinox gales, we all went to bed thinking nothing of it.

Paula and I were awoken about two in the morning with the whole house shaking as the wind suddenly rose to a fearsome force. At its height we actually felt the top storey of the cottage lift up and drop down again which we found out later left a crack around all the downstairs ceilings that is still there today although now filled with Polyfilla and covered with several layers of white emulsion. The sound of the wind that night was frightening as we battened down all the windows and sat it out. The electricity was the first to go and we did not get that back for over a week. Fortunately there was little structural damage to the cottage except for a few lost tiles and the cracks around the top of the walls downstairs although our TV aerial disappeared and was later found two fields away. Venturing out when the dawn arrived was a shock as two very large ash trees blocked the lane up to the road so no one was able to leave our end of the village.

I eventually cut the fences and drove my Subaru with its four-wheel drive over a couple of fields to the main road when we wanted to get into the village. Paula had built a stable for her horse in the paddock beside the cottage, this had been lifted completely and dumped at the far end of the next field 274 metres (300 yards) away in a thousand pieces but fortunately the horse was safe as she must have been outside the stable during the storm. My first trip to the river was a shock as an entire stand of 150 mature poplar trees, each several tons in weight, were laying all ways at contorted angles, some torn up by the roots, some snapped off half way, others with most of their branches shredded. It looked like a First World War battlefield. Amazingly enough, and as luck would have it, not one had fallen into the river so no immediate action had to be taken to save any damage to the low footbridges from drifting trees.

As the day progressed the radio informed us, no television of course, of the extent of the damage that this storm had wrought throughout southern England. The gale was in fact officially upgraded to hurricane force as wind speeds of 120 mph were recorded in the Itchen Valley and all along the path of the hurricane that ran from South Dorset through mid-Hampshire and Sussex into north Kent where the town of 'Seven Oaks' in Kent became 'Two Oaks' over night. The swathe cut by this storm through the stands of trees in Hampshire alone was a sight to behold and some hundred of thousands of mature trees were lost and there was structural damage to buildings. Four years later there were still teams of woodsmen clearing fallen trees. The replanting still goes on and in places regeneration has been excellent and wildlife habitat has been restored.

There were some long-term benefits from that storm for me on the river.

A Major Bank Restoration Project

In the 1990s a major bank restoration project was tackled to narrow the over-widened river channel by some 6.7 metres (22 feet) in places. Major structural engineering was involved.

[1 & 2] A new bank line was created with a line of tree trunks fixed firmly to the bed of the river.

[3 & 4] Many thousands of tons of chalk were required for backfill. The intensive work took several days with lorries coming every few minutes with 20 tons of chalk per load — a surprising amount to backfill such a large area.

[5 & 6] Nature quickly started to heal the area, helped with a layer of soil to cover the chalk, seeding and planting up with natural plants. A once-shallow stretch was re-energised with increased flows, healthier weed growths and less silt deposit. Trout used the improved habitat to spawn for the first time.

While work was in progress it looked like the mountains of the moon. We received a few initial complaints from some Valley residents who did not understand what we were trying to achieve and why. However, once everything settled and became green again it all blended in with the surroundings. Twelve months later it looked as though nothing had happened.

With help it was possible to salvage many tons of straight poplar logs, some almost forty foot in length. These were all cleaned up and hand-winched out of the woods with a 5-ton Turfer winch and stacked beside the riverbank. This clearance took over two years to move the damaged trees and burn all the woody debris but with all the usable logs stored it was then possible to plan some major riverbank stabilisation that had long dreamed of being done but up to then was impractical as there was never enough suitable wood available so close to hand to do the job. Thus started a very busy session over the following three years re-profiling a half-mile of riverbank along the carrier, which was also narrowed at the same time using the logs and backfilling with brush and soil, and chalk all of which was retained by a geotextile membrane. In retrospect the narrowing of this carrier stream was in my view overdone in places although at the time it looked fine as the water levels were still low but now good flows have returned I think less narrowing would have achieved a better result. In river work of this nature we won some and lost some and learnt from our mistakes.

To give a more complete picture of the river the water quality generally throughout the Itchen system was excellent with a majority of the Water Authorities sampling sites giving constant A1 readings. The base flows were being maintained, with abstraction being almost fully compensated for in normal times by the return of quality treated sewage effluent and with the standby in extreme low flow times of the ground water pumping compensation schemes at Candover and Alre sites in the headwaters of the river. Fishery management objectives throughout concentrated on salmonoid species primarily with the few coarse fish species considered a much lower priority. The lower reaches of the river, including the three salmon beats and the middle reaches up to Abbots Worthy, have historically relied upon regular stocking with trout to maintain viable sporting trout fisheries. The natural reproductive ability of the lower and middle reaches of the river for salmonoids was shown to be insufficient to naturally sustain commercial sport fisheries as it was in the headwaters where natural reproduction is more successful, so stocking was required in these lower reaches to bolster and maintain viable fisheries. Other species of fish reproduced naturally quite well in these lower areas. The majority of the upper reaches above Winchester due to geology and with good habitat management and sensitive controls on angling pressure, were able to maintain quality self-sustaining stocks of brown trout. The only reason that this status quo was maintained for so long in the upper reaches was because the fishery owners wanted it that way and had for the past 200 years or more managed and maintained the river system as a wild brown trout fishery, albeit semi-artificial. To achieve and maintain this objective many riverkeepers were employed over the years to protect, enhance, create and restore where necessary the right habitat for wild brown trout and they even controlled other species of fish that were, or were deemed to be, in the way. Between the two great wars there were employed a full-time riverkeeper for every mile of river, how times have changed.

History taught me that these chalk streams were not historically all that naturally productive for salmonoids but were, at best, just average dual purpose fisheries and then only when water quality allowed. Species diversity was rather poor even in the good old days before man's influence. The salmonoids only flourished well as and when man tended the river for them. The river continually tried its hardest to return itself to its former state whenever it was left alone but with the many man-made changes over the centuries some of which that have been very radical this is no longer feasible and quite unrealistic to expect. To allow, or encourage, the river to revert from its highly-changed state was foolhardy and a very short-sighted enterprise if the river system was to retain any social or natural beauty value for humans.

It is interesting to note that the ancient city of Winchester which straddles the River Itchen is honeycombed beneath the city with Roman stone-built culverts that then drained the city of surface run off water and domestic sewage all of which was discharged directly into the river. Many of these culverts are still in perfect working today although they now only drain the surface run off from rain that falls on the city. All domestic sewage is now disposed of through modern channels and is treated before it is discharged into the river as clean treated effluent. It was recorded in the 1530s that the inhabitants of Lower Brook Street, a street that runs alongside the river through Winchester, were evacuated back up the town to Middle and Upper Brook Street because the 'stench from the river was so great'. This leads one to wonder what the fish populations were like healthwise or if there were any fish at all in the river below Winchester in those days.

The construction and operation of a flood control hatch gate system that replaced Durngate Mill in Winchester during the early 1970s, selected very successfully against many of the anadromous species of fish from entering the now much under-used salmon and sea trout spawning areas of the upper river system. This problem has at last after all those years been addressed just recently and now a fish pass allows migratory fish access to the upper river.

To illustrate the historic use of the upper waters of the river by salmon I happened to meet Ray Hill on Easton road bridge one morning in the early 1970s when he was a very young keeper on the Itchen and before he took over from Mick Lunn at the Houghton Club. We watched spellbound as many adult salmon passed upstream during the short time we were stood there. One of these salmon I later found hiding under a footbridge and I estimated that fish to be in excess of thirty pounds. Pat Fox was sceptical of my story when I related it to him over our lunch time pint, until I took him down later to the river to show him and luckily the salmon had not moved. We were able to measure the length of this big fish quite accurately and from that measurement we were able to give a good estimate of its weight. It is and was the largest fish I have ever seen in the river.

The fishery management policies on each reach of the river were, and still are, set down by the individual fishery owners. Unfortunately at times, some of these policies were in my opinion hardly conducive to good catchment fisheries practice. There were also others that were influenced by the admirable Test and Itchen Association. Although this organisation had no legal powers it had the voluntary support of some of the major river owners within the catchment. The Environment Agency and English Nature had their legal remits but were mostly powerless to influence the overall objectives of the individual fisheries owners in their fish and wildlife management strategies.

Fortunately the attitudes and objectives of these agencies changed over the last few years with a definite move away from maintaining, at all costs, artificial salmonoid fisheries and in their policies towards stocking fish to maintain viable fisheries. The radical change in policies by certain Wildlife Trusts towards fishery management also created many an upset throughout the world of fisheries management not only on the chalk streams but countrywide. This was highlighted by the well-publicised contretemps that occurred at the very historic Abbots Barton fishery on the Itchen where the local Wild Life Trust imposed certain management requirements on the river beat that it owned that some felt, within a year or so, would degrade the habitat for trout – habitat that has been diligently nurtured successfully for brown trout by the fishery managers of this site for the past 150 years.

The introduction by the Wild Life Trust of the policy of benign neglect could in time alter the habitat into one with a totally different range of flora and fauna. I accepted that this was just Nature working and adapting but over time the river would try hard to return to its historical pristine state utilising the few natural elements that man had left in the system after inflicting many changes over the centuries, such as dredging and draining. This area was a perfect example of a totally man-made river system with cut high and low carriers and managed water meadows and a heavily canalised and dredged mainstream. If left it would have weeded and silted up and, if neglected, may have become overgrown with natural willow, reed, carr and sedge along with Japanese knotweed and Himalayan balsam both of which are dangerous exotic escapee species already now very visible in the catchment which, if not managed properly, could threaten surrounding land and property in and after any future flood events. Benign neglect is of course a very useful rehabilitation tool when used sensibly and in the right place and it can be shown to have great benefits, but in this circumstance I considered its use to be a very retrograde step that could well have had serious ecological effects not only on the adjacent fisheries but in time on the overall health and wealth of the whole River Itchen. It pleases me that things have at last changed and the Wild Life Trust have taken heed and the river at Abbots Barton is now returning back to a far better management regime under the guidance of the very knowledgeable previous tenants who had managed it so well for many years.

It was only within the last twenty years that the fishery management policies of this country have taken a change for the better by moving away from using stocking as the panacea for any reduction in the fish population strengths in our fisheries. As the cost of artificial fish production escalated, allied to the growing abhorrence by a growing number of fishermen of grossly over-stocked waters and the government agencies having their budgets reduced, fishery managers were encouraged to act to identify the limiting factors that were controlling the natural survival of our native fish populations. In so many instances it was soon found that the fish habitat qualities of many of the waters were abysmal and where once fish happily lived and naturally reproduced successfully years ago now many of these waters were unable to maintain self-sustaining stocks and could, at best, only support stocked fish of catchable sizes.

Thus dawned the present and growing desire to restore aquatic habitat not only for fish but also for all the other species of flora and fauna that had been either lost or were struggling to survive in the degraded habitats. This growing awareness stimulated several trout fisherman and fishery managers like me to get together and form the Wild Trout Society from which the Wild Trout Trust evolved and is now fully occupied in promoting aquatic habitat restoration.

~~~~~

Being a riverkeeper one inevitably became involved some time or other in many diverse discussions on fish, fishing, and all the many various topics fisherman like to talk about.

One of the more humorous discussions that was debated in the angling media for some considerable time was the pheromone effect that suggested reasons for some women catching more and bigger fish than men. These suggestions were applied mainly to salmon angling.

One of my personal observations on the reaction of trout to stress pheromones was an experiment I carried out after a discussion on the pheromone effect with some fishery management students.

To demonstrate a particular theory I had, I took a three-foot square plastic fish holding tank and rigged it up with a throughput of spring water and placed a dozen yearling brown trout into the tank. The tank was covered and the trout left for twenty-four hours to settle down in their new surroundings. The following day I took a screw-top plastic jar with a capacity of half a gallon and three parts filled it with the spring water above the tank holding the trout I netted out one of the trout from the tank and placed it into the jar and replaced the screw top and gave the jar a good violent shake which stressed the poor fish witless no doubt. The trout was removed from the jar and placed into another tank away from its original home. The contents of the jar which had held this trout was then gently drip fed in to the water intake of the tank holding the eleven trout and the trout were observed by peeking gently under the cover so not to frighten them and witness the affect. The trout were laying settled and unworried in an orderly group facing into the input flow of water. As the drip feed entered the water the first trout became disturbed and started to back away from the flow, as did the others as the water reached them. Within a few seconds the entire eleven trout became highly agitated and started to dart around the tank. When all the water had been passed through the tank it took just a few minutes for the trout to settle down once more into their original positions within the flow.

Now I would not say this was good science at all but as a one-off experiment it indicated to me that trout may, can and do detect and react to these so called stress pheromones exuded from other agitated or stressed fish. The scientists may draw different conclusions from such an amateurish experiment.

I came across another similar illustration of this in Canada concerning scientists who wanted to collect some cock Chinook salmon for their hatchery, and for some reason they were finding it difficult to trap sufficient numbers of males. To remedy this problem it was suggested that a ripe hen salmon was sacrificed and the body put through a commercial blending machine to liquidize the whole carcass which they did. The liquid was taken to the trapping site and a mechanism set up to drip-fed it into the stream. The results were quite staggering, as after a few hours the infusion drew upstream a mass of wild cock Chinook salmon and the scientists were then able to trap all the male fish they required. It was noted that as soon as the drip feed had been exhausted the numbers of cock fish in the vicinity of the site dispersed very rapidly. This indicated the strong sense of smell salmonoids possess as within that liquid I should imagine there were strong mating pheromones that could be associated with a ripe ready-to-spawn female salmon. Finally, as there were some recently tagged salmon in these males, it was noted from notes recording the tagging dates and times that some of those cock salmon had moved some 24 kilometres (15 miles) up the river during that period of liquid infusion of female salmon. One salmon had covered the distance in a matter of six hours. He must have been keen. Again, it was not good science but a very interesting exercise.

Over recent years, in the angling press, there has been unwarranted attacks on today's fisheries scientists claiming that they have and are to blame for the demise of the Atlantic salmon populations throughout the northern hemisphere. As salmon and brown trout are so closely related I also include brown trout in this statement. These were very strong words indeed and naturally the response was equally as strong.

For me it highlighted the problems that I faced throughout my career in fisheries management for almost forty years. I am largely self-taught and what knowledge I possess has been attained through experience, observation and a deep love for my work and an inquisitive mind, all of which drive me on to learn and understand more about how rivers work and how and why the fish within them live and survive. This thirst for knowledge has led me to delve into the libraries of the world to glean knowledge that has been researched and recorded by the scientists. I have sought out recognized experts in their field and talked to them and have taken their guidance where necessary. Anyone in fisheries management worth his salt would have done this for as the late Ken Loftus, a much respected fisheries scientist, so aptly stated, 'Yesterday's research is today's science and tomorrow's knowledge'. I doubt very much that there are not many of us in this world who have not and do not operate without some received wisdom. I have a tremendous admiration for many scientists who have a string of letters behind their names and yet still recognize the value of people qualified in practical experience alone. Unfortunately, there are also a few scientists about who are unable to acknowledge and value the worth of unqualified practical experience.

Prior to one of my early invited visits to Ontario when I was asked to have a look at some of the degraded river systems of that region and where possible advise and suggest which of my chalk stream habitat restoration methods could be adapted and used to address the perceived problems. I firstly queried with my host, The Ministry of Natural Resources Fisheries Department, my qualifications to undertake such a mission. I was told in no uncertain terms that although I had no academic qualifications they did require my practical advice out on the streams and to show them how my habitat restoration methods that had served me so well in UK could be adapted for use in Canadian river conditions. Furthermore, I was asked to talk to their young field biologists and discuss and show them out in the field how I read rivers and catchments and identified causes of habitat degradation and what remedial action could be taken. It was from these early visits that eventually a million dollar program of restoration was set in motion throughout Ontario, based on the use of my simple and practical methods. As to the answer to my question regarding my qualifications, which are none, I was told that it was the practical knowledge that was required and if I wanted a qualification they would give me one, a QBE, which as I was later to learn meant Qualified by Experience!

From that day on I have not looked back and have regularly visited Canada to assist in their various restoration programs, the last being recently advising the Toronto Region Conservation Authority on their catchment orientated protection and restoration program on Duffins and Carruthers Creeks. It was, and still is, so refreshing to work happily with highly qualified people who respected and valued the input that practical experience can at times offer. It is so unfortunate that in the UK I have found it such a different story and have for so long laboured under the effects of some of the misguided attitudes of some qualified biologists who operate under the veil of exclusiveness and that in their minds only qualified people are, or should be even allowed near a river let alone being capable of advising on fishery management subjects. Fortunately, this attitude is not quite so prevalent today, but there are still some dinosaurs out there in UK who will never change. Just as the real dinosaurs of the past died out due to climate change so these may soon cease to be!

A recent review of their membership regulations by the Institute of Fisheries Management, where I have been recognized as a registered member for many years, revealed that a registered member of the Institute required certain academic qualifications. Not having any I naturally expected to be reduced to the ranks and become a Friend of the Institute. On querying this I set the cat among the pigeons and after some consideration the Institute agreed that my status would remain as a registered member with the qualification of QBE that would meet the membership criteria. To be recognised and accepted as a member of such a respected professional organisation solely on practical merit makes me immensely proud.

Many years ago, in the early 1970s, Frank Sawyer suffered many brickbats from certain areas of academia who went out of their way to devalue much of Frank's work on his chalk stream, particularly his studies on the effects of added chalk on accumulated silt. Frank Sawyer knew more about chalk streams at that time than nearly all of his detractors put together and we have only to look closely at Frank's thoughts and observations which he set down in his writings for corroboration. Many of Frank's ideas and practices are still being used to advantage on the chalk streams today, even though some of the young implementers are totally unaware that they originated from Frank Sawyer. The chalk streams owe a great deal to Frank Sawyer. Frank was a very proud man and held very strong views about the way chalk streams were and should be managed, in his day for a riverkeeper to speak out as he tried to do and did at times was unheard of in those days. He bore the force of the rebuttals that he received constantly from many uninformed quarters with fortitude, much sadness and some bitterness I believe.

There was an eloquent editorial by Sandy Leventon in the Trout and Salmon magazine in August 2002 entitled 'Bad Science'. It pinpointed and identified at the time just some of the many generalities that plague much of today's understanding of the many factors that have brought about this perilous state in which we now find some of the Atlantic salmon populations today. There is hardly a fishing magazine edition throughout the northern hemisphere that does not at times refer to this perceived plight of a species of fish that means so much to so many people. I firmly believe we all should remember Charles Darwin's warning of 'the blindness of preconceived conjecture' and leave it at that.

I am firmly of the belief that the branch of salmonoid science that today deals with the Atlantic salmon is excellent and as time passes that science will be expanded and improved as more knowledge of the life cycle and requirements of the Atlantic salmon is attained. It entails understanding and identifying all of the required habitat needs, food and cover for every life stage of the fish both freshwater and marine. When this is fully understood then the next requirement is being able to look at any stream, river or sea to pinpoint and identify any feature or fish requirement that the system is lacking and acting as a limiting factor(s) that controls the survival of the species of fish required at any one of its life stages. The knowledge is attained by observation, experiment and induction. Undoubtedly there still are several areas that have yet to be investigated which leaves us to surmise what will happen to the salmon while we fill these gaps in our knowledge.

I am unable to agree with a reported statement in another magazine that fishery scientists are to blame for the demise of our salmon fisheries. It is down to the fisheries manager to interpret, understand and implement the available science and then be able to select the right science that will address the problems of the individual fishery. It is in the interpretation and implementation of that science by some of the fishery managers that the perceived problems in our salmon fisheries are to be found.

A good series of results can be obtained by careful observation and measurement over time by experienced and careful observers. Atlantic salmon can be observed at spawning and the deposition of eggs through to alevin, swim up fry and parr stage to give a good series of results for hatching and survival rates. The smolting stage is now being regularly monitored on many rivers and the numbers reaching the sea are now being counted quite accurately. The grey area of survival is from this stage onwards and to when the fish return as a one sea-wintered fish or a two or two-plus sea-wintered fish. The losses within a year class at sea appears to be on the increase as it is at this sea stage that man at present has only a perfunctory knowledge as to the causes of these losses although many ideas have been forwarded, such as by catch by drift netters through to changing temperature regimes at sea and over-fishing of fish prey.

Science has taught us a great deal and the future of each and every aquatic ecosystem that has a population of migratory salmon should be a concern. Whatever is happening within a system, be it good or bad, cannot be cited generally across the country as any reduced salmon run in a river system has to be treated separately as one entire ecological unit and managed as such. So many times it can be shown that each and every river system has its own individual problems.

Over recent years there has been so much hype printed about genetic integrity in the angling world. It must be understood there is not a strain of Atlantic salmon that maintains complete integrity. Although the majority of returning salmon to a river will have been born in that river it should be remembered that each run from the sea brings in individuals from other natal sources. This is beneficial as any natural inter-breeding improves and maintains the genetic variability of that stock. It is this genetic variability that is so vitally important in maintaining the health and strength of that stock. Salmon and trout have a great ability to adapt to changes and will naturally change as the generations evolve within a river system. Extreme situations, such as an escape of many thousands of farmed fish of mixed genetic backgrounds, could possibly super saturate and weaken an outnumbered resident population. To rectify this naturally may take several generations of adaptation. Trout and salmon have this ability by using natural selection and survival of the fittest.

The use of catch-and-release on a threatened run of spring salmon can do nothing but good to that run. Tagging and recording the numbers will give the fishery managers the information that will measure the numbers and quality of fish until such time as an allowed harvest of these fish can be taken that will not impair the sustainability of that spring run. People who complain about the benefits of catch-and-release in these circumstances should perhaps reconsider their views.

Taking eggs from wild fish and hatching and rearing them in a hatchery hundreds of miles away has been shown to be not very productive, as experience has shown. Eggs taken some years ago from the Test in Hampshire and hatched and reared on the Kielder hatchery on the Tyne, when returned to the Test, produced almost nil returns from fin-clipped Kielder fish. I would personally question the efficacy of hatching eggs at Kielder and planting the month fed fry or parr into the improved headwaters of the River Wye. Although the eggs were hatched on Tyne water the fry or parr survival through to smolt stage would only be successful if the fry were reared on Wye water from birth or at least at month fed stage. It would be far more useful, if stocking were to be used, to take eggs from wild Wye brood stock and hatch and rear them to the required stage in a hatchery using Wye water. Then only when all the identified controlling factors that are limiting survival in the wild on the River Wye have been addressed. There is a lot to say for the natural ability of wild salmon that have over the centuries adapted to the waters of their own natal rivers. There is nothing magical about hatching and rearing salmon so, if some form of stocking is deemed necessary, then build a small hatchery on the waters of the river that has to be stocked.

I do hope fishing magazine editors in future editorials will take a more positive view on the science that is available to all in the fishery management business.

I have said it so many times, that there is nothing in Nature more constant than change, and the Hampshire water-meadows are an excellent example of a habitat that has experienced a period of considerable human effort, then a period of human withdrawal and now a period of destruction. One has only to look closely at the Upper Itchen Valley to find that many of these historic sites have been destroyed or are being destroyed by infilling and these meadows are now being ploughed and treated with chemicals that destroy insect life and severely regulate the diversity of the plant life. I remember well walking the grass land meadows beside the river when I first arrived on the Itchen to work and the grass was populated by millions of grasshoppers, now I am lucky to find even one hopper in twenty acres. Other forms of land use that will look very different to the former irrigated meadows will replace many of these. Such is life.

~ 12 ~
More Philosophy than Science?

As the autumn of my working life approached my thoughts tended to centre upon the experiences of the early and middle years and to question what I had learnt along the way. Angling and fly-fishing in particular has spawned more books on the sport than almost any other human hobby activity. This may be because the love for the sport and the great contemplative pleasures an angler derives from a lifetime spent in pursuit of fish beside river or stream, loch, lake, pond or reservoir will never be erased from the mind. Silent contemplation, a recommendation given by Izaac Walton to Piscator centuries ago, is just as relevant today as it was then, and if in our contemplation we wander off into the realms of philosophy then so be it.

In the twenty-first century science-based fishery management principles were being implemented increasingly on our threatened fisheries and the time seems to be rapidly approaching when the trout fishing world will witness the partnership of the philosopher and the scientist, the seeds of which have already been sown in many places.

Having relished fly-fishing for fifty years or more I want to be around after this union has taken place because the progeny of this will result in trout fishing the like of which I have rarely seen before, let alone sampled. The scientist may be the breadwinner of this marriage but the philosopher will wear the trousers. It may have been dear old Izaac who wrote, 'Fishing is not a competitive sport but more a branch of philosophy'. Once the goals have been set by the philosopher the scientist will take over in order to achieve the desired result – quality fishing.

The demand for the finest possible fly-fishing stemmed from the dedicated fly-fishing enthusiast, the individual who really cares. He is the one who lavishes time and money on this recreation. As a tourist or as a regular customer he is usually a free spender and therefore of considerable value to others. When he hears of some quality fishing he yearns to sample it and when he finds what he likes he returns to it time and time again. Thus it is his desires that are so important to the many non-fisherman and particularly to the fishery owners who are involved in the economic interests related directly, or indirectly, to fishing.

To the dedicated angling enthusiast fly-fishing for trout never was, nor will be, a simple affair. The true greatness of this most delightful sport is due to many features: the fascination of the problems that Nature has presented; the beauty of the environment of wild trout; the accumulation of knowledge; the honing of the powers of observation; the analysis and the gaining of skill. All combine to meet the challenge of imitation, presentation and stealthy stream craft – all of which can be so darned complicated.

Each trout stream presents its own individual problems, and varied moods and mannerisms all of which need to be solved or understood by the angler. A rising trout of some proportions is the ultimate for which the dedicated fly-fisherman's eye is tuned, his ear cocked and his fly cast. Given this situation the discerning angler is kept in total and absorbed delight as time gently passes but unfortunately on many waters these days it is now increasingly becoming a hoped for, rather than an expected, event particularly on some of our chalk streams.

In the evolution of modern man the hunter-gatherer instincts are still latent in most of us, because each generation in turn produces offspring cast in the mould of its progenitors and there exists therein a strong desire at times to follow in their footsteps. Each generation in turn hears the call that has reverberated through the eons of time as fly-fishermen answer this deeply ingrained and powerful pull as his blood surges through his veins when he spots a large wild brown trout rising to a surface fly just within casting distance.

Today's discriminating descendant of early man now waves a featherweight carbon fibre wand as he stalks quietly up the banks of his favorite trout stream but here there is a very strange paradox, the strangest for any known sport, and which is positively confounding to the non-angling observer.

This fly-fishing angler sets forth to catch trout, but he does not want to catch them too easily. He likes to catch large ones, but he does not want them to be all the same size. He does not like the experience of fish getting away, but he does not want to be too successful in landing every fish he hooks. Just because he is hunting trout does not mean that he must kill all he catches as this is reducing every fish to a state of possession, which inevitably leads to that awful modern affliction called 'limititis'. There must be a certain degree of failure and a considerable uncertainty. The degree of personal satisfaction is realised and lies in the challenge of the natural problems and in the satisfaction of solving these problems – that is angling and fly-fishing in particular.

Almost all quality trout fishing in Great Britain is under great people pressure today that comes in very different forms. One form is reserved for holiday times that involve a dedicated destination trip to some dreamlike primitive place where the fish may not be sophisticated but there will be solitude and natural beauty in abundance, perhaps a remote highland loch. Such quality trout fishing is like gold dust – it is where it is. As enjoyable as these trips may be they will not suffice for the regular angler. He must fish more regularly than just at holiday time, so other fishing opportunities must be available within easy reach. This availability will cater for the one-day-a-weekers or weekenders or even for the odd hour in the evening after work. Indeed, it is a fortunate fisherman who can regularly ponder long on the banks of his favourite trout stream and fish through the ebbing pulse of a dying summer's day.

Harassment and danger is what fishing pressure is all about, it makes trout shy, observant, alert and resourceful and it encourages hypercaution within them. Trout have their ways of learning and here the laws of survival of the fittest prevail, as with all species. The common phrase for this in fly-fishing is 'leader shy' and that was not coined without reason. For anglers to understand we must allow wild trout to become sophisticated by giving them a second chance to benefit from their youthful exuberance and misjudgement. Now add to this the economic truism that wild trout are too valuable to use only once.

It is at this stage that the philosopher swings into action as the scientist searches out the facts, and as and when the two travel paths cross there will be a union resulting in a new dimension in the management and production of quality fly-fishing for trout.

It is understood from discussions with fly-fishermen that the chief among the frustrations and vexations of today's distraught fly-fisherman is the matter of where to go for some quality fly-fishing for trout. This perceived union would therefore address this problem by stimulating special trout management.

The whole purpose of this philosophizing is to explore the possibilities that will result in the improvement of our trout fishing in spite of diminishing natural resources, modern development and poor land use practices in our river catchments.

History and experience teaches us that the most important fish to the fly-fisherman are the surface feeders, as they become prime targets as they advertise the fact that they are on the feed. One of the major and most common place problems that has to be addressed is what happens when the most valuable wild fish both catchable and the natural brood stock are removed and replaced by flaccid fleshed stock fish that have little or no experience of feeding off the surface.

The angling philosopher will continue to philosophize and, as like breeds like, so let the scientist apply Mendel's law and encourage Nature to produce the right strain of free rising trout. Once the scientist understands the problems and recognizes his assignment his task is not all that difficult and, besides, he likes the idea as it is of interest to him and good for the future. The philosopher has to realize that there is more than the quality of our trout fishing and the trout that has to be subject to control.

The greatest predator of all is man himself and at times he does present a problem. By intellect though he is still the ardent conservationist, so the required plan must be explained clearly to him so there will be support and understanding to achieve the goal.

The education will start by asking that there shall be no killing of the undersized free risers and that they are returned to grow on. To start with the take home rewards may only consist of the odd trophy fish that would be past its sell by date if returned to overwinter once more and also the odd non-rising fish that remains constantly bolted to the river bed and can only be taken with a deep weighted attractor.

The angling philosopher will at this stage quote the patron of all aquatic conservationists, Aldo Leopold, who wrote, '*There must be conservation management which will positively produce rather than negatively protect – wildlife is a crop which Nature will grow abundantly provided we furnish the right seeds and the suitable environment*'.

Anyone who has spent the best part of their working life on and around a river like the Itchen will understand that Nature is a hard taskmaster, but Nature is also a willing servant and the opportunities she offers must be recognized before they can be grasped.

Trout fishery management frontiers and philosophy must spill over into biology and other related sciences including the management of man himself if there is to be any positive development in trout management. From this, many problems can be solved and the main one, better fishing, is simplicity itself.

Our precious trout streams need special attention because new ones are just not being made any more. The character and value and quality of many of our revered trout streams are in jeopardy. In the name of progress they could suffer ruination by over-exploitation, mismanagement and poor land use practices. There must be recognition of their monetary value for quality recreational pursuits besides solely for preservation and conservation for biological reasons only.

Since my arrival in Scotland I have detected a general feeling that the wild brown trout populations north of the border are mostly still in excellent condition and I have little doubt that is the case in many catchments. However, similar thoughts were held in southern England just after the last war and history has taught us that we have since paid the price for this complacent attitude. I believe very sincerely that fishery managers should look towards building future strategies based on the premise 'protection before restoration'. A pennyworth of protection is worth a £100 of restoration.

The discriminating fly-fisherman is a tourist by nature and the hope and care of our natural resources are just the antithesis of resource bankruptcy so from here on in on all our rivers it has to be 're-creation for recreation'. There should be no fear that the fishing tackle of our grandchildren will be a computer and a reality software package on fly-fishing. So it is suggested what is needed in the trout world is a meeting of the minds, the philosopher and the scientist.

The River Itchen, up to the middle 1990s, had been in better overall health than it has been for many years and this state, despite the substantial threat of some present day problems, has to be regained, maintained and protected although it is a very artificial system. With the use of good fisheries science and the other branches of rivers and earth sciences that are now available and, more importantly, given there is a common will throughout the communities within the catchment, I am confident that the future quality of these artificial rivers could be secure. Good science and a sensitive use of Nature's own regeneration powers will guide us to produce and maintain a quality aquatic system from the sustainable use of all the available remaining natural elements that man has left unsullied, and that includes self-sustaining fish populations, albeit limited, which we have within the system and are at our disposal.

<hr />

'Always look on the bright side of life' as the song goes; so one must think positively and look to the future with a strong sense of optimism. The last few years of the twentieth century has seen many changes within the management and controls that the government agencies are now implementing on the aquatic ecosystems of these isles.

Once again I say there has to be conservation management that positively produces rather than just negatively protects. This situation would not have arisen had there been an agreed integrated catchment management plan in place for the Itchen catchment. Anything less will spell disaster in the long term for the future of our rivers and the plan has to be a live plan. Only when an integrated management plan for the whole aquatic ecosystem system that is the River Itchen with agreed objectives for the *whole* system will it become clear what has to be done, if anything, for its protection and rehabilitation.

Given that it is unrealistic to return the river system back to its pristine natural state, thought has to be directed to positively identify what actual state is required and how that state can be achieved and maintained economically for the future to protect the very existence of our fisheries, and therefore the sport we love so much. The answer may lie in the forthcoming EU Legislation enshrined in the Water Framework Directive, impending legislation that will be eventually translated by government into domestic legislation. It should be the baseline strategy for the future.

Within this transition lies the greatest and most unique opportunity for man to redress the past trend of degradation of our river systems and of their ecosystem functions upon which society depends. The opportunities are vast but so too are the risks of government agencies and the frailties of their local advisors not interpreting and implementing this legislation effectively. Government's duty is to translate this Directive in a cost-effective manner which is fine as long as the envisaged cost constraints do not emasculate the vision of the Directive or they do not retreat from the task and deem that the frailties of the existing approach to water management in the UK are satisfactory.

The whole Directive is a weighty tome. To summarise its five main purposes are: (1) the prevention of further deterioration and the protection and enhancement of the status of aquatic ecosystems; (2) the promotion of sustainable water use; (3) the enhanced protection and improvement of the aquatic environment; (4) the progressive reduction of pollution of groundwater; (5) the mitigation of the effects of floods and droughts.

These five purposes are given teeth by the recognition within the Directive of the designation of river catchments as 'the area of land from which all surface run off flows through a sequence of streams, rivers and possibly lakes to a particular point in a water course'. The Directive follows up these five points with a requirement for Integrated River Catchment Management which recognizes the need to treat river catchments as one whole dynamic land–water system, including all interconnected water courses, water bodies, ground waters within the bounds of the designated river catchment.

The basic intention of the Directive is to ensure that all ecological problems are addressed in an integrated cross-disciplinary fashion linking water quality, water quantity, all land uses and other parameters within the management process.

It should be understood that the Water Framework Directive, if and when implemented by the Environment Agency in England and Wales and SEPA in Scotland, will have an impact on every river in Britain and affect every riparian owner in one way or another. Although it might take about 16 years to complete it is the right legislation that incorporates all of the necessary aspects of environmentally sustainable economic development within individual aquatic ecosystems as represented by whole river catchments. That gargantuan mouthful means to say that each and every major river catchment will become the basic unit of aquatic management with no political boundaries cutting through or across.

Within this very brief outline of this impending legislation lies the future of our rivers and our sport that is associated so closely with clean wholesome rivers. The legislation is vast in scope, complicated and will be very expensive to carry out. It is within our hands to ensure that our Government translates and implements this Directive into good legislation, creating the national building blocks for the protection, maintenance and restoration of every single one of our aquatic ecosystems in the future. This could very well be the last chance we get to achieve this objective and it involves us all.

The Water Framework Directive gives to all who reside within the Itchen catchment and every other river catchment in the UK the opportunity to ensure that our favourite river and its entire catchment are managed as one complete aquatic ecosystem. Great concern from the very outset is being shown that questions the ability and the will of the relative agencies and in particular their local advisors to fully interpret all the objectives of this legislation before its implementation.

These basic ecological management philosophies, principles and concepts are ones that I have supported and promoted for many years now and in my opinion when implemented will have more beneficial affect in the future protection and enhancement of our rivers than any previous legislation, but only if it is implemented correctly. To see this Directive implemented before my close of play would just make my day, time only will tell!

Whatever transpires we have to be prepared to invest in a truly sustainable future that recognises water as a vital resource that should be managed for the good of the whole population and the environment. Indeed it is difficult to conceive of a more pragmatic form of investment in a genuinely sustainable future for the human race than the quality of the water environment which, once achieved, will pay back to society in terms of its supportive capacities – our precious fisheries. There may well be costs that may even entail some social changes and reforms in the areas of exclusive land usage but that may then lead to further innovations and productive multi-disciplinary thinking. One thing for sure is that whatever comes out of this Water Framework Directive it has to be a live and active plan and not another mighty tome to gather dust like many previous plans.

It is pleasing to note apart from the Water Framework Directive the movement towards the conservation and the restoration of our inland freshwater aquatic resources continues to grow with excellent work being undertaken not only by the Environment Agency and English Nature in England but also by other charitable organisations like the Wild Trout Trust and the Game Conservancy and Salmon & Trout Association who are all at last working closely and in harmony with these government agencies together to restore and protect some of our threatened waterways and fisheries. Science based restoration and enhancement and habitat protection cannot be undertaken solely by any one agency so the formation of partnerships are and will be very important in the future.

The rivers Test and Itchen have the greatest ever opportunity available to them now that will ensure the future of these two wonderful rivers because their future is in the hands of all the river owners and the Test and Itchen Association. This association formed many years ago in 1907 by the riparian owners of both rivers, and now supported by many fisherman who fish the various beats of both rivers, has the ideal opportunity and latent political and financial strength to establish and implement the right management strategies in conjunction with the Water Framework Directive that will secure the future for the two rivers and all the fisheries they support. With the necessary employment of some experienced and qualified scientific assistance and complete and total support from all its members, a worthy strategy for the future integrated catchment management of the central Hampshire Basin could then be set down with confidence.

With some infusion of young blood and a good science-based strategy to follow, guided by an experienced river scientist, then the Test & Itchen Association could go from strength to strength. The chalk streams are entering difficult times so I wish the Association well. Their future policy surely has to revolve around their ability to gain complete agreement between their members and to build partnerships between all fishery owners and land owners, all the user groups and communities within the catchments of the Test and Itchen, as well as the relative Government agencies They need to grasp the nettle and come together to form a single working partnership with the relative government agencies that will address partners' requirements and that includes all aspects of habitat protection, restoration and fisheries management. When achieved the two catchments will then be managed together as one entire ecological unit using a common strategy put together and agreed by all the partners under the scientific guidance of the government agencies.

Some of the present fisheries management policies now operating within the chalk streams of Hampshire are in my opinion unsustainable as each and every individual fishery still appears to have its own, and often, different management ideas on each beat of the river. It is in the formation of a comprehensive working partnership that the Test & Itchen Association could and should take the leading role and exert its full potential.

I was very fortunate over the years to have attended and have been involved in many meetings, seminars, and conferences on the subject of the restoration of degraded rivers. One thing that I have gleaned over that time was how well the scientists have honed their skills in their assessments of our degraded freshwater ecosystems in the UK in particular.

While all this was happening, the 'river menders' got on with the practical and more specific restoration works and bandaged many of our seriously wounded rivers and streams. Looking back, many of these restoration projects, despite being beautifully engineered, focused on restoring local features in damaged streams, often without really understanding the underlying causes of the degradation. They were treating the symptoms rather than the causes. Despite a great deal of money being poured into some of these programmes, the overall catchment health in some of these instances still continued to deteriorate.

Catchment management plans were not a new idea, some had been around for a few years and many of our major river catchments in the UK had one. I suggested that maybe a new approach to the application and implementation of these plans was required which was broader and more integrated and which was plugged into the right process and spatial scales, because I thought that the implementation of catchment management plans had almost ground to a halt in some areas.

Catchments are the logical units for the management of land, water and aquatic resources. The catchment integrates the chemistry, water flow characteristics and human activities. Streams and rivers within the catchment reflect all these interactions and abuses. This should not be the only scale of interest. Although the interplay of catchment geology, topography and climate create the potential for specific fish communities within the catchment, this potential is realised at a more finer scale within specific valley segments, or river reaches. The river reach scale is the next logical level for fisheries management, engineering, and geomorphological planning. Most restoration workers are familiar with this site scale because to date most of the traditional restoration work occurs at this level.

Having been an advocate for adopting the basic principles of holistic catchment management for 20 years or more I have often been criticised for these beliefs even by some river menders or people involved in restoration work who do not appear to understand or are willing to accept the principles of the whole catchment philosophy, citing as one of their main reasons as being, 'they are impossible to implement'. I am convinced that it is possible and can be achieved.

During my working life I was able to visit countries where river restoration and fresh water fishery rehabilitation was being undertaken and I was able to glean practical knowledge and information on many small and large catchment orientated projects, some of which were mediocre but many were excellent. I felt that we in UK should be more willing to learn and profit from the results and experiences of the good, and not so good, projects conducted elsewhere.

We have to realise and understand that Britain is blessed with abundant rivers, some of which are of unsurpassed beauty and quality, such as the River Itchen, but remembering also that these waters are finite. So many of our rivers have been damaged by past land use practices and many more will be further damaged by future ill-conceived, poorly planned and badly implemented development and along with threat of possible climate change, many of our waters in the UK are now at serious risk.

There are also other problems that will have to be resolved besides development. Many who are involved in river management will be aware of an ever-increasing pressure for the multiple uses of our rivers and river corridors from an ever-diversifying array of users. Besides fishing there is, for example, walking, bird-watching, mountain biking, photography, rafting, canoeing, kayaking, bug-hunting, picnicking, and the 'right to roamers', to name but a few. Experience alone teaches that often these activities, either alone or combined, spark conflict with not only the riparian owners but also other interested users.

There have been court actions over the usage of the rivers by canoeists. There were regular and almost daily confrontations between landowners and walkers, canoeists, bird watchers, photographers, artists, dog walkers and the like. There were even many arguments and disagreements between fishery owners themselves on local river and fishery management policies. The list was endless. These problems did not go away but one thing was certain – that every single faction would willingly come together to fight collectively against any action that would have even the slightest detrimental effect on the quality of the whole river or any part of its surroundings. If the interest groups who wish to use a particular river and its valley do not eventually come together amicably under one umbrella and resolve their differences a variety of outcomes may occur.

One possibility is degraded fishery quality and a general decline in the abundance and diversity of the natural flora and fauna resulting in areas of a river being closed off completely with all groups being excluded with the possible exception of one exclusive group. In the future there will probably need to be a revision in the way our historic strictly private ownership system operates on many of our rivers in this country. This situation has at times not only prevented many people the opportunity to see and appreciate what the wonderful beauties our rivers and river valleys can and do offer but also at times this system has even compromised the diversity of the natural flora and fauna.

If this is the sad outcome of this thorny problem the whole community ultimately loses out and many of our treasured aquatic resources will be left with very few friends. History teaches us that past management practices provide little guidance for us to solve these problems so we will need to think of new ways of doing things, as we appear unable to solve today's problems with the same level of thinking that our forefathers used to create them.

The social fabric and the establishment that has dominated the countryside for many generations has to adapt and fortunately many have. The times, they are a-changing.

A way has to be found whereby this could be done, if we are to gain the support of more of the population of this country in our efforts to protect and enhance and restore our precious aquatic ecosystems. Fencing them off and barring people from the riversides will not help and in the long run will certainly not in the long term protect these rivers. Society in my opinion has and will need to change in the future, maybe not in my lifetime though. There has to be a system devised whereby everyone shares the beauties, the responsibilities and costs of protecting these places. The archaic head-in-the-sand, strictly private, single-use attitude of some riparian owners groups has to change. Twenty or more, different river management strategies on one river system will not work efficiently for the overall and common good of a river and its catchment. Sadly, this is a system that is still all too prevalent today on many of our streams. As inherited money runs out, and costs overtake income, much has to be yet invested in protection, maintenance and restoration work. Without this investment rivers start to decline, particularly the man-made chalk rivers, if they are not regularly maintained. I detect that it has already started in the Itchen Valley.

On the other hand total open access would at times be detrimental so a properly managed, controlled and balanced access scenario is needed. Inevitably the cry will go up 'Who pays for it all?' One has only to take a look at some other countries in the northern hemisphere to find some answers to that question.

If we are to develop new approaches it may be worthwhile to take a brief retrospective look at how fisheries and rivers were managed in the past here in UK. Generally speaking from the middle 1800s up to the mid-1960s fishery management in particular used basically three management tools: stock fish; control of harvest (bag limits); catch poachers. The various management agencies of that early period also liked the idea of hatcheries as it provided a simple solution to local fish population depletion.

From the old River and Water Boards, through to the regional Water Authorities, National Rivers Authority, and now the Environment Agency, fishery and all the other river sciences have flowered. These new science based professional agencies finally came to realise the vital importance of habitat management and restoration and so many major strategies for scientifically based management have and are now being produced. These do also include catchment management planning. Unfortunately, catchment management has yet to really manifest itself successfully in many areas, mainly due to stringent central government financial cutbacks, where agencies have been forced to downsize staff and drastically reduce budgets so they are now doing less. All this despite the inevitable population growth within our cities and of the increasing human movement out of the cities to the greener pastures of our already pressurised countryside and its natural resources.

My travels to Canada brought me in touch with a good and successful working example of integrated catchment management which is the Grand River Fisheries Catchment Management Plan (GRFMP) from Ontario, Canada. Their innovative plan came about when fisheries professionals and anglers began to realise that, due to Federal and Provincial government reductions in funding, to progress they had to expand their partnership processes to encompass the whole catchment and include all the other active or potential river user groups. The GRFMP has now been developed for the entire 6,800 square kilometre catchment of the Grand River in Western Ontario and is in my view an excellent working example of a community agreed and community based catchment management plan. The plan, begun in 1995, was completed in 1998 and was developed with not only the community of anglers but in partnership with all the other interested groups leading the process along with the two government resource agencies, the Ontario Ministry of Natural Resources and the Grand River Conservation Authority, which are the equivalent to our Environment Agency and English Nature in UK playing the role of facilitators and supplying technical support.

A spokesman for the GRFMP told me that they wanted to start the process with a blank sheet of paper, and use all past plans as background information. They wanted the anglers and all the other potential user groups to come together and create the plan, and then to commit to it. Create and commit they did. The anglers from the entire catchment were represented on the committee along with representatives from all the other user groups. They worked with the agencies to develop an open, transparent process and established a core set of principles to guide the process. They requested readily available scientific and technical data to determine what fish community objectives were possible, preferable and ideal. The first meeting sought confirmation of present known fish distributions and asked anglers what they wanted. Some people thought this was a very dangerous question to ask. The second set of meetings determined whether the plan answered all of their questions.

In order to determine realistic and achievable fish community goals, the catchment was divided up into three zones, based on geology. The three zones defined the potential for specific fish communities. The zoning also enabled anglers to understand what was possible and what was not, in any particular part of the system. The three zones helped to explain the opportunities and constraints there were on each zone by geology. From this, the plan then elaborated on the following format for each zone: Fish Community Objectives; Issues; Management Strategy; Tactics.

Increasingly it will be found that Government agencies alone cannot and, will no longer, be expected to totally look after the quality of our aquatic environment. It must and will be down to the dedicated individuals, anglers, fishing clubs and associations, riparian owners, conservation groups and communities, that will need to come together and form a partnership with Government agencies to formulate a more strategic and integrated approach to our aquatic resource management.

If we look at all of the Government Agencies here in the UK it will be found that they also cannot now do it all by themselves. So what is needed is a new paradigm that uses an integrated catchment management approach to set context and direction to cement a single strong partnership between all river users, anglers, local communities, businesses and conservation groups and riparian owners. Once established this single partnership will identify, design, plan and implement these directions both at the catchment and local levels. These community-based initiatives are the property of, and in the keeping of, all who live within the catchment, albeit though the resources may occur on private lands. The first and overriding priority is that we all must learn to work together. I do foresee some very high-powered inertia being exerted by some riparian owners towards this approach but I do believe that in this country we must find a possible starting point for this to happen. For no other motives other than ensuring the future protection and conservation of our rivers and aquatic resources.

Among some of today's river workers there is a growing awareness of the need to protect certain reaches of rivers that still exhibit exceptional quality and productivity this follows the Leopold maxim of 'protect the best and restore the rest'.

The waters of the River Itchen at Martyr Worthy are an ideal example of this maxim. For some time now, some anglers, many river keepers and other fishery managers have recognized that some reaches of river due to specific combinations of geology, topography, man's land use practices and good annual maintenance practices have created waters that contain strong self-sustaining wild populations of highly sought after fish species. These areas are more naturally productive and aesthetically pleasing than other reaches within the catchment.

From this awareness an 'exceptional waters approach' could be initiated to develop a community-based process to protect, manage, and enhance and maintain these identified fragile 'centres of excellence' from which a high standard can be identified and used as a good practice for the rest of the catchment. Once understood, this approach will assist and encourage landowners, community groups, angling clubs and associations and all the other interests within the catchment to come together and work in unison to develop a planning process on a workable stretch of river in order to protect ecological, economical and recreational interests that make the 'centres of excellence' so special.

Although not all portions of a catchment are, or can be exceptional, the exceptional waters approach will automatically use the more holistic ecosystem concept that ensures that all waters within the catchment are maintained at a level of health that ensures the overall health of the whole catchment and contributes to the protection of these 'exceptional waters' in the catchment. It is a continuum in which anglers, communities, agencies and all the user groups together must strive together to avoid degraded waters and achieve healthy or exceptional waters.

Depending on the outcome of the necessary decision-making that directs the future, if the status quo is required then, yes, there is work that could be done on the future management strategies of the whole Itchen river system. To achieve this requires the maintenance and enhancement of the habitats of the lower and middle reaches to improve and encourage more natural reproduction and rearing on of not only salmonoids but also other species of fish.

Unfortunately, I have that awful sinking feeling at times that total agreement between all the riparian owners to manage the river as a whole ecological unit successfully may never come about so all the best laid plans of mice and men could go by the board and the river will continue to suffer from the wide diversification of ideas held by some of the owners as to how the river should be managed now and in the years to come. If we do not know where we are going then almost any road will get us there!

The immediate and future causes of any ecological problems that face many of the chalk streams and other rivers may not all lay between their riverbanks but may well relate to the effects of man's land use practices within the river catchments. These in my view are now clearly manifested in the insidious and growing problems of the possible effects of diffuse pollutants within the sediments carried into the watercourses from surface and subsurface run off. A symptom of these effects could well be illustrated in the already observed and documented slow but regular annual decline in the volumes of insects that have and do maintain the natural wonder and value of the historic fisheries of many of our beautiful rivers. Maybe it is more protection that is required, not rehabilitation.

I may at times have painted a rather dismal picture of our rivers and I believe that some of my prognosis up to now may well not be well received yet I do detect a positive upwelling from many quarters that gives me consolation from the fact that there are now an ever-increasing number of people and organisations who realise that if they do not get together and work in partnerships with each other then our aquatic resources will continue to deteriorate.

'Protect the best and restore the rest' could be a good thought to dwell upon.

To illustrate this fact one has only to look back twenty-five years or more to remember the condition of many of our rivers in the industrial heartlands of the country. Since the decline in the heavy manufacturing industries that grew from the Industrial Revolution and which enabled Great Britain to become a wealthy and great product producing nation the rivers that supplied the power, cooling facilities, effluent disposal opportunities were no longer required to fulfil these functions. Over time many of these waterways have started to clean themselves up naturally. As part of the Advisory Visit scheme, run by the Wild Trout Trust, I have been invited to look at several of these rivers and have been excited by what I observed.

The Bradshaw Brook for example that runs through the heart of Bolton in Lancashire is an excellent example of a stream that had been for many years totally wrecked by all the effects of the heavy industrial operations that were situated along its length and had over the years discharged huge amounts of toxic effluents and sediments into the stream. When I was conducted along this stream early in 2002 I discovered a beautiful green oasis. I was amazed at the natural healing that had already taken place and all this right in the centre of Bolton. I was able to find masses of young of the year wild trout fry in the margins of the stream amongst the debris of past industry right beside a line of now disused derelict factories that had for years been discharging toxic effluents into the stream. The river was telling me that it was able to do it and so with a bit of thought I was able to give some constructive advice to the new fishing club who had recently acquired the fishing rights from the city fathers on measures that could be taken to further help Nature to continue its good work.

Only just recently this club has had its five year plan agreed to by the Environment Agency and the Wild Trout Trust has given the club a further leg up by awarding them the annual Sage Bursary which will help further in their planned work on the brook. It is so encouraging to find that there are people out there who really care about our rivers and the fish that live in them and most important of all are prepared to roll their sleeves up and get out on the rivers and implement restoration work under the right guidance.

Another and similar situation I found was on the River Yarrow between Chorley and Leyland again in the heartland of industrial Lancashire where the demise of the heavy polluting industrial activity had again encouraged the once heavily polluted river to start to clean itself up. A local conservation group have taken up the cause and have now with help from the Environment Agency produced a conservation plan for the river that will aid the natural improvement and assist in improving the resident brown trout and the return of the sea trout and salmon that once historically used the river. There is some way to go but it is so encouraging that projects like this are being planned and implemented by volunteer organisations that have the forethought and drive to retrieve lost aquatic ecosystems like the River Yarrow. Again I was pleased to visit the river on several occasions and give some practical advice on an already excellent plan of action. If I can continue to encourage people and groups like the Bradshaw Brook Club in Bolton and the Yarrow Conservation Group in Lancashire or the Nar Angling Club in Norfolk or the Turriff anglers in Aberdeenshire and various others in between in their work and stimulate more to do the same then I think I may have contributed something to the future regeneration of some of our most degraded rivers and streams. I do not like generalisations in fishery talk but I believe that our river systems throughout UK are now in better condition than they were fifty or hundred years ago. That does not mean we can afford to become complacent as there is still a long, long way to go yet in restoration and whatever we do it must be remembered that the protection work will never end!

True fly-fishermen know that there can be no fly-fishing without pure waters in which our game fish can live. There can be no such waters without proper management of the rivers and their catchments or without good controls of pollution, erosion, industrial and human waste and the infilling and hardening of the flood plains. Therefore, each fly-fisherman should be deeply concerned with all measures to conserve and restore quality waters and must involve himself whenever possible in any effort to promote such measures and be able to recognise that all these efforts are inseparable from the conservation of all our renewable resources.

Finally to sum up all this philosophizing it might be well to bear in mind the words of a wise old Ojibwey Indian Chief in Ontario who remarked after witnessing the clear felling of all the trees within his tribe's ancient hunting grounds, *'This land belongs to my people, some of them are dead, some are living, but most of them have not yet been born'*.

~ 13 ~

The Wild Trout Trust
~ Stocked vs Wild Trout ~

hen I was invited in 1996 by Charles Rangley Wilson to a meeting to discuss the possibilities of forming an organisation that would do something to avert the decline of the wild trout in this country I was naturally intrigued with the idea straight away. For many years I admired the way Trout Unlimited in America had developed and had not only spread its doctrine far and wide throughout the North American continent but also did some excellent on- and in-stream restoration works on many river catchments in the USA. During one of my trips across the Atlantic in 1979, I was made an honorary member of the Cumberland Valley Chapter of Trout Unlimited. I have, for many years, been a great advocate for wild brown trout, their protection and enhancement of their habitat, so to be invited to be part a plan to do something tangible about the plight of this species was something I could not resist. I was confident that, with the years of working with wild trout both here in the UK and North America, my experiences could well be of some help.

It was early in 1996 that we met down in deepest Dorset at Richard Slocock's house and where we spent hours deliberating over how and what should be done to firstly organise and find a name for our new baby. By the third meeting there were five of us: Charles Wilson, Richard Slocock, Mike Weaver, Ronnie Butler, Roger Mills and me. That third meeting will be well remembered by all who attended as we spent most of one day discussing and debating what to call the new organisation followed by a long and protracted discussion trying to define what actually a wild trout was. We came up with 'The Wild Trout Society' (WTS) to the first question but it took rather longer to come up with a full and clear definition of what we considered a wild trout to be:

> *A wild brown trout is a trout that completes its life cycle without direct help from humans after hatching in a largely natural environment from eggs deposited there by its mother. Wild trout rear to maturity, spawn and have offspring to produce the next generation of wild trout.*

Although these trout may have come from stocked trout originally they were deemed wild under this description. Native trout were trout that continued to complete their breeding cycle annually, totally uninterrupted by man or by any stocking introductions, and have done so continually since the end of the last ice age when brown trout naturally first found their way into our rivers. Therefore wild trout were not necessarily native trout.

As the WTS progressed and the membership grew the Society became involved in several trout habitat restoration projects and, with some good media coverage, we slowly became recognised as an organisation that actually did something rather than just talked about it. It was a team effort and, although we all had day jobs, things continued to go from strength to strength. Those were hectic, frenetic, frustrating days and although at times things went wrong there was one saving grace and that was the sheer dedication and enthusiasm between the members of the founding committee that kept us going. We all were amateurs at all we tried to achieve, yet somehow we did it.

Time passed and as things changed the Society evolved into the Wild Trout Trust (WTT) which, being a charitable trust, eased the administration and sought to attract suitable levels of support and funding to allow the Trust to achieve its aims of conserving more of the wild brown trout populations of the UK through the protection, enhancement and restoration of their habitats. The Wild Trout Trust's approach to conservation was, and is, proactive and committed to promoting and encouraging active improvement to wild trout habitats in a variety of ways.

Following the formation of the Wild Trout Trust it became very noticeable that the Environment Agency and other conservation groups were increasingly interested in the management of wild trout. This change in management emphasised habitat protection, enhancement and restoration besides including a subtle change in fishing regulations. Catch-and-release became very popular within tailored regulations that were geared to the productive capacities of waters and which at the same time isolated the hatchery-orientated stocking programmes that impinged so much upon wild trout stocks.

The Trust went from strength to strength, guided by a growing band of volunteers whose dedication to the cause and objectives of the Trust was boundless. It was decided that if progress and growth was to be maintained at the rate the Trust had achieved in its initial three years of existence then a employed Chief Executive was needed to take up and ease the ever growing burdens that were been loaded on the shoulders of the volunteer founding committee. To this end, after a great deal of discussion and sorting out of applicants, a CEO was appointed. The Trust was very fortunate to have acquired the services of Admiral Fred Scourse who took on the onerous duties of plotting the right course. Simon Johnson, who has taken the Trust forward, now holds this position and is doing a great job.

It was particularly pleasing to me that as the Trust grew so did its reputation. It was recognised by the Government Agencies as an informed well-run organisation that was beginning to fill the niche that we perceived was the void between science and its application on the rivers and lakes of UK where protection, conservation and restoration of trout habitats was needed. The Trust worked very closely with these agencies and partnerships were encouraged between owners, fishing clubs, the Trust and these agencies to develop and guide the planning, designing and implementation of protection and restoration projects.

The Trust blossomed and a great deal was achieved but only through the dedication and enthusiasm of its volunteer committee members and our small band of membership contributors. To continue and maintain this growth and success the Trust needed not only more subscribers but also more support from other areas. The Trust was fortunate to attract solid support from some areas of industry including the fishing tackle manufacturers and this valuable support was directed into practical conservation and restoration projects with none taken for infrastructure costs.

The future indicated to me that if our fishery resources were to be protected, maintained and restored where necessary then it would cost money and due to the downsizing and reductions in grant aid funding, the government agencies did not have the manpower, let alone sufficient funds, to do the job. So it seemed that these agencies would become coordinators and it would be increasingly down to Non-Government Organisations, like the Wild Trout Trust, to be the instigators and facilitators in forming partnerships between these agencies and the owners and clubs. The Wild Trout Trust has a very important role in the future of our game fisheries, yet it has to be remembered that if we tend the game fishing areas of our aquatic ecosystems then we also have to tend the habitats and water qualities for all the other natural flora and fauna that live in the system.

As part of the growth of the Wild Trout Trust activities it formed an Advisory Service that I was proud to have pioneered in its infancy that operated a system of sponsored Advisory Visits that were carried out by a team of experienced trout habitat advisors. If a visit was requested a member of this team would visit the fishery to undertake a walk-over study of the conditions of the habitat for trout and then provide a report that explained what problems there might be and suggest and advise on the right procedures that could and should be taken.

Any work was planned and implemented in conjunction with agencies, such as local government, that needed be involved in any rehabilitation work that was deemed necessary. This service proved to be very successful in encouraging riparian owners, fishing clubs and associations to look at the habitat within their fisheries with a view to its protection, maintenance and restoration for self-sustaining populations of trout. I undertook 36 sponsored advisory visits country-wide from which many have since developed into successful restoration projects for the enhancement of wild trout. Now I am retired several of these projects still contact me for advice and it gives me great pleasure to continue to help wherever I am able. Unfortunately due to a policy change and political correctness creeping in regarding insurance all WTT Advisory visits have now to be undertaken by qualified biologists only. So it was decreed that I was no longer required to undertake any advisory work for the WTT which has saddened me no end after all the time and work I voluntarily gave to the organization from its fragile beginnings. However I wish the Trust well in the future and I now rest in my retirement knowing that I had the privilege of being a fundamental building block upon which the WTT has since gone from strength to strength.

It was interesting to note that among the many agreements on targets for the environment that were agreed and signed by 187 nations at the 2001 Earth Summit in Johannesburg was the agreement on the need for governments to form partnerships with non-government organisations and businesses. The Wild Trout Trust had already done its bit, now it was down to the government agencies and UK businesses to play their part. As a non-profit making charity the Wild Trout Trust channelled all sponsorship monies into well-planned aquatic habitat protection and restoration work.

No angler should expect in the future to go fishing for nothing if quality trout fishing is the objective, as quality trout habitat and fishing in most waters costs money to protect, maintain and restore where necessary. True wildness is increasingly hard to find these days and will be a commodity that will become harder to find in the future. Even the wildest hill loch will require some form of management protection particularly if it becomes a sought after fishery. The days have all but gone for the angler who wanders the hills in the hope of stumbling across a rugged, heather-bordered, dream loch full of wild and free-rising brown trout. These destination dream fisheries are now few and far between and are just sweet pipedreams that only come to light in fishing magazines and books for the average trout fisherman. To actively protect the best and restore the rest of what we have got left has to be the best way forward in my opinion. Unfortunately some angling journalists seek out these dream wild fisheries, write about them and extol their virtues to such an extent in the well-read angling magazines that these fragile gems are now in serious danger as they suddenly come under heavy pressure from the over fishing that has been generated from all this thoughtless over exposure. Some angling journalists should show more responsibility and be more aware of the damage that can be inflicted on some of these very fragile wild trout fisheries by their thoughtless over-hyped reporting.

I have long been an ardent admirer of Orri Vigufsson, the Icelander whose drive and deep passion and boundless enthusiasm that he has sustained for so many years in raising so many millions of dollars and pounds for the protection and rehabilitation of the threatened Atlantic salmon populations throughout the northern hemisphere is surely a great lesson to us all. If we trout fishermen are unable to find a similar dedicated person in this country to undertake the same for our indigenous brown trout populations then surely the passion, drive and boundless enthusiasm shown by the Wild Trout Trust's 'Dream Stream Team' must come very close to it. If we think about it there are approximately 2,000,000 anglers in the UK that trout fish at some time or other during the year and if each one of them contributed only 50p per year then that would enable the Wild Trout Trust to fund £1,000,000 worth of much needed and valuable habitat protection and restoration work on our trout fisheries nation wide. It is not just for us today it is for our children and our children's children that we must provide for if there is to be any quality aquatic habitat in the future that supports self-sustaining fish populations for them to enjoy.

Over the years I developed rather strong views upon the subject of stocking hatchery-reared trout into rivers that had even a vestige of a remnant stock of self-sustaining wild trout. I feel it is vitally important to communicate something about the things I learned and witnessed regarding the real and potential effects that stocking had on a fishery in an attempt to convince some fishery managers to reappraise their future stocking policies.

Wild trout matter because they are of far higher quality than trout that are bred and raised by humans. There is a growing band of trout anglers, especially experienced trout anglers, who hold all wild trout in high esteem. These anglers also value highly the naturalness of the setting more than the catching of trout. As this experience grows they place less value on harvest and more on the skills involved, the natural beauty of a wild trout, and the personal escape provided by the water bodies that support wild trout. To provide this fishing experience requires good fishery management and the late Bob Jackson defined this as 'giving people what they want to the extent that the ecosystem can support it'.

These anglers also would most probably subscribe to that Leopold theorem that may incorporate economic as well as aesthetic logic: *The recreational value of a population of trout is inverse to the artificiality of its origin and hence, in a broad way to the intensiveness of the system of fishery management which produced it.* Therefore, logically, a wild trout is opposite to artificial.

The meaning of wild trout management is, in itself, another paradox, as is angling. The practice of managing wild animals is called domestication and if we think about that then we can cite many examples; a wild horse is not managed and a manageable horse is not wild. Our trout brood stocks in trout hatcheries have been domesticated from wild stocks, through management. Even the wary greylag goose and pink-footed geese are being domesticated on a rather large scale across this country, through management, by the construction of refuges and sanctuaries, by feeding and by various aids to existing stocks, including predator control and sporting bag limits. One has only to go and see this in action at the Wild Fowl Trust site at Slimbridge on the Severn estuary. This wildfowl management is a process of domestication. I think that managing wild fowl with a little less intensity, through wider protection of more of their native habitat is a better idea.

Management of this nature however does come in various degrees of intensity. The following list highlights my perception of the order of, and relationship between, the various levels of management intensity and the wildness of brown trout.

1/ The least wild and most intensively managed trout populations are of catchable trout or, as more commonly called, put-and-take trout. These trout are of domesticated parents, raised in the sterile confines of a hatchery, fed on special food and when of required size are then ferried to a river, lake or stream or reservoir and released. Classic domesticated animals, just like broiler house poultry.

2/ Next come populations of trout sustained by the planting out of growth stock of fry or fingerlings from domesticated hatchery stock. These trout are then allowed to grow on natural foods for a few months before they are harvested. They are still highly domesticated and it is a similar concept to the artificial insemination of hill cattle.

3/ The populations sustained by planting growth stock from wild brood stock come next. Good examples of this practice are the salmon programmes similar to the ones carried out on the River Test in Hampshire and the River Beauly in Scotland.

4/ Next are the self-sustaining populations which are aided by such manipulations as gravel importation for missing spawning shallows, the importation of adult brood stock from the wild, non game fish control, habitat improvements and even food introductions.

5/ Fifth in the ascending scale of wildness and descending scale of management intensity are populations solely aided by habitat protection. Protected habitat needs to be maintained, as near as possible, to its original form so that it supports self-sustaining populations of trout. This can be compared with the preservation of our diminishing natural wetlands for wildfowl and other wildlife.

6/ Sixth are populations aided only by catch restrictions, size limits, creel limits, fishing closures and now catch-and-release methods.

7/ Finally there are the true wild native trout populations totally unmanaged. These are the trout populations that are still unfished, or possibly even unknown to man. Maybe there are still trout populations in some such rivers in northern Canada and Russia that man has yet to find let alone fish. If there are such rivers then surely any trout in them must be *the* true wild trout.

It will be noticed that levels 5 and 6 are man-made restrictions, with trout being the beneficiary. In this form of predator control, man manages himself as well as the trout.

~~~~~~

I have had a lifelong doubt over the benefits of stocking trout in some waters and I now note an intensification in the criticism by many anglers of stocking and a growing preference toward managing for wild trout. To add weight to my views on stocking I have trawled through some of the many studies that have been undertaken on this subject from which some main facts came to light.

The physical, chemical, and biological environment in trout hatcheries differs markedly from the environments of wild trout and native trout. Trout that do well in hatcheries typically perform poorly after release into wild environments, especially streams. Inevitably, the artificial surroundings and experiences within a hatchery alter trout unfavourably for post-stocking and survival and reproduction although it can be shown that this domestication may improve them for fish farming that supply direct to the food processors and super markets. This disparity between wild trout and farmed trout results from one biological phenomenon – adaptation. These hatchery trout are ill-adapted to perform in the wild because, in addition to the intentional and inadvertent selection that fish farmers do, the hatchery environment itself selects for anatomical, physiological, and behavioural features that make the trout especially suited to survive and reproduce in hatcheries. In contrast, wild trout have been naturally selected to survive and reproduce in a particular water body and are uniquely adapted to that local environment. There are several forms of anatomical problems that are known to arise in trout hatchery fish; inappropriate gross body proportions; malformed body parts like gnarled fins, worn fins from nipping and fin rot and disease infections from crowded conditions and hyper-buoyancy derived from obesity brought on by overfeeding and lack of exercise that in turn encourages gas bladder abnormalities.

As for physiological features in hatchery trout it has been found they have at least nine instances where they are less successful than wild trout. They show poor traits of stamina, temperature tolerance, and stress resistance. They experience rapid decline in energy stores and a high susceptibility to disease. Hatchery trout tend to have reduced abilities for coping with the normal variation in the natural environment such as natural catastrophes as droughts, cold snaps and low flows or flood events, and for many hatchery trout other than triploids very early sexual maturity in females occurs.

In the behavioural features there are between 10 and 15 problems that have been observed depending on how one groups or splits them. Eight of the problems are well documented and the rest are probable but still speculative. The most important are the complex aberrant behaviours that cause high vulnerability to predation, inept foraging, inappropriate habitat occupation and breeding failure. Hatchery trout have also been found to waste energy in fast water, lack appropriate social behaviour, have weak territorial behaviour, exhibit social disorientation and undergo great stress when placed in unfamiliar surroundings. Other traits include: abnormal tameness towards humans and predators; hyper-aggressiveness towards their own kind; inappropriate timing of spawning; coping poorly with the changing seasons, especially winter; being more susceptible to angling than their wild counterparts.

Trout genetics is an intricate science, part of which has been described to me as the ecological memory of a population that shows the way a population fits itself into or adapts to its environment better and better in each generation via heritable traits. It is with sadness that I note that such significant genetic disruptions have been shown to occur in hatchery produced populations of trout in just one generation removed from the wild (Reisenbichler and McIntyre 1997). Hatchery trout among their other shortcomings, do not know how to behave properly in natural surroundings, a trait that works to their disadvantage and that of the wild trout populations into which they are stocked. At times it has been proposed that there are positive effects to be gained from stocking hatchery trout over wild stocks whereby these stocked trout will buffer the wild stocks from harvest by absorbing fishing pressure but this hypothesis can only apply if the stocking does not stimulate increased harvest of wild trout as it often does. So the positive effect is overshadowed by the negative influences.

Predation, competition, social disruption and the Pied Piper effect are the other downsides to stocking.

A problem that was suggested by some riverkeepers on the River Test concerned hatchery planted trout eating wild fish if the trout were stocked at sizes that were physically capable of doing so. It is still uncertain whether predation by recently stocked trout occurs often, even where the capacity for it seems to exist. Predation studies are difficult to undertake and so are seldom contemplated. Predation by hatchery trout may be a lesser problem than their competition with and social disruption of the wild trout.

Hatchery trout are usually stocked at local densities far exceeding those that occur in nature. Such stocking creates overcrowding that can cause social disruptions along with a suppression of the normal behaviour of the resident wild trout.

The stocking of smolts of migratory salmonoids over wild stocks of a similar age and size, has been suggested to create a Pied Piper effect by inducing the resident wild fish to migrate to the sea at smolt stage before their natural time which could be very detrimental. It has been observed that sea bound smolts do tend to migrate towards the sea in shoals rather than individually. Righting the problems of the long overemphasis on stocking will require a re-focusing upon the ecological management of wild trout; where by man and his activities will need more managing than the trout.

Managing for wild trout is necessarily habitat based. Protection of existing good habitat from human abuse is the first priority. Protecting against over-harvesting and the harm from hatchery stocking is fundamental as well. Restoring degraded habitat is also important. Some of the best restoration work has been achieved solely by identifying the man-made causes of the degradation, removing them and allowing Nature to regenerate normal stream features via natural plant growth, water current and sediment redistribution. In many such situations major benefits happen naturally in one to five years. Unfortunately there are situations where streams have been heavily manipulated by past severe dredging, canalising, straightening and or widening so even after several decades, natural regeneration has yet to take place, so man has to act to re-profile the stream channel by diverting it back into more natural meanders. Such re-profiling of a stream or river requires not only approval from the consenting agencies, such as the Environment Agency, English Nature, but well informed expertise in the design by experienced fluvial geomorphologists who understand how water and soil can work together to re-create sound river channels.

Having looked at the many and various adverse effects that fish farming and stocking can have on our trout fisheries helps define the areas where stocking can be used properly. Given certain local conditions and management objectives, and a willingness of the beneficiaries to bear the costs, some kinds of stocking can be quite appropriate. One area that has yet to be tried in this country is the rescue hatchery for endangered races and species of fish including trout strains that could be saved from extinction by capturing and breeding them on correctly for later reintroduction to their restored habitat. Other kinds of stocking are usually used to provide for fishing in waters where none existed, such as man-made lakes and reservoirs, and in put-and-grow situations where young of the year are planted in waters where there are no natural spawning facilities but growth conditions are good. Also there is the put-and-take stocking of harvest-sized trout for instant recreation. Unfortunately this latter form of stocking is becoming less economical and less popular with the more discerning anglers all of which is amply illustrated by the demise and eventual closure of so many put-and-take trout fisheries around the country.

Stocking is just a fishery management tool that can be used either to kick-start a population or to bolster it and only after the limiting factors that control natural survival have been identified and suitably addressed. If stocking is done without the knowledge of knowing why and what the causes of the reduced productivity are then stocking will only mask the problem and most likely exacerbate it. Stocking has its valuable uses but to stock a system, that for some reason cannot and never has naturally supported the required increase in stock, is making a very expensive rod that breaks the back of good sustainable fishery management. The potential holding capacity of a system has to be fully identified before any stock enhancements are carried out.

Wild and native brown trout matter a great deal not just biologically and economically but culturally as well. They are valued by anglers and by those people with a concern for Nature. Wild brown trout represent what Nature really is and to fish for them is to have a genuine experience in and with Nature. This experience is something to be treasured in this new millennium, increasingly characterised by artificiality and a lack of genuineness.

~ 14 ~
What of the Future of our Rivers?

One thing I realised after almost forty years involvement with rivers and streams in the UK, USA and Canada, but mostly on the Itchen, was the need to address the subject of stream improvements and fish response from a bio-engineering perspective and to establish a more integrated and comprehensive approach.

Stream improvements for restoring or enhancing fish environments can take many forms and history teaches us that only some of these projects have been successful and many more have been less successful or outright failures and, unfortunately, some have even compounded degradation. I believe that this is because we have not:

- ✧ Developed or applied in depth, scientific (biological) and physical (engineering) criteria for the design of so-called stream improvements.
- ✧ Trained people during their formal education to think in a multi-disciplinary way.
- ✧ Taken into consideration the fact that some people who, although willing and keen, are inexperienced in the practical and/or scientific aspects of stream rehabilitation.

Stream improvement effort in both the public and private sectors, is now on the upswing. Increasingly, programmes are being developed, funding is being allocated, many projects are planned and many people are gearing up to capture the opportunity to enhance Nature. But I wonder at times if they are approaching these opportunities from the five-stage process of assessment, planning, design, construction and evaluation, without which the impact of such crusades could be both frustrating and devastating. The frustration that will emanate from frequent project failures and the crusade could be devastating in terms of too much effort and concern being applied in the wrong place. For example, a stretch of stream might be modified to how we think it should be for fish – a 50% riffle to 50% pool ratio – when surely it should be modified so that the natural fluvial geo-morphology of the stream dictates the riffle to pool sequence. This is especially true given the fundamental ethic that no two streams are the same, and each has to have its own tailor-made re-habilitation strategy. Perhaps a stronger, more united and consistent, bioengineering approach is needed by professionals to emphasise to others when discussing the importance of reducing damages to fish habitat as well as playing catch-up for past degradation. We cannot continue to bandage parts of wounded streams while other parts are being wasted in the name of land management at a faster rate than the natural healing process.

The evaluation of habitat improvements and historic and present day maintenance programmes is usually done in terms of increased spawning area, rearing volume, cover area or an increase in biomass. This evaluation phase must be incorporated into the scheme of things during the planning stage. Comparisons made on nearby untreated control stretches have little value if consistent pre-assessment and post evaluations are not made on the catchment and on the stretch due for habitat modification. The time and period of evaluation is a function of the species involved, such as wild brown trout on the chalk streams, and two complete life cycles of 8 years is suggested. The timing and methodology of evaluation has to be questioned. In some cases today sampling is done at low water flows because it may be easier. All assessments of habitat conditions that should be carried out before any re-habilitation works, and monitored afterwards and be conducted in a standard, repeatable manner.

Improvements or changes in annual maintenance regimes are expected to cause an increase in value and an assessment involves determining how much this increase has been. This raises three basic questions about evaluation.

◇ Whose set of values is to be applied?

◇ What methodology will be used to apply them?

◇ Are the values and methodology constrained by real or artificial constraints?

For assessment itself to have any real value the unconstrained aspects must begin in phase two of the scheme, the planning stage. For example, statements such as 'we have £5000 to do the project' or 'we have the money, now lets do it' are both artificial constraints. If such attitudes are in force during project planning, it is guaranteed that the project will be constrained throughout its design, construction and evaluation and project efficiency will be reduced. Projects must be properly structured, be multi-disciplined and be approached in an open-minded and unconstrained, manner.

Value judgements and economic constraints must be applied after all the design options have been completed. Design must also include the monitoring and evaluation schemes for the whole project. By considering all the various modifying terms which are linked with habitat projects such as modification, improvement, restoration, re-habilitation, mitigation, enhancement and, hopefully not, degradation, it has to be determined whether or not these various activities have been achieved and this requires that some frame of reference such as habitat quality objectives, are established.

Given enough concerted co-operation and interdisciplinary effort it is possible that the various forms of classification of streams, now available to us, can be blended into a useful process whereby habitats can be assessed, improvements planned, construction carried out, effects and responses predicted, monitoring designed and performed and post project evaluation completed, all in one repeatable methodology.

One of the most important objectives of a classification system is interdisciplinary communications. This is especially true when dealing with what is a bi-disciplinary problem; stream improvement should be made from a biological perspective and stream improvement should be made from an engineering perspective. The results of this bi-disciplinary assessment, without a set of standards to follow, can be constrained by each perspective based on professional training and experience.

There are many professional people who are available and committed to stream improvements, the conservation and improvement of our native wild trout populations: ecologist; zoologist; fisheries biologist; environmental scientist; earth scientist; fluvial geomorphologist; forest hydrologist; hydrologic engineer, river engineer, fluid mechanics engineer, hydraulic engineer; civil engineer; scientific hydrologist.

In an ideal world these highly-motivated people could form a pool from which a designated 'dream stream team' of four could be selected to lead a nationwide inter-agency programme with carte blanche to correct the fishery ills in our streams. Perhaps someone from a different discipline is needed such as a computer whiz kid, or a systems analyst, a resource analyst or resource economist. What might be needed is an integrator or a generalist and not so many specialists.

One shortcoming of this approach is the fact that there are, at times, uncertainties of appreciation in the levels of skills between those disciplines and so there is a strong feeling of uncertainty and risk, yet by analogy, the selection of a 'dream stream team' can be compared to the selection of the appropriate habitat improvements on a stretch of stream because both must be approached in an integrated, systematic and procedural framework which guarantees a high probability of success, especially when considering the methods planned for use in the evaluation process.

Probably the most complex aspect of any habitat improvement on a chalkstream lies in the characteristics of all the stages in the life cycle of the wild trout. We are able to monitor biophysical conditions on a site over time and space, yet experience indicates that this is rarely done effectively so it is imperative that past monitoring and evaluation history has to form the foundation stone of any new project. Added to this there has to be analysis of the data from hydraulic and hydrologic and hydro-geomorphic evaluation of stream modification structures. Strong emphasis has to be given to the need for considering a total catchment management perspective when performing project evaluations instead of keeping to a more limited one. Stream improvements require skills and knowledge to address the problems of stream degradation – *Quo vadis et quo modo – Where are we going and in what manner*? To date, on our chalk streams many habitat improvement projects have been guided by a programme that is dictated, opportunistic and on a short-term construction schedule which is too site specific rather than from a long-term well-designed catchment management plan of staged action that has been worked up by a multi-disciplinary team using an integrated, systematic, procedural and standardised framework which guarantees a high probability of success. To be successful in any river work a team approach is all important and a set of standards needs to be laid down for all the five phases of any river re-habilitation project.

The suggested options to guarantee that our future efforts to save, help, manage, restore and to husband our fisheries resources will be successful at a higher degree are:

- ✧ Start at source and implement stronger and even more effective lobbies, laws and policies over catchment management and catchment land use and stormwater run off management and pollution of streams.

- ✧ Inter-agency and inter-departmental co-operation and communication is in place but tenuous in some areas because habits, missions and policies are, at times, in conflict and this problem needs to be resolved.

- ✧ Encourage, support and utilize riparian owner and riverkeeper and public interest and volunteer groups by improving public communications.

- ✧ Incorporate stream improvement project history, planning, bioengineering design, monitoring and evaluation strategies into student teaching programmes.

- ✧ Promote and use the multi-disciplinary team approach.

- ✧ Develop more inter-disciplinary seminars, workshops and courses for the inexperienced workers.

✧ Do what we can individually to increase our own appreciation for the perspectives of other disciplines by keeping an open mind and concentrating on effective communications. Avoid poor inter-disciplinary communications. Understand the other person's point of view.

✧ Strive as bioengineering colleagues to nourish a co-operative resource ethic whose goal is the restoration, maintenance and management of our streams.

✧ Develop a set of standards for each of the five stages of any re-habilitation or restoration scheme. Make use of the right data, methodologies, models, monitoring and evaluation and case history studies that are available and apply the latest knowledge. Publish a usable manual that sets out procedures and standards to be applied by the profession.

✧ Blend the various available forms of stream classifications into a useful process whereby habitats can be assessed, improvements planned, effects and responses predicted, monitoring designed and performed, constructions assessed and project evaluation completed, all in a repeatable and standardised form.

It is essential here to reiterate and to describe once again the fundamental philosophy of catchment management.

The aquatic ecosystem concept of holistic catchment management has been the foundation stone upon which my river management philosophy has been built upon for most of my working life's involvement with rivers, yet even today I perceive at times there are people involved in river restoration who still, at times, forget, or are not fully acquainted with or understand, these fundamental principles.

There is little that is new in all the various restoration techniques that are used up and down our rivers and streams today, most of which have been used in various forms by professional riverkeepers for 200 years or more. The difference between then and now is that today we are beginning to use more efficient methods of implementation, mainly in the use of natural materials and modern equipment but, more importantly, we are learning more about when and why restoration and good ongoing maintenance is needed and how, why and where the degradation processes occur.

Traditionally, riverine habitat conservation, annual maintenance programmes and restoration projects have been conducted with a tight focus on the stream itself. This approach fails to address the reality that a stream and its catchment function as one ecological unit. Projects that do not account for the interactions between the stream and all the adjacent lands are much more likely to fail or, at the best, yield only short-term results. To date, many works on restoration projects have been conducted on individual sections, beats or reaches, call them what you will, when these projects should have been developed with an eye to an in-depth understanding of where the project fits into the big picture for the health of the entire catchment.

To better comprehend a streams relationship with its catchment, an understanding is needed of all the natural means through which the stream and its catchment form trout habitat, because these are the critical processes that the restorer and riverkeeper in his maintenance program will need to imitate or repair in the best possible way. By understanding the way Nature produces trout habitat will help us design projects and maintenance programs that provide or repair habitat in a manner appropriate to the stream. The science and discipline of fluvial geomorphology deals with the natural interactive land and water processes that shape streams and their catchments.

Streams naturally strive to achieve a state of dynamic equilibrium where the whole aquatic ecosystem is in balance and where the amount of water and sediment leaving a stream section is equal to the amount of water and sediment entering it. Whenever the stream or its catchment is altered, the stream will change naturally to a new state of dynamic equilibrium. As the name suggests, this equilibrium condition is not static but is constantly changing as the catchment changes.

There are many physical characteristics that influence the way a stream achieves equilibrium, such as the amount of sediment provided by the catchment through to the peak and base flow levels, the gradient and stream bed type and the nature and make up of the bank materials. A stream that is subject to heavy stormwater run off events will look very different to the stable spring-fed flows of a chalk stream and a stream with a bedrock bed will be different to one with a sandy stream bed. Therefore, restoration projects must be designed accordingly. Land use and changes in land use within a catchment can have a great influence on the character of a stream. For example, as more impervious surfaces are added to a catchment such as roads, motorways, new housing developments, business parks, megastores leisure areas and golf courses, all with their car parks, runoff from all these areas will be channelled rapidly to the nearest stream and there will be less water soaking into the ground. Also, agricultural land use and changing agricultural and forestry regimes, abstraction and hydro operations, the effects of which have all to be taken into account. In such circumstances, it would be expected that peak flows increase during storm events while base flows that are maintained by groundwater discharge into the stream would decline. During these increased peak flows, the stream will possess higher levels of energy and will be more likely to erode its bed and banks. When the stream returns to its lowered base flow level sediment deposition may well begin again. If catchment changes are so traumatic a stream may be thrown out of equilibrium to such an extent that a restoration project may not be feasible.

It is vitally important therefore, to incorporate the basic principles of fluvial geomorphology into any restoration project and by so doing it will help in several ways. For example, it provides a technical basis for addressing catchment impacts on the stream; it incorporates the reality that streams are dynamic and not static entities. It will focus attention on the natural processes that a restoration project should imitate and it will pinpoint and highlight and enable us to address the causes of habitat change and not just the symptoms.

By understanding these fluvial and hydrological processes we will then determine what can and cannot work on the stream. If a restoration project is designed that works against the natural forces that are striving to bring the stream towards equilibrium rather than with them, then the project will almost certainly fail.

It cannot be over emphasised how important it is to thoroughly assess the stream and its entire catchment before a restoration project or even establish a maintenance program is developed and to consult with a person or persons who has knowledge about fluvial geomorphology, thus increasing the understanding of all the physical characteristics and processes both historical and present, that are at work or have been, in the whole catchment.

Looking at the stream alone will not give the information needed to cure the streams apparent problems. Only by conducting a thorough catchment reconnaissance that identifies all the various land uses and changing land uses within the catchment will it be possible to identify the changes that have, or are, causing degradation, will it then be possible to contemplate any meaningful rehabilitation or plan any meaningful maintenance programmes.

There are many common land uses that effect aquatic habitat. Unless action is brought to bear to change or mitigate the effects of these land uses, and this includes abstraction, so many site specific projects could well fail, or be ineffectual. On the other hand, merely by changing, or mitigating the effects of the land use practices or reducing abstraction alone may be all that is required as once protected by these actions, some streams will heal themselves with little further help from the restorers.

There are many sources of information on rehabilitation of cold water streams but so many of them address the scientific and technical aspects of habitat restoration only or merely explain how to build stream improvement devices and structures. The Wild Trout Trust (WTT) since its inception for example came to realise and recognise the need for more general guidance on the process of organising and coordinating volunteer habitat restoration projects and I am proud to have been an integral part of establishing this recommended process when serving as their first projects officer.

Although no document can provide the answers for every situation, the WTT offer a general framework in their literature that can be used to plan co-operative fisheries habitat projects. It is emphasised that this framework is not a replacement for expert professional public and private sector assistance, because streams and their catchments are complex systems and developing a successful project will require assistance from qualified professionals who have the training and experience in working with aquatic ecosystems.

It is suggested that the complex process of planning and conducting a stream habitat restoration project can be set down in the following six major steps:-

- ✧ Define the purpose of your re-habilitation project.
- ✧ Recruit your partners and find the experts who are familiar with your stream and catchment to assist with the project.
- ✧ Assess the current conditions in the catchment and stream and pinpoint and identify the factors that limit trout production.
- ✧ Plan the project, raise the money, obtain the consents, negotiate access, recruit a volunteer workforce and build local support for the project.
- ✧ Organise and conduct the project on site.
- ✧ Monitor and maintain the projects results.

These basic guidelines that are now used by the WTT offer a useful conceptual framework to work from. However, in practice, projects may develop very differently, these six steps are not as distinct as they may appear on paper as there may well be places where one step overlaps and feeds back into another. There are many paths that lead to success.

If I have any fears for the future they would be that with all these guidelines and apparent attendant bureaucratic constraints that are now involved and required in any aquatic restoration project the enthusiasm to carry the project through to completion by the instigators and implementers will be blown asunder before any progress is made.

~ 15 ~
Winding In

When I started out as a riverkeeper in the early 1970s there were 21 full-time riverkeepers on the River Itchen and I believe over 50 on the River Test and its tributaries. Today there are about six full-time riverkeepers employed on the Itchen and the number of riverkeepers on the Test has been reduced in recent times. This makes me feel very concerned, and certainly saddened, about the future of these unique rivers and fisheries. It has been the dedicated work carried out by a host of riverkeepers over the last two centuries that has maintained the fragile quality of these famous rivers.

The common cry from some owners today is that full-time keepers are now too expensive to employ. This statement carries little weight if one considers if the total rod rental income per annum is kept directly in proportion to the costs of employing a full-time keeper, as it was when I first started. Commercialisation has now invaded many fisheries on the chalk streams as the owners and lessees are now looking more to make profits from their investments and fishery assets. It is sad to see well-keepered beats, that have historically fished well, go rapidly downhill when local poachers get wind that there is now no full-time keeper so they can regularly go in and strip the unguarded river of wild trout. The damage can be so acute that the owners have to resort to regularly stock inferior stew-bred trout each year to provide any sport at all. With the best will in the world part-time contractors will not be able to nurture these rivers and maintain them so lovingly to the high standard of expertise as did so many of the experienced and dedicated professional riverkeepers. Furthermore the intensity of repair and annual upkeep of a beat cannot be maintained efficiently by a part-timer so the habitat in and around the river will gradually deteriorate. To see any beat that used to provide first-class, self-sustaining, wild brown trout fishing deteriorate is heart-breaking. To me it is almost criminal that owners are allowed to let this happen. I use the analogy that if you can afford to buy a Rolls Royce motor car you must be able to afford to service it properly and fill it with petrol.

The most valuable asset that any fishery has is its reputation, and if this declines so will the demand to fish it. In turn this will reduce, in the same ratio, the level of tenant fees that can be levied. It is an ever-increasing downward spiral. It is essential in these forbidding monetary times for a fishery to be successful financially that its reputation is maintained by good fishery management and that the fishing is adequately protected and its fishing marketed properly. If our quality fisheries are to survive and the wild trout fishing within them we have to move swiftly into the twenty-first century.

My experience indicates to me that much of the fishery manager's or riverkeeper's education must be completed on the job. I do believe this is as it should be. So if the fishery manager or riverkeeper can make fishery management, trout fishing and the quiet observation of life in and around the stream part of his ongoing self-inflicted learning process our fisheries would undoubtedly be the better for it.

Unfortunately it appears that there are fewer youngsters being encouraged to become professional riverkeepers which for me is and has been one of the most rewarding occupations known to man especially for a person as myself who just loves rivers and nature. I remember remarking to my employer before I retired that whoever took on my position he or she would have to love the river because without that love the river would suffer.

In the early 1970s and by the late 1980s the Hampshire Farm Institute at Sparsholt formed new courses for gamekeepers and riverkeepers. These courses expanded to cover not only game and riverkeeping but also fish farming and other country-based subjects culminating today with a degree course in fish culture and various other fishy subjects. For several years the game and river students were expected to spend some of their time out in the field working alongside experienced riverkeepers and gamekeepers in order for them to learn the down to earth practical aspects of both professions.

So it was that a constant stream of budding riverkeepers who would appear on my doorstep at the crack of dawn on Tuesdays and Fridays. As I had been so eager to learn and absorb as much knowledge when I started on the river I expected all these students to be the same way inclined, although not all of them were. I would happily spend hours talking to them, showing and sharing my growing knowledge with any student who showed an interest and who obviously wanted to learn. I derived a great deal of pleasure from students who decided to come for a block release period to undertake a study project. This entailed choosing a relevant course-work subject and preparing a full and comprehensive thesis to be handed in to the course tutors after the practical time spent with me on the river. Many a student would raid my library to read up on their chosen subject and I found it stimulating to help them with any research, or in obtaining information from other sources from not only this country but from my ever-growing array of contacts from around the world. Several students, who chose to work with me for their study projects, won several end-of-term trophies that were awarded to top students for exceptional work.

Many of the students became my, and Paula's, good friends. On several occasions over the years there was a knock at the door and a 'Hi remember me? I was a student with you back in 1986'. We usually went to the pub for a drink and a chat to catch up with all that the student had achieved since leaving college.

I derived many pleasures from my work over the years and the one thing in particular that gave me more pleasure than most was guiding and instructing young riverkeepers and seeing them take on responsible jobs as riverkeepers and doing well. The mere fact that at least some of my ideas and riverkeeping philosophy will be carried on to the next generation of riverkeepers gives me a great deal of satisfaction in the knowledge that I may be putting something back into a profession that gave me so much pleasure for so many years.

It is inwardly amusing at times to listen to the young buck fisheries biologists fresh out of university expounding upon their scientific remedies for solving all the problems related to our fresh water resources. I admire their energy and enthusiasm for the job in hand and some of their thoughts for the future. I do not have the heart to say they have still a great deal to learn, the good ones will very soon find that out without me having to tell them. Many biologists have asked me over the years why I did not train to become a fisheries biologist. My answer was that if I had done so I would not have been able to spend my working life on the wonderful River Itchen and done all the things that I have had the good fortune to do. I am sure I would have retired with more security and a paid up mortgage but that is about all.

It was a college student who finally led me to retire to the Scottish Borders. It all goes back to the early 1980s when there was a group of eight students who had arrived for a morning's session of practical riverkeeping tuition. As it happened I had just received delivery of ten tons of chalk that was to be used to make up a stretch of riverside bank that was in need of repair. So with eight healthy young and keen lads I armed them with the necessary tools and wheelbarrows and we set to move the lot in the three hours that had been allotted for their visit. Among this group was a tall, noisy young Scotsman with hair of many colours – yellow, blue and orange and, if I remember correctly, also with the obligatory earring. The team had vowed to finish the job before the bus arrived to take them back to college but after an hour's hard work several were showing signs of slowing down. The 'hair of many colours', who had worked very hard, chivvied up the others to keep going and doubled his input so the job was completed just in time. Hamish Wilson, it turned out, was the name of the 'hair of many colours' and he asked if he could come back to do some more practical work on the river. I agreed readily and told him to ask his course instructor to put his name down to come to Martyr Worthy on the next block practical.

Hamish returned and worked with me for a month or more. During that time I was able to allow him to dry-fly fish on the odd occasion after he had completed his tasks for the day. We soon became firm friends and I discovered that under the colourful exterior was hidden a deep passion for rivers, fish and fishing. A great deal of his spare time, when not spent doing things that boys do at college at that age, was spent on the river with me. Students who volunteered to help me were usually rewarded with a good plate of food from Paula and a few pints of quality ale from me. We rarely found a student who was not agreeable to this type of arrangement. We were to discover that Hamish ate and drank for Scotland. My Grandad would have described him in his inimitable way as able to 'eat a dead horse between two bread vans as a sandwich and come back for seconds'.

Hamish hailed from the Tweed Valley and told me that his folks had just purchased a property on the banks of the lower River Teviot, a major tributary of the Tweed. After he had completed his two-year course at college he returned to the Borders leaving me with promises to keep in touch and his intention to invite me to visit and fish the River Teviot for a salmon. Albeit all such farewells are often laden with great well meaning so I did not think any more about it. How very wrong I was. After a few months had elapsed I received a call from Hamish inviting me to the Borders to have a go at the salmon on the Teviot that autumn. I couldn't wait and delved straight away into my fishing cupboard to see what state my salmon tackle was in, as it had not been used for some considerable time. After a few visits to the Rod Box, that well-known fishing tackle shop in Winchester, to replace and restock the contents of my salmon bag I was ready to go and it was only August.

The middle of October arrived and Hamish would ring almost every Sunday evening to update me about the conditions on the Tweed and the Teviot and what the prospects were for the following week. Eventually I received the green light and off I motored to the Borders. I shall never forget that drive, it was 390 miles of ever increasing excitement and anticipation so by the time I arrived I was a gibbering wreck and needed a pint or three to reduce the tension. Unfortunately on the journey passing over Moss Paul, the high spot between Carlisle and

Hawick on the A7 it started to rain and it rained steadily all that night. So much for Hamish's weather forecasting I thought. All was not lost as Hamish said the rain wouldn't bring the river up until later the following day and if we got out of bed early next morning we were still in with a chance of a fish.

Hamish, I have learnt over the years, is always the greatest optimist I know when it comes to fishing prospects. We managed to get down to the water at about 5 o'clock next morning and although there was a little colour in the water it was still very fishable. Hamish, being the perfect host, led me to the right spot and explained how to fish the stretch of water and settled down to watch my efforts. Having taken more than a few minutes to once more get used to wielding a fifteen foot rod and mastering a sinking line with a 3 inch brass tube fly attached to the end I started to cover the water Hamish had indicated that could be holding a salmon and a fish showed in the very place at just the right time. I worked my way down the beat as directed systematically covering the river in front of me. I soon got back into the rhythm and even Hamish complimented me on my casting. To this day I don't know if he really meant it or was just being polite to his guest.

Three parts of the way down the beat just in front of a large beech tree on the far side of the river something heavy gave the rod a jolt in my hands and by the time I realised that this might be a salmon I had given enough time to allow the fish to hook itself before I lifted the rod – it was a salmon. Hamish was anxiously pacing up and down the bank complaining that I was playing the fish too hard. I eventually drew it into a shallow gravel-covered beach where Hamish tailed it and we took it up the bank and dispatched it. I believe that this was the first autumn fish that had been taken on their newly acquired beat for that year, it also was my first ever Teviot salmon. We both had a cigarette while we admired the fish and then decided to go up to the house for some breakfast and to come back afterwards to catch some more fish. We bolted down the huge breakfast that Hamish's mother had kindly prepared as we were both looking forward to a good morning's fishing. As we walked back down from the house to the river something was not quite right. The river had risen three feet since we had been away and was now totally out of order as it was the colour of milky cocoa.

So ended my first, memorable visit to the Teviot as Hamish's guest. Many happy and enjoyable visits were made over the following years and these visits became an annual autumn ritual for me to look forward to especially during the hot steamy weed cutting days on the Itchen. Hamish would return to the Itchen Valley as my guest to play the return match each year in the springtime to tackle the wary wild trout with the dry fly.

It was through my friendship with Hamish that my wife and I came to move to the Tweed Valley when I finally retired from my work on the Itchen. For many years I had said to Paula that I would like to retire to Scotland, a place I have always loved.

Coming to the Itchen Valley almost thirty years ago and having worked as a riverkeeper on the wonderful River Itchen for most of my working life, was the best decision I ever made. It is not without a great deal of sadness therefore that Paula and I found it necessary to depart the Valley and move to the Scottish Borders, in the little village of St Boswells, on the banks of the mighty River Tweed between Kelso and Melrose.

A young lassie who was working for Hamish in the office of the smokery was getting married and moving away to live near Glasgow and kindly offered to show us her cottage at Magdalenehall Farm, about a mile and a half from St Boswells. The cottage was rented from the Duke of Sutherland and was part of his Mertoun Estate. We took one look at it and were immediately sold on the idea of moving north, the cottage and surroundings were just perfect for us and we were very fortunate to be accepted as tenants and moved in on 2 March 2001 in two foot of snow and with temperatures of –15°C (5°F). Luckily the central heating system was very efficient.

Our relocation to the Borders of Scotland was the most traumatic upheaval in our lives and it took some considerable time to come to terms with our totally new environment. The analogy to illustrate the way I felt at the time was as if I were a wild trout taken live out of the Upper Itchen, transported up the M6 and stocked into the mighty Tweed at St Boswells. I now know how that trout would have felt. Like a good Itchen trout I survived the journey and have now adapted to the conditions of my new habitat although it took several months to regain body condition.

Fortunately, our ex-farm worker's cottage has been tastefully modernised and we are only 100 yards from the banks of the River Tweed. We both love it. Good neighbours, little traffic and lots of peace and quiet – what more could we ask? Coming from central Hampshire the indigenous broad Borders accent we have found does take time to fully understand – you ken?

I was soon to learn that the Borders have their own supreme beauty but very different to the beloved Itchen Valley. During the first year it took some time to understand and appreciate my new surroundings in the Tweed Valley, however I soon became aware of the supreme peace and quiet that reigns here. On the banks of the Tweed, it is possible to listen to a blackbird delivering its evening recital from some half a mile away unsullied by any extraneous man-made sounds

Our new abode in the Borders.

of twenty-first century. Thirty years ago the Itchen Valley at Martyr Worthy was likewise an oasis of peace and quiet and at most times then around the river all that could be heard on a still summer's day was the sleepy drone of the insect life and the bass baritone hum of a distant bumble bee as it searched for food among the wild flowers and the near and distant alarm calls of the coots and moorhens as they argued over some territorial dispute. Human-made sounds were a rare interruption to life on the river in those days.

There is one thing I have learnt since my move north and that is I am now in a far better position to comment on the differences between a chalk stream riverkeeper's work and the work of a Tweed boatman. I have had the pleasure of becoming acquainted with many of the Tweed boatman and a grand bunch of people they are and, as with the keepers of the chalk streams, there are some great characters among them. The leg-pulling that goes on between us is great and I take it as a compliment that it does. The impression that some boatman had of the 'soft southern riverkeeper' took a little time to alter but when I described my work as a keeper they began to realise that a chalk stream riverkeeper's job was not so soft. Our work is very different and I fully realise and appreciate all the hard physical work a boatman has to do, particularly when trying to hold the boat over a salmon lie in strong currents with a force 6 gale blowing across the river. I would say that equates equally energy expenditure-wise with a days weed cutting with a hand scythe on the Itchen.

Since arriving in Scotland there has been a continuous stream of friends and relations from not only the south but abroad including many of the past and present tenants of the Martyr Worthy fishery all of who were so concerned for Paula and me after our sudden move and were all so anxious to make sure that we were comfortable and safe in our retirement surroundings. It is at such traumatic times of one's life that one really discovers who and what good friends really are. One couple, who live in New York and still fish my old water on the Itchen, came all the way up to Scotland to visit us solely to make sure Paula and I were OK.

~~~~~

Having now spent the early years of my retirement living on the banks of the River Tweed in the beautiful Scottish Borders the fond memories of my life on the River Itchen are still very much in my mind. I sincerely hope there always will be these fond memories. After all the best part of my working lifetime has been spent working on the river. Regrets I have but few, although it may be apposite at this stage to apologise for my obvious obsession with the principles of integrated catchment management within these pages but it is a passion of mine.

I remember clearly my late employer, after I had been working for a few years for him, ringing me up one morning and asking *my* permission to allow him to come down and fish *my* river. I must have created some impression on him of the devotion I had for the river.

Over the years I have been very passionate about the River Itchen and what the future may hold for it, and many times I have spoken out in no uncertain terms and have been rebuked by many folk, many times for it. In retrospect I do not regret one word. No doubt I may also have upset some people along the way by not agreeing with their views on river work but I have always 'said it as it is' when it comes to rivers. At times I may have treated the River Itchen as being more important than people, for that too I do apologise, but still I have no real regrets.

If I have made any reputation for myself, whether good or bad, I owe it solely to the River Itchen itself. I am also very grateful to the family who originally employed me for 30 odd years to look after it.

There is one of life's great pleasures that I can and do still indulge in and that is brainstorming over fishery management problems with like-minded people. There is now ample time for me to share a beer or three and poke holes in the air with our fingers as we discuss all that is happening, good or bad, in trout fisheries around the world. I have been very fortunate to get to know so many of the unsung heroes from around the world who have dedicated their lives to wild trout and trout management. If it were not for some of these wonderful people sharing their knowledge with me this would be a very thin book.

~~~~~

Although my travels are less frequent than they used to be I am now still able to discuss fishy things with my friends from many countries via the intricacies of electronic mail. If someone would have said to me five years ago that I would be semi-computer literate I would have certainly told them there was little chance of that ever coming about. The same goes for the use of mobile phones.

Having now arrived in the autumn of my fishing life, or more positively described as the 'springtime of my senility', where my eyesight is not quite so sharp as it was and my body joints keep telling me they are unable to sustain too much damp activity I tend to become more contemplative about fly-fishing. I find that I seem to spend more and more time in and around the fishing hut or bothy than I do actually fishing these days, and when not fishing I am usually found discussing some finite item of tackle, clothing or casting technique. I love fly-fishing and do spend a lot of time at it yet I seem to get to cast very little these days. I now watch the others fishing and, if they are inexperienced, I enjoy sorting them out and getting them among the fish. Just being in a fisherman's company is enough and at most times such a pleasure to me, although I suppose some of my fishing friends might not agree.

In retirement I have been following, with great interest, the progress of the Millennium Fly Survey that has been coordinated by Peter Hayes and Dr Allan Frake, and despite some early flak from some quarters suggesting that it was not science based, good investigative work continues a pace.

Even now, when a fishing trip has been planned with days of meticulous preparations and after more than fifty years fishing, the sense of anticipation that comes over me is still as strong as ever within me. The anticipation may be even stronger now than those fishing trips that my father and I shared during, and just after, the last war. I find these days the further one has to travel to the fishing and the more friends in the party the more intense the excitement and anticipation seems to be. However there is still that awful sinking feeling when after a long journey the destination water is viewed for the first time and it is found to be out of sorts and the ghillie's or fishery manager's first words in reply to the question, 'What has the fishing been like?' are 'Bloody awful, but you should have been here last Thursday' – words that really sorts the men out from the boys. Anyone that has fished for as long as I have will have been there and

Playing a salmon on the River Spey at Arndilly.

done that. I remember one instance having left home in Hampshire directly from a shoot day in November and driving up to Kelso on the Tweed arriving there at midnight and, after a can or two of beer and a quick forty winks on a sofa, being awakened by Hamish at 6 o'clock in the morning to fish the river only to find it had risen four feet overnight and was still rising and carrying the colour and consistency of liquid Mars bars. So after a quick egg and bacon sandwich and a mug of tea in the local greasy spoon café the car was turned around and driven the 400 miles all the way back to Hampshire arriving home without even having taken the rod out of the car. These were the days before the informative 'Fish Tweed' on the internet and more reliable or believable weather forecasts. The excitement was still there even then as all the way up the M6 I would be thinking to myself and wondering what the fishing was going to be like on the Tweed and then again all the way back down the M6 I was imagining what the salmon fishing would have been like if the conditions had been right had all that overnight rain fallen on the other side of the Cheviot Hills.

Living as I do now many miles away from the Itchen Valley, time and place can never remove the memories of those years spent working in and on the river at Martyr Worthy. The love and appreciation of that wonderful place grew as the years passed and at times it became an increasing burden not to show and share the beauties with others. Nothing gave more pleasure than taking an appreciative friend or even a total stranger around the river and on the journey explain all that was happening in this busy world of 'managed' wilderness that is Nature's gift to man. I do believe so strongly that these beauties should be shared with other appreciative people a little more often and to me it is a crime for it to be locked away and kept solely for the use of just an exclusive few. Unfortunately however to maintain the right balance between protecting this unique wilderness which allows Nature to go about her way uninterrupted and a sharing of the appreciation of her efforts can be a conundrum that is so difficult to resolve in this modern age. The pressures that come with the increasing population growth, and the more leisure time people seem to have these days, fuels the ever growing divide between the dedicated conservators of this landscape and the growing band of right-to-roamers who do not seem to appreciate that these wilderness areas that are so appealing to them are there solely because man has dedicated and protected these areas from the ravages of any detrimental human influences.

The unique characteristics of the Upper Itchen Valley are there because the long-term owners of this originally man-made landscape decreed that large areas of the Valley floor would be left to Nature and only managed by man where Nature could be assisted to produce the fruits. This in essence was the riverkeeper's job who knew where, with experience and thought, the natural evolution could be protected and at times assisted by applying a knowing and helpful nudge here and there.

In my early years I often would have long discussions with total strangers who when passing by on the public footpath would stop and ask if they could walk around the riverbanks. If it was during the fishing season I had to say no because my job was to ensure the paying anglers had their privacy when on the river. To explain why to total strangers who had very little knowledge about the river and all it stood for was at times very difficult and some rather heated discussions would sometimes ensue. I can to a certain extent sympathise with these people as I have said I feel in some way these beauties should be shared with our fellow humans.

At times one would meet a person who held very strong views on the subject of the exclusive use of private land who would point out in no uncertain terms that he had fought for King and Country in the last war just to ensure his freedom and that freedom included the right to walk wherever he wanted to and that includes all the riverbanks of every river. There may be a moral issue here but

I had to explain at that time that the peaceful wilderness that is the riverside at Martyr Worthy was only there because the owners and the keepers had kept it that way and all the wildlife that abounds within it is only there because we have protected the right habitat for them. I would explain that if I had allowed free access then all the wildlife that did live there would soon move out but if they just waited for a while quietly on the footpath and with the use of a good pair of binoculars then the wildlife would come out and show itself quite happily. The problem is that there very little wilderness left in this country and far too many people. This is a further conundrum that future generations and we will have to resolve.

The angling challenge that wild brown trout offer to the dry-fly fisherman is now legendary and is reflected in the great demand there is for the opportunity to fish these waters. The social and challenging conundrums of the future will no doubt revolve around how this wonderful resource can or will be allocated and used in a way that the beauties and fishing experience are not compromised yet enough revenue is derived to continue to protect and maintain these qualities. Instinct tells me that legislation controlling access and use and management of such resources may well alter in the years to come to allow a more open attitude rather than the exclusive use that has prevailed for so long but, unless sensitively implemented, it could also spell the death knell of the river as we know it today.

Unfortunately, it appears to me that there are, in this modern day and age of computers and other electronic diversions, fewer young people with a real interest in the natural world or even are showing any interest in taking up the sport of fishing in general or fly-fishing in particular. The present, and older angling generations, should I believe be addressing this situation by encouraging and teaching, and allowing youngsters to at least taste the delights of the natural world around them and to encourage all forms of angling.

I am convinced that I was very fortunate to have lived through, in my opinion the last of the very best of the quality fishing experience that prevailed for two hundred years or more in the Upper Itchen Valley. The signs are there for all to witness, with the increasing smell of exhaust fumes, the continuous roar of traffic the drone of the jet planes and the cancerous growth of economic development along with the ever-growing problem of diffuse pollutants which put together is threatening this priceless fragile gem that was once the most green, serene and peaceful part of Hampshire.

Fishery owners and managers have to recognise the fact that social and environmental economics are now essential fishery management tools to use if we are to ensure the health and quality of our rivers and the fisheries they support are to survive and that are maintained in an environmentally sustainable manner.

I believe unrestricted open access could well be the final straw.

Over the years most of us experience in life the ups and downs in dealing with the traumas that circumstances throw up. Coping with them has been made so much easier for me due to the very nature of the work I did over those years. Working on and living by the River Itchen, observing and learning how the river works and studying all the animals and insects, fish and flora certainly kept life into perspective and I have come to regard it as the greatest healing balm ever devised by Nature.

So many times I have found myself reciting quietly to myself many of the lines from Alfred Tennyson's poem, *The Brook*, particularly on those perfect spring days of May and June. These happy words have stayed with me since learning them long ago at school and even today they remain quite clear although some verses do come more readily to mind than others. These three verses will always remind me of all the happy times spent in and around the River Itchen at Martyr Worthy.

I wind about, and in and out,
With here a blossom sailing,
And here and there a lusty trout,
And here and there a grayling,

And here and there a foamy flake
Upon me, as I travel
With many a silver waterbreak
Above the golden gravel,

And draw them all along, and flow
To join the brimming river:
For men may come and men may go,
But I go on for ever.

We made and treasured many friends over the years. I have spent countless memorable days with many fishermen, both past and present, with whom we shared friendship and kindness. We had to bid them all *au revoir*, not goodbye, as we both intend to return to visit the Valley we both love. Looking back, now that we are retired, we were very lucky to have such an interesting and happy life and neither of us, I'm sure, would have cause to change it.

Having moved into Martyr Worthy in 1972 the charm of these villages that looked as natural and as one with the scene of chalk downland and green valley it was found that they had an air of tranquillity that allowed a human to be part of nature's life, so calm, slow and sweet and which had not then been greatly disturbed. Unfortunately now the Valley is fast becoming the Xanadu of the mighty ones of the money markets with houses of four bedrooms changing hands for a million pounds or more. Happily in the early years the downland slopes and the green valley had mainly been neglected by modern development and remained 'ours' and by that it is meant all those who love and revere this wonderful valley. Sadly it is irretrievably being eroded away and much as I love it and miss it I would not go back to live in it and I now just want to remember what it was like when I first moved into the Valley.

The physical magic and beauty of the Itchen Valley is still there – just.

The construction of the M3 motorway across the Valley put for me the final nail into the coffin of the tranquillity and serenity that was the Itchen Valley of my youth. The constant 24-hour smell of diesel fumes and roar of traffic along the motor way and Easton lane and the regular flights of jet aircraft in and out of Southampton airport over head all of which can only increase in intensity as the years pass and can only further erode the quality of life in the Valley. The only time I had noticed real quiet in the Valley for many a year was when I exercised the spaniels at 3am on millennium day morning when the roar of traffic along the M3 was almost non-existent. Once again, but sadly only so very briefly, the silence in the Valley was deafening.

How things have changed was brought home to me very forcibly when recently staying in the Itchen Valley for a day or so when visiting friends and family. I was awakened one morning at about 6 o'clock by the constant roar of traffic and sound of low flying aircraft. I suppose having been resident in the Itchen Valley for all those years I grew with the ever-increasing demands of modern development and all the noise it brought and so I tended to block it out of my conscious hearing. Being subjected to it after having been away a while was quite a revelation. It illustrated the problems I had when trying to participate in radio or television interviews on the riverbank. To record a minute's dialogue could take an hour as 'cut' was constantly called with every passing car or lorry or low flying aircraft besides coping with the constant background roar of the never-ending flow of traffic along the busy M3 that cut across the Valley some 1000 yards below the bottom boundary of the fishery.

Although I have returned to the Itchen Valley on numerous occasions since it was not until the very last visit when departing from the banks of the Itchen after a good look around my old stamping ground did I say quietly to myself – 'she still looks well, but I want to go home now'. Although my heart will always be alongside the River Itchen my home is now in the Tweed Valley, Scotland.

During my last visit to the Itchen Valley the impending tragedy that over-population brings is evident in the defences that are now being erected along some of the most beautiful areas of the riverside. The social and moral conundrum that has yet to be resolved over access to 'wilderness' areas and the exclusive use of certain lands apart it is still difficult to understand the need and full reasons for the erection of ugly fencing along such natural and beautiful areas when regular policing by a full-time riverkeeper would be easier and far less offensive to the eye. However I do not dispute for one minute the need to protect the fragile wilderness habitat that is so unique in the Itchen Valley. The secret is in the answer to the question 'how can this habitat be conserved satisfactorily and yet still be shared by all those who care'? The word balance comes into the equation somewhere within the answer to that question but exactly where I am as yet unsure.

Sadly, at the end of my visit, I returned to the Borders this time without looking back. As Paula and I motored up the M6 back to our new found home I contemplated in my mind Tennyson's words in his short poem, *A Farewell*, the riverkeeper's farewell to *his* river:

> *Flow down, cold rivulet to the sea,*
> *Thy tribute wave deliver:*
> *No more by thee my steps will be,*
> *For ever and for ever.*
>
> *Flow, softly flow, by lawn and lea,*
> *A rivulet then a river:*
> *Nowhere by thee my steps will be,*
> *For ever and for ever.*
>
> *But here will sigh thine alder tree,*
> *And here thine aspen shiver,*
> *And here by thee will hum the bee,*
> *For ever and for ever.*
>
> *A thousand suns will stream on thee,*
> *A thousand moons will quiver,*
> *But not by thee my steps will be,*
> *For ever and for ever.*

There is a large part of me that will forever reside beside the Itchen and its glorious waters. Not many people can say that they have been able to lay in bed on a still hot summer's night with all the windows open and be lulled to sleep by the sound of trout rising to nocturnal hatching sedge flies.

Nobody and nothing can ever take away that unforgettable smell of fresh cut ranunculus, the sweet dank odour of the sedge beds on a warm summer evening, the calls of the ever fractious coots and moorhens, the screaming swifts skimming the river during an iron blue hatch, the purple flags and yellow iris and the singing toads and the call of the first cuckoo and song of the reed warbler and blackcap in spring time. The strong scent of the meadow sweet in summer the vibrant colour of the yellow musk, the chatter of the little grebes and above all the exciting heart stopping sound of a rising trout part hidden within the whispers of the waters of the Itchen as its flow argues gently with the piles of the footbridge. Not forgetting that evocative sound of an old well-worn Hardy Perfect reel as it gives line to a trout that has taken off towards the far bank. All this followed at the last ebbing light of day by the pop of a cork departing from a bottle of wine. The unforgettable savouring of a river chilled classic white burgundy shared on the riverbank with a friend and angler all this and much more will forever remain with me. It has been a wonderful life… so far!

To quote the song: *Regrets I have had but a few, but yet, too few to mention, the record shows that I took the blows*, and, as I have written this tale, '*a river runs through it*' and I did it *my* way!

At the end of the bottom beat, communing with the River Itchen from Easton road bridge.
Where it all started ... and ends.

For men may come and men may go...

Easton road bridge has featured in several of the landmarks in my life, not only as my first introduction to the River Itchen at Martyr Worthy upon which I was to spend a large part of my working life.

I became a riverkeeper by the chance meeting with Frank Moores on the bridge on a summer's day in the late 1960s. Frank was the riverkeeper of the Martyr Worthy beat of that river, and whose position I eventually took when he moved on to pastures new.

I first met Pat Fox, on this bridge in the early seventies, as I did my great fishing friend Peter Kane in the eighties.

In 2004, a couple of years, after my retirement, I was on a brief visit from Scotland to collect a new motorcar in Winchester. I could not resist the opportunity to visit the bridge again to commune with the river. By chance George Mann happened by and he asked about my manuscript of this book that I had told him I intended to write before I moved away to Scotland. If I had not met George in the new millennium on Easton road bridge this tale may never have been told.

Some Terms Explained

acidification / an increase in acidity (decrease in pH) usually due to atmospheric pollution.

alevins / trout fry with their yolk sacs still attached.

aquatic plants / plants that grow in the water.

aquifer / water bearing strata; for example, sandstone.

baetis / a sub-genus of ephemeroptera.

bank / permanent side to river, top marked by first major break in slope.

bank full discharge / discharge that fills a channel without overtopping the banks.

bar / an accumulation of sediment in a river, formed underwater in floods and subsequently exposed at lower flows

berm / shelf at the base of the bank that is the level of normal flow and gives extra channel width in high flows.

biomass / a quantitative estimate of animal and/or plant matter.

buffer zone / riparian strip of vegetation left uncultivated to intercept agricultural pollutants, such as silt and agrochemicals.

catchment area / the area of land from which rainfall flows into a river.

channelised / a channel that has been artificially modified by widening, deepening, straightening, embanking or concrete lining for the purposes of flood alleviation, drainage of agricultural land or stabilisation.

coir rolls / biodegradable products, which may contain growing plants that can be installed on river margins.

coppicing / traditional management of trees and shrubs for wood production by culling stems close to the base and removing new growth periodically.

current deflector (groynes) / a structure built into the riverbank to deflect current from erosion or to enhance fishing.

corridor / that part of the flood plain or land either side of the river extending from bank full bank top to 50 metre width.

cut-off meander / a loop in a previously meandering river that has been cut off from the river naturally or during engineering works to straighten the channel.

diptera / gnats, midges, reed smuts, houseflies, bluebottles etc.

diversity / relates to the number of species present and their abundance.

drowners or meadsmen / experienced men who could control the exact depth of the flood level of a water meadow using a series of carefully constructed ridges and furrows to manage very accurately the input, throughput and output of water.

ecosystem / any system in which there is an interdependence upon and interaction between living organisms and their immediate physical, chemical and biological environment.

emergent vegetation / plants that grow in water but have leaf structures that emerge above the surface; for example, bulrush.

enhancement / small scale environmental improvements.

environmental assessment / requirement to assess possible impact on the environment of any significant project.

Environmentally Sensitive Area (ESA) / where the landscape wildlife and historic interest are of national importance. MAFF administer the scheme.

ephemeroptera / up-winged flies or mayflies.

faggots / bundles of long branches or brushwood placed along the waters edge and pegged down, to protect the riverbank.

flood capacity / the capacity of a river, and/ or a flood plain, to contain floodwater.

flood plain / the lowland relief area of valley floor adjacent that is periodically inundated by flood waters.

flood protection standard / the standard of protection afforded by a flood defence structure or system is expressed in terms of the frequency with which a breach is expected. For example, a 1-in-50 year standard affords a higher level of protection than a 1-in-20 year standard.

fluvial geomorphology / the study of the physical features of the earth's surface and their formation, as effected by rivers.

geotextiles / natural or synthetic permeable fabrics used in conjunction with soil for the function of erosion protection.

habitat / the natural home of an animal or plant.

habitat bottleneck / the habitat of whichever life stage of trout has the greatest constraining influence on the population.

hurdles / panels made of woven coppice stems, usually hazel, and used as a traditional bank revetment.

hydrology / the study of the distribution and dynamics of water.

incised / where a river has cut downwards into its channel, producing raised banks.

indigenous / native or occurring naturally in a particular area.

invertebrate / animal without a backbone; for example, insects, worms, spiders.

larvae / young stage of aquatic organisms, especially insects.

macrophyte / mother term for higher plants.

main river / rivers designated as 'main' on a map held by MAFF; generally defined as a watercourse of strategic nature, carrying flows from an upland catchment of significant size to the sea.

margin / a term used to describe the junction of the water and the bank.

Mendel's law / principles developed in the 1800s, by an Austrian botanist called Mendel, that were the basis of today's understanding of modern genetics.

multi-stage channel / most commonly two stage, with berms cut above normal water level to contain flood waters, increasing channel capacity in times of flood.

niche / where a plant or animal lives within its community, which determines its activities and relationships with other organisms and its environment.

nursery grounds / fish spawning areas.

ova / fertilised trout egg.

overshading / shading by bankside trees which is severe enough to suppress in-stream and emergent plant growth.

parr / a young trout or salmon with finger or 'parr' marks on its flanks.

pH / a scale of 14 points indicating the degree of acidity or alkalinity of water; 7 is neutral.

photosynthesis / production, in green plants of organic compounds from carbon dioxide and water using light energy from the sun.

plecoptera / stoneflies.

point bar / bar formed on the convex side of a channel bed.

pool / a distinct feature of naturally deeper water in a river. Sequences of pools and riffles are most commonly found in unmodified gravel bed rivers.

reach / a distinct length of river channel.

redd / gravel excavation used by salmonoid fishes to protect incubating eggs.

rehabilitation / the process of restoring some of the physical form of a degraded river.

reprofiling / modifying the slope and shape of riverbanks.

revetment / a facing structure built to protect a riverbank from erosion. Materials used may be either natural or man-made.

riffle / an area of shallow water over gravel deposits on a stream bed.

riparian / zone area adjacent to a riverbank.

run / generally fast-moving water with a rippled surface.

slob trout / brown trout that live in the estuarine waters of a river and come and go with the tides.

sinuosity / the degree of meandering in the river channel.

spate / flood flow that is of high magnitude but short duration, characteristic of upland streams after heavy rain.

spiling / willow twigs woven around willow stakes used to protect steep or vertical banks. Usually twigs are alive and grow to form a living bank protection measure.

substrate / riverbed material.

SSSI / Site of Special Scientific Interest.

swim-up fry / an alevin that has made the transition from dependence on its yolk sac to reliance on external food supply is called a fry and goes through the process of 'swim-up' which means leaving the protection of the stream bed and swimming up into the open water to establish a feeding territory.

tiger trout / a cross between a American brook trout and a brown trout.

trapezoidal channel / an engineered channel with a flat bed straight banks that usually slope at a uniform angle of 45 degrees.

trichoptera / caddis flies.

watercourse / includes all rivers, streams, ditches, drains, cuts, dykes, sluices and passages through which water flows.

water table / level below which the soil or rock is saturated with water.

weir / an artificial submerged baffler across a watercourse forming a step in the natural slope of the river bed.

wetland / an area of wet land, for example marsh, fen, and shallow ponds. Such areas provide valuable wildlife habitat and can act as a 'reservoir' to hold water in times of flood.

water meadow / common 17th, 18th and early 19th century systems of flooding chalk streams and other limestone rivers to produce good quality grass for grazing sheep and cattle. Traditional management involved riverside fields being flooded and then drained by a series of sluices, carriers or feeders (ditches taking water from the river) and return drainers (ditches returning the water to the river).

woody debris / twigs, branches and trees that have fallen into the river channel which form valuable habitat in creating a diversity of current speeds and depths.

Further Afield

Of all the many books written about angling, and fly-fishing in particular, each and every dedicated chalk stream fisher will have his or her top chosen dozen or more books that regularly find their way back to the bedside table. Over time, many books written about fly-fishing have become classics in their own right not only for the information they contain but also for the atmosphere they create in the mind of the fly-fishing reader. Such classic books have that ability to take one onto the chalk stream river bank to identify, tackle and overcome the many and varied challenges presented by Nature for the fly fisher that are played out, time after time.

It would be an interesting exercise to invite a 100 regular chalk stream fly-fishers each to list their top twenty fly-fishing books. Of these chalk stream anglers it would not be surprising to find there were certain individual books that appeared on almost every list made. The books of Halford, Skues, Sawyer and Wilson et al would no doubt feature prominently. These gentlemen were the great true innovators who set down the principles, ethics and methods that are still so much part of the evolution of chalk stream fly-fishing. There have been many great books written over the intervening years about chalk streams and about chalk stream fishing. Plunket-Green, Edward Grey, Waller-Hills, and more recently Peter Lapsley and Tony Hayter to name just a few who have contributed so much to the chalk stream story. The list may appear to be endless and each personal bookshelf will also contain some lesser known books that in their own individual way have become personal treasures because they engender or capture some aspect of fly-fishing on chalk streams that no other book can or does deliver.

For me I treasure one little book written during the latter part of the Second World War and published soon after which paints a wonderful picture of the Upper River Itchen. Maj. R.D. Baird wrote his delightful book, *A Trout Rose,* from his experiences he encountered along the river while he was recuperating from his war time injuries. This little known book away from the chalkstreams, now long out of print, captures through the eyes of a dry-fly fisherman who fished his way along the many and varied beautiful beats of the river. The appreciation of the beauties of Nature he encountered beside the river and in the surrounding countryside away from the River Itchen and his battles with wild brown trout within it are described to perfection. The atmosphere Major Baird creates so vividly reminds me of my earliest experiences on the river and within the Upper Itchen Valley as a young riverkeeper. Having had the great privilege of fishing many of the wild trout waters on the Upper River Itchen at some time or other over thirty years at no time did I fish those waters without imagining that Major Baird was at my side. As I cast a dry fly to a rising trout I would frequently wonder whether I could, or did, cover that fish as expertly as he did some sixty or more years before. It is interesting to note also that the gallant dry-fly fishing Major became Secretary of the Test & Itchen Association in 1948 and held office until 1951. There is one other book to go with *A Trout Rose* which together are equal top of my book list and that is Sir Edward Grey's classic, *Fly Fishing*, first published in 1899. This book in my opinion is not only one if not the most informative ever written on chalk stream dry-fly fishing it is also regarded as a literary gem in its own right. It is indeed a joy to read over and over again as I have done over the years it is such wonderful, simply written English.

Compiling a list of favourite fly-fishing books is very much a subjective exercise so many may not agree with my personal choice overleaf!

My Top Twenty Fly-fishing Books

R.D. Baird	*A Trout Rose*
Sir Edward Grey	*Fly Fishing*
F.M.Halford	*The Dry-Fly Man's Handbook* which includes *Fisherman's Entomology* and *The Making and Management of a Fishery*
F.M Halford	*Dry Fly Fishing in Theory and Practice*
F.M.Halford	*Floating Flies and How to Dress Them*
G.E.M. Skues	*Minor Tactics of the Chalk Stream and Kindred Studies*
G.E.M. Skues	*The Way of a Trout with a Fly and Some Further Studies in Minor tactics*
G.E.M. Skues	*Side Lines, Side Lights and Reflections*
Dermot Wilson	*Dry-Fly Fishing*
Oliver Kite	*Nymph Fishing in Practice*
Frank Sawyer	*Keeper of the Stream*
Frank Sawyer	*Nymphs and the Trout*
Tony Hayter	*The Dry Fly Revolution*
Peter Lapsley	*River Fly Fishing*
Harry Plunkett-Green	*Where the Bright Waters Meet*
Izzac Walton	*The Complete Angler*
John Waller-Hills	*A Summer on the Test*
Col. E.W. Harding	*The Fly Fisher and The Trout's Point of View*
J.R.Harris	*An Angler's Entomology*
Dr Winnifred Frost & Dr Margaret Brown	*The Trout*

Even now in the 'springtime of my senility' I rarely find that is one of these books at least laying open on my bedside table or my computer desk. To delve into recent or past fly-fishing literature and search for some obscure fishing fact or forgotten dry-fly pattern from a book is a delightful time-consuming, but necessary, pastime that becomes second nature to fly-fishermen.

Organisations Needing Your Support

The Wild Trout Trust (WTT)

A charitable trust that is dedicated to raise funds by membership and fund raising events the proceeds of which are channelled into giving advice to fishery owners on trout habitat protection and restoration and funding on site restoration projects.

Contact: director@wildtrout.org

The Salmon & Trout Association (S&TA)

The S&TA are an organisation that lobbies in the corridors of power for the benefit and good of all game fishers and fishery owners nationwide.

Contact: hq@salmon-trout.org

The Environment Agency (EA)

If you find or notice anything wrong in your local river, stream or pond contact your local EA office immediately, they are there to help keep our precious aquatic ecosystems healthy.

The important and far-reaching EU Water Framework Directive is in the hands of the EA for implementation and they have the plans for your local river catchment.

Contact: your local EA office

Eight Core Rehabilitation Principles

Look at the big picture

Do not focus solely on in-stream habitat but also look to the riparian zone and the larger catchment. Successful rehabilitation projects will be designed with an eye to the larger aquatic ecosystem in which a stream functions.

Learn from nature

The goal of your projects should be to restore the natural qualities of healthy streams. Learn and identify what those qualities are and work to restore them to the degraded system.

Focus on the limiting factors at work in your stream

Identify and address those factors that are most important in keeping trout populations below the potential capacity in your stream. Focus on the causes of problems not just the symptoms. i.e. Think like a wild trout

Each stream is an individual – treat it that way

Carefully plan your project with an eye to your streams particular physical, hydrological and biological characteristics because what will work well on one stream may fail dismally on another.

Work with not against the natural capacity of streams & their catchments to restore their own health

By changing the land use practices or protecting a stream corridor, may be enough to set a stream back on to the road to recovery.

Involve a wide range of experts

Include different disciplines from Environment Agency professionals through to riparian owners and river users who are familiar with the history of the stream and its catchment.

Strive for a natural appearance

Select projects and materials that blend into the natural setting of your stream.

Finally...

Enjoy! If you and your volunteer workforce and your professional partners are not enjoying the effort, your and their commitment will be short-lived.

Illustrations

Illustrations (continued)

Page

Index

Hardy Itchen 9ft 6in 2
Hardy Itchen three-piece 12
Hardy Jet fly rod 13
Hardy perfect reel 2
hatchery-reared trout 237
hatchery trout 240
Hawthorn 80
Hay, Col. 'Scrappy' i, 39, 135
Hayes, Peter 259
Hayter, Tony 94, 100
Headlam, Gus i
hedgehog 70
Heede and Rinne 57
hen harrier 73
herons, grey 74, 75, 126
Hewitt, Ed 103
high water temperatures 52
Hill, Ray 207
Hills 100
Hills, John Waller 94
Himalayan balsam 209
Hiscock, Mr 185
holistic catchment management 146
hooking stress 112
Houghton Club 177, 208
house martins 70
Howat, 'Jock' and Anne i
hurricane, 1987 47, 73, 202
Hursley Park 47

I

Ice Age 20
indigenous vegetation 55
Institute of Fisheries Management
    147

Integrated River Catchment
    Management 221
interdisciplinary communications
    245
iris, wild yellow 77
Iron Age 22
iron blue 59, 95, 96
iron blue dun 85, 96, 127
Isle of Wight 20
Itchen 900 fly rod 186
Itchen Abbas 17
Itchen Stoke 16

J

Jackson, Bob 237
jack pike 178
Japanese knotweed 209
Jennings, Preston 104
Jones, Jack 40
J M Loveridge Ltd 13

K

Kane, Peter i
Kavanagh QC 130
Kemp, Fred 40
Kielder hatchery 215
Kilmeston Down 16
kingfisher 76
Kite, 'Ollie' 113
Knight, Alec 78
Krey, 'Lefty' 142

I wind about, and in and out,
With here a blossom sailing,
And here and there a lusty trout,
And here and there a grayling.

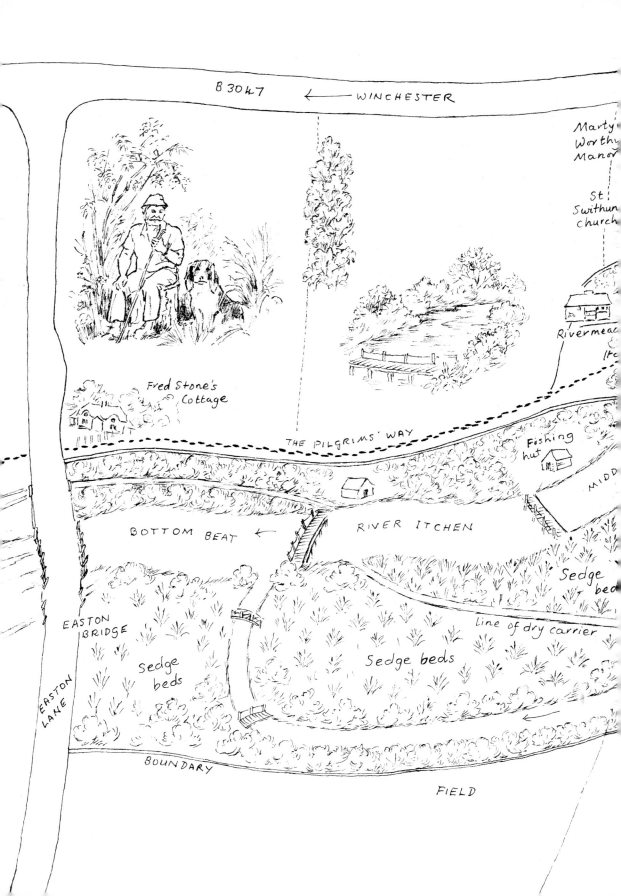

B 3047 ← WINCHESTER

Marty
Worthy
Manor

St.
Swithun
church

Rivermead
Fred Stone's
Cottage

Fishing
hut

THE PILGRIMS' WAY

MIDD

BOTTOM BEAT ←   RIVER ITCHEN

Sedge
bed

EASTON
BRIDGE

Line of dry carrier

EASTON
LANE

Sedge
beds

Sedge beds

BOUNDARY

FIELD